Educating for the Twenty-First Century:
Seven Global Changes

IBE on Curriculum, Learning, and Assessment

Series Editor

Mmantsetsa Marope (*IBE UNESCO, Switzerland*)

Managing Editor

Simona Popa (*IBE UNESCO, Switzerland*)

Editorial Board

Manzoor Ahmed (*BRAC University, Bangladesh*)
Ivor Goodson (*University of Brighton, UK*)
Silvina Gvirtz (*Universidad de San Andrés, Argentina*)
Hugh McLean (*Open Society Foundations, UK*)
Natasha Ridge (*Al Qasimi Foundation for Policy Research, UAE*)
Joel Samoff (*Stanford University, USA*)
Yusuf Sayed (*Cape Peninsula University of Technology, South Africa*)
Nelly Stromquist (*University of Maryland, USA*)
Felisa Tibbitts (*Teachers College, Columbia University, USA*)
N. V. Varghese (*National University of Educational Planning and Administration, India*)

VOLUME 3

The titles published in this series are listed at *brill.com/ibe*

Educating for the Twenty-First Century

Seven Global Challenges

By

Conrad Hughes

BRILL
SENSE

LEIDEN | BOSTON

All chapters in this book have undergone peer review.

The ideas and opinions expressed in this publication are those of the authors and do not necessarily reflect the views of IBE UNESCO.

Library of Congress Cataloging-in-Publication Data

Names: Hughes, Conrad, author.
Title: Educating for the twenty-first century : seven global challenges / By Conrad Hughes.
Description: Leiden, The Netherlands ; Boston : Brill Sense, [2018] | Series: IBE on curriculum, learning, and assessment ; volume 3
Identifiers: LCCN 2018025929 (print) | LCCN 2018032777 (ebook) | ISBN 9789004381032 (E-book) | ISBN 9789004381025 (hardback : alk. paper) | ISBN 9789004381018 (pbk. : alk. paper)
Subjects: LCSH: Education--Aims and objectives. | Education and globalization. | Education--Philosophy. | Postmodernism and education.
Classification: LCC LB14.7 (ebook) | LCC LB14.7 .H856 2018 (print) | DDC 370.11--dc23
LC record available at https://lccn.loc.gov/2018025929

ISBN 978-90-04-38101-8 (paperback)
ISBN 978-90-04-38102-5 (hardback)
ISBN 978-90-04-38103-2 (e-book)

Copyright 2018 jointly by IBE-UNESCO and Koninklijke Brill NV, Leiden, The Netherlands.
Koninklijke Brill NV incorporates the imprints Brill, Brill Hes & De Graaf, Brill Nijhoff, Brill Rodopi, Brill Sense and Hotei Publishing.
All rights reserved. No part of this publication may be reproduced, translated, stored in a retrieval system, or transmitted in any form or by any means, electronic, mechanical, photocopying, recording or otherwise, without prior written permission from the publisher.
Authorization to photocopy items for internal or personal use is granted by Koninklijke Brill NV provided that the appropriate fees are paid directly to The Copyright Clearance Center, 222 Rosewood Drive, Suite 910, Danvers, MA 01923, USA. Fees are subject to change.

This book is printed on acid-free paper and produced in a sustainable manner.

*To my father, Professor Geoffrey Ian Hughes,
and my mother, the late Dr. Jean Marquard*

CONTENTS

Foreword	ix
Mmantsetsa Marope	
Introduction	xi
Chapter 1: Mindfulness	1
At One with the Cosmos	1
Jacobo	2
The Mindfulness Craze	3
Views of the Sceptic and the Cynic	4
Other Avenues for Peace of Mind	6
Walking and Running	8
Mind Wandering	10
The Arts	11
Schools and the Arts	13
Three Points	14
Jacobo Again	15
Conclusion	16
Chapter 2: Singularity	23
Meaning of "Singularity"	25
Can Human Intelligence Be Simulated?	27
Can Computers Take on a Life of Their Own?	30
Points Made Thus Far	33
Educational Responses	33
Ethical, Consequential STEM	34
Integrated Technology	35
Post-Singularity Higher-Order Thinking	37
Conclusion	39
Chapter 3: Terrorism	45
9/11 Onwards	46
What Is It That Drives People to Become Terrorists and How Can Education Prevent or Reduce It?	47
How Should the Education We Design for Young People Present the Phenomenon of Terrorism Historically, Politically and Philosophically?	53
How Do Schools Prepare Young People Psychologically and Spiritually for a World in Which Terrorism Exists?	55
Conclusion	57

CONTENTS

Chapter 4: Sustainability	63
Introduction	63
The Catastrophe of the Environment: What Research Tells Us	65
Human Responses	68
Conclusion	79
Chapter 5: Post-Truth Politics	85
Lucian	87
What Is Truth?	88
Postmodernism and Truth: Relativistic Discourses	90
Historical Revisionism	92
Propaganda	93
Contemporary Political Approaches to Truth	95
Lucian Again	99
Conclusion	99
Chapter 6: Knowledge	107
Skills versus Knowledge	108
Bloom's Taxonomy Revised ... Again!	112
The Role of the Teacher	114
Rote Learning	115
A Twenty-First Century Education	116
Sarah	119
Conclusion	120
Chapter 7: Character	129
Discipline	130
Ethics	132
Values in Schools	135
Emotional Intelligence	139
Bringing the Pieces Together in Character Education	142
Conclusion	145
Chapter 8: Conclusion: The Framework	151
The Purpose of the Framework	152
Note 1: On Character	174
Note 2: On STEM Criteria	174
About the Author	181

FOREWORD

A considerable number of factors place unprecedented pressure on education and learning systems to change swiftly and profoundly. These include rapid advances in communications and information technology; growing urbanization; concerns for environmental sustainability; shifts in geopolitics, demographic patterns and labour markets; increasing unemployment, especially of young people; new waves of violent extremism; and the growing divide between rich and poor.

The emergence of the fourth industrial revolution is fully acknowledged as a formidable accelerant of change and complexity in the twenty-first century, and as having significant implications for education. Industry 4.0 is pressuring learners to develop a wider range of multifaceted, multidisciplinary, complex, and integrated competences, for which many education and learning systems are unprepared.

The rapid pace of change in the twenty-first century amplifies the pertinence of education and learning systems as foundations and key sources of lifelong learning and human resilience, and, by unleashing the potential of the human mind, as foundations and key sources of development.

While policies that address the role of education in development are commonplace, specific and concrete instruments for enacting these policies remain both scarce and ineffective. In today's world, the perception of education's heightened role in human and societal development coexists with heightened frustration about the irrelevance of educational practices to modern challenges and opportunities. Evidence for this frustration includes young graduates' functional illiteracy, their lack of digital skills required by their labour markets, their alienation from their cultures, and so on.

The International Bureau of Education (IBE) is deeply involved with these issues. The IBE's work highlights the crucial role of curriculum in enabling learners (young and old) to acquire competences for effective uptake of opportunities and for the effective addressing of challenges across fast-changing, and sometimes disruptive, twenty-first century development contexts. In this setting, the IBE also aims to improve access to the evidence-based knowledge needed to guide curriculum design and development as well as to guide teaching, learning, and assessment.

This is, therefore, a particularly opportune time for the IBE to publish this important book, which stresses the need to re-evaluate education and learning and to prepare learners for an unknown future.

Conrad Hughes comes to the subject as an educator and school administrator, a standpoint entirely different from the academic perspective usually featured in publications of the IBE. Educated in South Africa and England, Conrad has worked in schools in Switzerland, France, India, and the Netherlands. He is now Campus and Secondary Principal at the International School of Geneva, La Grande Boissière, the oldest international school in the world, which has learners from over 130 different

FOREWORD

cultures, and strives to make the world a better, more peaceful, open-minded place through education.

Drawing on his extensive personal and professional experience, and on his substantial contributions to thinking and writing about future competences, curriculum, and learning, this book bridges theoretical scholarship and applied work relating to education policy and practice.

Conrad Hughes is at home in this century – in his own words, an "exciting, chaotic, fast-moving era" – which is about to fundamentally change education, teaching, and learning.

His power stems, I believe, from a coherent, historically-and-personally-informed world view. Conrad knows more than a little about most things under the sun, and he expresses an entire world view through his writing – an intellectual landscape that encompasses art, current events, economics, fiction, history, music, philosophy, politics, and science. His previous works (including *Guiding Principles for Learning in the Twenty-First Century* and *Understanding Prejudice and Education*) can be reread in this light as a single, continuous, coherent theoretical undertaking, a commitment to the idea of sustainability, public good, and community, laced with his feeling the burden of responsibility for the future of our planet. In the world according to Conrad Hughes, there is always a moral edge and there is always something to be done.

Conrad Hughes' book is emblematic of the amazing potential and the excruciating limitations faced by education in the twenty-first century. However, for all of Conrad's stern seriousness about the state of the world, his writing also evidences a merriness; it is morally serious but never drearily earnest, as he returns again and again to life and work events, with humour and wisdom, often veiled with introspection and internal conflict, to support his arguments.

His ability to fuse history, futuristic thinking, and personal experience is exceptional. His personal history becomes the history of our times, and his book, a walking chronicle of the twenty-first century in the making.

Mmantsetsa Marope
Director, UNESCO International Bureau of Education (IBE)
Geneva, Switzerland

INTRODUCTION

BLIKSIM

When I was a boy growing up in Apartheid South Africa, I went to an all-boys private Catholic school. I hated school with a passion. Every morning when my parents would drive me to assembly under the open African sky, I would start to become nervous because I had not completed my homework or was not ready for a test.

The teachers would hit us. It was called getting caned or jacked. This was in the late 1970s and early 1980s. In most countries, corporal punishment in schools was illegal, yet in South Africa we would get the cane.

One of my teachers was a small, dark-haired man. He had bright blue eyes that would bore into your soul when he spoke to you. He smelled of cigarette smoke mixed with musk and would work his way up and down the aisles of his Afrikaans lessons with an aura of power. His cane was called "Bliksim", which in Afrikaans means lightening. When he caned us, he would spend time aiming the stick correctly and incisively across the buttocks and then bring Bliksim down with a clean whipping sound that cut through the crisp morning air of Johannesburg with a singular purpose. "Sheuuw" … "Whack". The boys would tense up, fear darting all over their freckled faces, and then they would go back to their seats with tears invariably welling in their eyes. I was in deep fear of that teacher, and I remember more about him than anything we learned in school.

Whenever I was caned – and it happened a lot – the physical pain was not what stayed with me; it was the humiliation and the feeling that some terrible injustice was being done and that no one cared or would stop it. The billowing cumulonimbus clouds strewn across the Highveld horizon looked down at our corporal punishment in commiserative silence. The only ointment to address the pain and dry the tears was the dry heat of the copper rays of the sun.

My driving forces were, on the one side, my ongoing hatred of school, its teachers and the cane Bliksim, and on the other, the rhythm of life that came out of the pounding vinyl albums of Zulu rock. I would listen all weekend instead of doing my homework.

I'll come back to Bliksim later.

I'm the headmaster of a school. Every day, when I look at a wayward student, a disciplinary case, when I need to reign in one of our students, I remember how I would get the cane at my own school, and I make sure that everything I do with our students keeps their confidence intact, protects their dignity, honours their souls and the development of their values.

Teachers can do damage to young children at school, and you don't need a cane to do it. All it takes is to look at a young person with an expression that signifies judgement and disbelief. All it takes is to strip them of their confidence, tell them they will not succeed, that they are bad. Much damage can be done. It can happen unconsciously, the throwaway phrase or action, the unthoughtful gesture. We need to be careful of young children and adolescents the way we would bathe an infant or hold a newborn to our chest. A good teacher empathises with her students, a bad one treats them as registration numbers.

You have to love your children as parents, and you have to want the best for your students as teachers, because the meaning that they give to their lives and the way they will construct themselves comes directly from the picture you draw of them, the picture you draw on the sketchpad of their minds. It does not take a lot to damage a child's self-esteem. A single statement or scornful look can sear the hippocampus – the part of the brain where we store the deepest memories – and remain there like a scar for life.

But the tricky part is that, as we all know, character is formed by adversity. We have to care for our children and care for our students, but we must not spoil them. To spoil a young person today will not prepare him or her for a world that is more complicated than it has ever been in human history. In fact, to spoil young people will prepare them for a life of depression and low performance. Since they will be competing with children who have gone through hell and high water to gain their place in the sun, our children need to be challenged. How do we round that square? What is the balance between an education that strengthens young people and equips them to take on the world and an education that crushes their confidence?

My job is one of the most complicated but also one of the most rewarding imaginable. Education is the most exciting professional area of the twenty-first century, not just because it is diverse, but also because you are dealing with the engine of the future: youth.

This is a book about education. However, it is not a book that can only be read and understood by specialists in education. This is for two reasons.

The first is that the research and references, the studies and the theory that substantiate what I say, I packed into endnotes. I did this so that you don't have to read through long in-text citations and academic references to get the point. I go straight to the point. For the academically inclined, however, the endnotes are thorough. They back up what I say with evidence.

The second reason, more important than the first, is that everybody is, and should be, interested in education, not just teachers, heads of institutions and researchers in education. Your life is a long education, and the people you are in any way responsible for will seek some sort of education from you no matter who you are or what your job is. If they do not, or if you do not feel that you are an educator as a parent, supervisor, aunt or uncle, big sister or brother, then think again. It takes a village to raise a child. Education goes beyond school and university, and everybody should feel connected to education.

Before we dive into the heart of the matter, let's stand back and ask ourselves some big questions about the purpose of education.

INTRODUCTION

BIG QUESTIONS

Where do we come from and where are we going?

What is it we should do to our children and to ourselves to ensure that the lives they, and we, lead are productive, happy, beautiful and purposeful?

What of the world we are living in? How are we to carry the cultural and intellectual legacy of ten thousand years of history on our fragile shoulders? As the world gets older and the means of communication expand, there is more to know and more to transmit. How do we ensure that young people carry the past into the present?

At the same time, how do we prepare young people for the opportunities, openings, extraordinary diversity, threats and challenges of our times?

These questions linger, and many scramble for answers, some turning to the past, others to the future; some design experiments (never an easy thing to do with the complexities of living, in-situ human beings as they learn); others page through theory; while others, still, rely on the media, on hunches, intuition and hearsay.

These big questions raise various wormhole-like additional questions, most ending soon after they have started. These include myths, neurotrash (findings in neuroscience that are half-baked or are not telling us anything specific about education), sales pitches, cheap speculation, dramatic conference keynotes by academic pop stars and attention-seeking politicians, sound bites gone viral, unfounded research claims and bestsellers putting a spin on old ideas, often platitudes and tautologies.

At the end of their taking or considering these various pathways, each person has formed an opinion on education and an idea of what we should be doing to prepare young people for the future. None is entirely complete; none is without contradiction or error. In the twenty-first century, there is enough information out there to confirm just about anyone's bias, and most people have a fixed idea of what an education is and will not venture all that far from it no matter what they encounter.

Discourses

An increasingly common assertion – one that has in fact now become banal – is that education needs to change to meet the complex needs of the twenty-first century. Whereas science and technology, medicine and travel, multinational corporations and economic development have all followed revolutionary trajectories in the last decades, in most instances the world of education, most especially in schools, seems to have stayed the same.

Different sources point to different global megatrends, involving urbanisation, the creation of wealth, resource scarcity, planetary problems. The world has changed incommensurably in the last century: the world population has quadrupled since World War II (from two billion to nearly eight billion); artificial intelligence now effectively has the computing power of a human brain; we are exhausting over 150% of the planet's biocapacity; while globalisation and social media have made

INTRODUCTION

the world far more accessible than ever before. At the same time, increased and increasing income disparity and new forms of terrorism have created further division and polarisation within the planet's population.

The world of today is one of VUCA (volatility, uncertainty, complexity and ambiguity). Our great-grandparents would find society unrecognisable (at least in its technical aspects). And the intuitive response is that the education we are providing for young people should therefore change radically. We are now in the fourth industrial revolution, commonly known as Industry 4.0. It is characterised by exponential change, the Internet of things and highly developed artificial intelligence. Human beings no longer merely use technological tools; they interact with, and in, intelligent systems.

Over the last few decades, there have been major changes in the planet's political, social and environmental landscape, and experts suggest that change will be even more pronounced over the decades to come.[1]

There is a need to re-evaluate education. It would be absurd to put our heads in the sand. This does not necessarily mean that everything should be changed; it might be that older strains of education need to come back into focus, that other strains need to remain as they are or experience further emphasis. Change for the sake of change is the error that comes from a lack of serious analysis. Often systems are in place, and have been for a long time, for good reason.

Indeed, one curse of educational reform is the pendulum effect created by constantly rewritten legislation that reflects political agendas and belief systems that vary from one government to the next. Education becomes the ever-morphing target of leadership hyperactivity.

It is true that in schools children tend to still be grouped by age and are still subject to a knowledge-based learning experience with little in the way of transdisciplinary, project-based, relevant learning that prepares them directly and explicitly for the challenges of our time. A tired, overused statement is that the classrooms of today resemble the classrooms of yesterday, that between the nineteenth century and the twenty-first century, schools are still essentially identical in layout and in terms of what young people learn.

This assertion is almost always meant as a criticism. It expresses the idea that education should be moving with the times, not frozen in the past. However, anyone who knows anything about the history of education knows that for the majority of human beings' collective experience over the last few thousand years, the whole idea of education has been strongly traditional and conservative. The idea has been that the primary purpose of an education is to transmit history and culture to young people, to make them knowledgeable about the past and to ensure that a transmission of skills, knowledge and wisdom is at the centre.

And any parent knows that a good upbringing goes back to old-fashioned principles: children need to be taught to respect their parents, to be polite and kind to those around them; they should not be spoilt or simply left to do as they please. At the same time, parents across the globe are struggling to cope with social media, new technologies and what exactly they should be doing to prepare their children for a complex, challenging world and unknown future. Are we getting it right? Will our children find, once it is too late, that we did not equip them with the right values and approaches to life to be successful?

If we focus on schools, however, the traditionalist view seems far from the normative discourse in education today: the convergence of lines of thought all promoting the pressing need to reform schooling has become something of a cliché.

Of course, many schools and examination boards, universities and colleges will claim that they are not locked into the past and that there are tangible examples of educational philosophies and institutions that have changed the shape of instruction and learning quite emphatically.[2]

What this "winds of change" frenzy has led to is a collection of overused words, phrases and ideas in education. Here are some better-known examples:

- The jobs of the future do not exist yet, and therefore the educational experience must somehow prepare young people to be able to enter a number of different professional fields rather than one narrow area.
- Schools of the past focussed on content, whereas the schools of the future will focus more on skills.
- Social media and the rise of technology have revolutionised knowledge acquisition to the point where learning facts is fairly pointless, as students can access facts directly through the Internet, essentially without teachers.
- Good teaching is not about teaching, it's about learning: what is important is not what is being taught but what is being learnt.
- Neuroscience allows us to understand the biology of learning in such a way that practice can, and should, reflect contemporary scientific developments rather than non-scientific ideology.
- Children learn when they are emotionally engaged and see the relevance of what they are learning.

Whilst some terms that have currency include:

- flipping the classroom (meaning that you frontload knowledge at home and go over what you have learnt in the classroom);
- group work;
- project-based learning;
- critical thinking;
- creativity;
- character;
- collaboration;
- entrepreneurship;
- student advocacy;
- social and emotional intelligence;
- digital literacy;
- STEM;

INTRODUCTION

- grit;
- relevance;
- mindfulness;
- kindness;
- self-agency or decision-making.

On the other hand, words, phrases and ideologies that are less appealing and will perhaps be held up as examples of nineteenth century bad practice tend to include the following:

- lecturing;
- facts;
- rote-learning;
- punishment;
- humiliation;
- manners;
- dictation;
- multiple-choice tests;
- pure theory (without relevance);
- lack of emotional intelligence on the part of the teacher.

Plus ça change, plus c'est la même chose

E. D. Hirsch, a bold and perspicacious force in education, has pointed out that much of this ideological shift is nothing new: it started towards the last quarter of the twentieth century and was influenced by a change in thinking about education at the turn of the twentieth century.

In fact, for the better part of the twentieth century, we lived with reforms and intended reforms that were rooted in an essentially similar romantic, naturalist perspective on learning – inspired first by the eighteenth century philosopher Jean Jacques Rousseau and embraced by his successors (Dewey, Montessori, Piaget and Vygotsky). These thinkers collectively promulgated the idea that what matters in education is how you work around the psychology of the learner.

What appears new and contemporary is in fact rather tired. The recent additions to this romantic, naturalist, constructivist approach are scientific and technological shifts, which have accelerated the discourse but not actually changed it fundamentally.

The discourse of the early twenty-first century is thus not actually markedly different from that of the twentieth century. We are still in a dualist controversy, which opposes an academic, insensitive and content-heavy approach, that cliché of a Dickensian nineteenth century, to a learner-centred, constructivist, skills-based approach that aims to motivate students and make them feel comfortable to be more creative in their thinking.

What has changed is a sense of urgency to change the classroom and the now widespread belief that education can change the world.[3]

INTRODUCTION

Parents also realise that what is important is not just what their children know and how well they understand what they know, but also the development of character, lifelong learning, confidence, a strong work ethic and interpersonal skills (knowing how to negotiate with other people, listen to them, work together).

Part of what I do in this book is examine some of these modernist discourses (modernist, not postmodernist, because they are not particularly new). I point out that the less-politically-correct, comfortable assertions about education relating to discipline, hard work and well-established traditions (content learning and the importance of classical subjects such as history and philosophy, for example), are not to be thrown out simply because they are old. I will, on the contrary, argue that in many ways they are needed more now than ever.[4]

Central to the discussion is the unavoidable and timeless truth that a good education comes from the person learning more than from the subject being taught or even from the style of the person teaching it. Perhaps we have fallen too deeply into the trap of obsessing over what should be taught and how it should be taught when, in truth, what is important is the passion, intelligence and dedication of the student, no matter what is taught.

Even the simplest of messages can be used to extract great meaning if the student is motivated to learn deeply,[5] hence a plethora of writings on motivation, "mindset", character and what have you.

Furthermore, education is not a monolithic entity or a static field. It is in constant evolution and development, responding to changing times and contexts. It is ongoing, never stops.

For these reasons, among many others, education remains the most stimulating and fascinating, but also the most frustrating and inaccurate practice of human beings. We search, we probe, we hope and we dream. Sometimes we react angrily and assert. But we never reach the bottom of the rabbit hole; it just gets deeper.

While most education experts and researchers agree that grading systems are not effective, schools continue to grade students, creating aggressive grade-centred competition, a lack of interest in comments on performance (the grades wash out the effect of the comments) and a "grade junkie" ethos. We know now that homework in the primary school years does not add any real gains to learning, but most schools continue to drown their students in homework. While many are pointing out that the purpose of education should be to be intrinsically rewarding, rather than a mere means to an end, many parents pressure their children to simply use school to get the best scores, get into the best universities and secure high-status jobs.

It is as if we want the best of two very different worlds: excellent academic performance, the type one usually associates with high levels of stress and rote learning, and at the same time a compassionate, creative and student-friendly way of facilitating learning.

INTRODUCTION

WHAT CHALLENGES OF THE TWENTY-FIRST CENTURY SHOULD EDUCATION ADDRESS?

The question in this book is this: to what exactly we should be directing education? Which challenges should education address?

The challenges I discuss in this book[6] span divers fields: they bring together some of the major tensions and problems the planet is facing.[7]

This book outlines seven areas that I believe are important to the world we are living in and towards which we are moving.[8] These areas represent a summary configuration of some of the trends and strains elaborated by various voices in the world of education as well as those of social commentators, journalists, scientists, sociologists and philosophers.

Whether you are a parent, a scholar, a teacher or a head, this book is for you, as we need to think together about what an education for the world we are living in should comprise.

AREAS TO BE TACKLED

For over a decade and a half, I've been researching the theme of exactly what types of knowledge we should be learning in the twenty-first century, seeking a pattern out of a myriad of seemingly endless statements, examples, experimental research results, naturalistic research results, positions, hypotheses and arguments.

I feel ready now, in 2018, to finally answer the question through this book.

What should an education in the twenty-first century entail? The response to our question relates to subjects, domains, tasks and assessment. I have divided this response into seven chapters that investigate critical areas of human planetary activity, as follows.

Mindfulness

In many so-called developed countries and in most schools, human beings are complaining about high levels of stress, as they carry out their lives in hyperactive lifestyles that can become unhealthy and compulsive. This problem has led to a number of responses, especially in schools, in the area of mindfulness. What are schools doing, and what should they be doing, to promote happy, focussed, calm and appreciative people? And how well does the mindfulness movement stand up in this respect?

Singularity (Artificial Intelligence)

The machines that humans have built and the algorithms that drive them are challenging the uniqueness of some of the essential constituents of human intelligence. Human beings, including young people, appear increasingly attached to devices and dependent on them. What are the implications for education?

Terrorism

International terrorism, particularly that related to Islamic fundamentalism, has become a global problem. Few societies feel completely sheltered from the risk of attack, whilst a climate of fear, mistrust and xenophobia grows in response. How can schools work with young people to face the problem of terrorism and, hopefully, reduce it?

Sustainability

The planet's biocapacity is being depleted at an exponential rate, and if current behaviours do not stop soon, our planet's resources will have been exhausted and humans will be faced with a scarcity of resources that will make life intolerable, if not impossible. What can schools do to slow down this time bomb?

Post-Truth Politics

Political developments in the middle of the first quarter of the twenty-first century have led some to argue that truth does not mean what it used to, that we are entering a type of post-truth era in which communications strategies are more important than the verity of what is being discussed. I argue that whilst it is true that twenty-first century democratic politics seem saturated in a number of areas, at their core things have not changed much; rhetoric, oversimplification and mendacity have been standard tools for political gain as far back as we can think. We should, nonetheless, be careful about how we grapple with information in the twenty-first century: there are approaches to knowledge construction that are essential in an age of sound bites and alternative, often false, positions broadcast on social media.

Knowledge

Because of new technologies and the way that knowledge is made available and distributed in the twenty-first century, some believe that we need to rethink entirely what is taught in school and perhaps teach less content, opening up time and opportunities for skills development. This debate is becoming more and more acute. I grapple with it by pointing out some essential features of knowledge that cannot be given short shrift. I argue that knowledge in the twenty-first century is more necessary than ever and that skills-over-knowledge proposals, depending, of course, on how they are construed, tend to be misguided.

INTRODUCTION

Character

At the core of any response to the global challenges that face us is the age-old question of a person's character: the moral fibre that will determine the scope and style of their response. Today's world is fast-changing and uncertain and therefore requires a particularly developed level of resolve and sturdiness. Character can be determined through six core concepts: mastery, discipline, respect, beliefs, confidence and adaptability. These are fleshed out in this chapter.

***

All these chapters suggest choices that schools can make to ensure that students learn to grapple with these seven issues in age-appropriate, informed ways. Each area is looked at in detail first from personal and professional perspectives and then in relation to existing theory and research.

The final chapter brings my positions together in a framework, made up of summarised suggestions for educational institutions. The points in the framework can be adapted and adopted according to context.

THE FATE OF BLIKSIM

I need to come back to my own primary schooling and what eventually happened to Bliksim, the cane that whipped our young hides.

I stole it.

One day when the master was not in the classroom, and with a friend of mine on the lookout, I took it from its cabinet, threaded it into my right trouser leg and carefully made my way to the car park to be picked up, walking as if I had a wooden leg. Because the cane could bend (the teacher used to make each end touch, in order to demonstrate its flexibility), I managed to bend my leg in the passenger seat of the car without the cane being noticed by my father.

I kept the cane at home for a number of years, eventually cutting it into smaller sections to use in an art project. My parents knew I had taken it but were on my side. Eventually I left the school and went to an institution that was completely different: co-educational, multiracial, open-minded. There teachers did not cane the students, and we learnt about how we could live together in peace. There I learned not to hate school but to love it. That changes everything.

NOTES

[1] Current planetary goals can be well summed up in the United Nations' Sustainable Development Goals. The fourth, on education, focusses on lifelong learning and access to quality. Visions of the near future of education point to loosely related directions: The Organisation for Economic Cooperation and Development (OECD) has developed a 2030 "learning compass", which focusses on self-agency and well-being; Singapore's 21st Century Competences Framework focusses on values; whereas

INTRODUCTION

UNESCO International Bureau of Education's "future competences" include lifelong learning, self-agency, interacting with others and interacting in and with the world.

2   Universities are in a slightly different situation – after all, universities are there to contribute to knowledge and should therefore be leading the dance. Many technical subjects, such as STEM, are evolving at an extraordinary pace with the development of technology, whilst a number of well-respected universities are experimenting with different types of online learning platforms. However, I would argue, the average university is still rather staid and traditional, with large amphitheatres in which lecturers speak for hours on coursework that has not evolved significantly over the last 60 years. I include among the institutions that are changing the forward-looking examination boards, like the International Baccalaureate with its emphasis on educating the whole person while focussing on values; the United World Colleges movement with an emphasis on service learning; High Tech High with its interdisciplinary approach; and the Whittle group of schools with a focus on actualising every young person's passion. I could add a mention of the phenomenon of online learning that has swept through a number of universities, such as MIT and the University of California. In fact, many education institutions are trying to change if they are not trying to get on the bandwagon of change.

3   "Education is the most powerful weapon which you can use to change the world" (Mandela, 2003).

4   I should add that there is something ironic and contradictory in the fabric of modern education-speak, for at the same time that constructivist discourses continue to proliferate, extremely academic and content-heavy approaches – in many ways extremely traditional – are celebrated too. This schizophrenic tendency can be seen through references to international tests such as the OECD's PISA, which celebrates high scores from countries such as South Korea, where it is by no means unheard of for students to work till 11 in the evening in order to achieve superhuman results in mathematics and the sciences (Chakrabarti, 2013).

5   As the great Chinese philosopher Lao Tzu said in his *Tao Te Ching*:

> The superior student listens to the Way
> And follows it closely.
> The average student listens to the Way
> And follows some and some not.
> The lesser student listens to the Way
> And laughs out loud. (Lao Tzu, 41, Taoistic.com, 2018)

6   I came to the number seven not for any particular reason. One might be tempted to see a resonance with mystic, religious or historical numerology, but this is not the case. These areas are fundamental, and, while they might not cover everything that an education should do, they address issues that affect many other areas of the development of young people, issues that cannot be put to the side in contemporary society. Seven is also a number that the human mind can hold onto easily, as we know from cognitive psychology.

7   I should point out that the premise of this book is that the purpose of an education is threefold: it should fortify the individual and group with a body of knowledge, for knowledge leads to an appreciation of culture, beauty, truth and goodness; it should empower the individual and group with a set of skills that can be used in a variety of contexts, professional, social and physical. Finally, but perhaps most importantly, a good education should provide the individual and the group with a set of values and belief systems that give life direction and any decision a clear moral purpose. One might call these three overlapping areas three types of knowledge, as Gilbert Ryle did in 1946 (Ryle, 1971), namely declarative knowledge, procedural knowledge and dispositional knowledge.

I believe that these three areas can be related to the objectives of any educational experience in the world, modified only by context and specific application: all educational institutions are trying to develop character, competences and knowledge.

8   I have already written on the topic of prejudice and how education can respond to it (Hughes, 2017). This is one of the overarching challenges of our time, for no sooner do we believe that a certain set of prejudices has become a historical archaism and left behind us than it re-emerges, creating conflict and even war. As I write this, right-wing extremists have driven a car into a crowd of protesters in

INTRODUCTION

Charlottesville in the United States, while thousands of Americans rally behind the Black Lives Matter movement – this half a century after the Civil Rights Movement. Prejudice is a massive educational challenge that deserved a monograph all to itself, which is why I wrote *Understanding Prejudice and Education: The Challenge for Future Generations*.

REFERENCES

Chakrabarty, R. (2013, December 2). South Korea's schools: Long days, high results. *BBC*. http://www.bbc.com/news/education-25187993

Hughes, C. (2017). *Understanding prejudice and education: The challenge for future generations*. Oxford: Routledge.

Mandela, N. (2003). *Lighting your way to a better future.* http://db.nelsonmandela.org/speeches/pub_view.asp?pg=item&ItemID=NMS909

Ryle, G. (1971). Knowing how and knowing that. In G. Ryle (Ed.), *Collected papers: Collected essays, 1929–1968* (Vol. 2, pp. 212–225). New York, NY: Barnes & Noble.

Taoistic.com (2018). *TTao Te Ching (Ch. 41): The Taoist classic by Lao Tzu, translated and explained.* http://www.taoistic.com/taoteching-laotzu/taoteching-41.htm

CHAPTER 1

MINDFULNESS

AT ONE WITH THE COSMOS

I am sitting in a stone village house deep in the countryside of France. From the bay windows I see ears of golden wheat spread in a gently undulating blanket beneath a pale blue sky, not unlike one of Van Gogh's emblematic paintings of the south of France. The landscape, so pretty and simple, seems to contain many solutions within its bucolic framework. The dreamy summer atmosphere makes me think of the great Stoic philosophers, Zeno, Chrysippus, Cleanthes, Epictetus, Cicero, Marcus Aurelius and Seneca, and that ancient idea they all expressed: that moments of peace with the world, moments when we feel a light-footed harmony within us, moments redolent of the natural elements, allow for a feeling of eternity; that they connect us with an endlessly good, beautiful and true cosmos.

Surely this is what we should teach young people above all else: to live out the present with a joyous intensity; to look beyond that which appears ugly, unfair or false; to strive for an existence that puts these ills into perspective and allows us to rise above them and to realise, as Spinoza taught, that evils are temporal and temporary pains that will not last in the larger scheme of things, the larger scheme of things being good, beautiful and true.

So rather than dwelling on fear of the future or futilely musing on the past, let us live each day to the fullest – *amor fati*, as Nietszche said, or *carpe diem*. Let schools teach young people to appreciate the beauty and goodness of the world. Just as I feel a soft whisper of eternity come to me in the thoughtless serenity of the lazy summer day before me, I should try to enjoy this heavenly feeling as much as possible and make it last as long as possible each day, to learn to be happy through a philosophy that allows me to see the world from the perspective of eternity (*sub specie aeternitatis*, as Spinoza said). If this is my guiding principle, then so too should it be that of my students: they should be taught to love life and appreciate the present, not to squander their existence through anguish and regret. Trials and tribulations will come but will subside, and peace of mind will return if we have the strength of mind to will it so.

Great stories of human wisdom support this model of existence. Think of Kazantzakis' *Zorba the Greek* (1946), a larger-than-life fictional figure who lives not in quiet desperation, but entirely and freely. Think of the book of *Ecclesiastes* in the Bible, with its adage that there is a time for all things. It suggests that life should be lived with patience and appreciation, even for its vicissitudes: for all its parts of a rich

© JOINTLY BY IBE-UNESCO AND KONINKLIJKE BRILL NV, LEIDEN, 2018
DOI:10.1163/9789004381032_001

CHAPTER 1

and unavoidable tapestry. Each chapter of *Ecclesiastes* prescribes a different approach, but the whole is marked by an underlying acceptance. Think of the Buddha with his subtle smile, enlightened by the inner harmony of things. Think of the Swahili saying *Hakuna Matata* (meaning "no worries") or the Muslim dictum *inshallah* (meaning "God willing"). These all point to the same idea: a type of fatalism and acceptance of the unravelling of events; a realisation that human suffering comes from trying to oppose the world, to change it, to roll back the inevitable – in sum, from not accepting one's mortality. Inner peace, on the other hand, comes from a constant effort to embrace the world and to reach to fathom its underlying harmony and goodness.

Perhaps this model of living is more necessary today than ever before because the planet's overpopulation, its unsustainable modus operandi and its endlessly complex configurations of political, economic and social tensions mean that young people must seek within themselves the ability to live without fear and with some degree of acceptance of volatility, uncertainty, complexity and ambiguity.

Young people are under huge pressure as they enter a challenging, paradoxical world. University places are increasingly scarce and difficult to obtain, while the guarantee of future employment from such an education is slight. In order to thrive in such a world, young people will need to be focussed, able to block out the noise around them and to remain lucid and confident.

Today's learners need to exercise mind over matter. They need to be able to steer the ship through the storm whilst remaining concentrated on their goals. Distraction comes not only from the media, but also from video games, e-mail, YouTube and the thousand other temptations that lurk in the Pandora's box of the Internet. By learning to harness thinking in a controlled, careful fashion, students will gain the discipline to put away their androids, switch off their screens, disconnect from virtual reality and engage with the here and now.

At another level, mental illness is on the rise. Reports tell us that one out of three families in the UK include someone considered mentally ill,[1] while 21.4% of children between 13 and 18 have suffered from a severe mental disorder (NIMH, 2016). The most commonly diagnosed disorder among US children is ADHD (attention deficit and hyperactivity disorder).

JACOBO

I'd like tell you a short story about a student at a school where I worked. The name is fictitious, but the character is real. Jacobo, 14, with a long blonde wave over one side of his face, sporting jeans, basketball trainers and a hoodie, was always getting into trouble. He could not keep still at assemblies. His incessant chatting in class would drive his teachers up the wall. Even when left to his own devices, he managed to get into trouble. He would play with the fire extinguishers and at one point sprayed an entire wall with foam.

When Jacobo was in my office, he would shift fretfully from one foot to the other, his small brown eyes darting everywhere and rarely settling into a firm, confident gaze. He would speak in nervous, high-pitched, rapid-fire half-sentences, his hands twitching or hidden in his pockets. His cell phone was never far from him, connected via Bluetooth to the headphones around his neck. I liked Jacobo despite his constant excesses and infractions, because he had character and a healthy 14-year-old-boy naughtiness about him.

Once when Jacobo was in my office for having thrown paper balls behind the teacher's back, I asked if he read. "Yes, sir", he shot back. "What sort of books do you read?" I asked. "All sorts", he said. "We have books to read in English". "Such as?" I asked. "Um, I've forgotten the title, but it's a story about World War II, no World War I". It was clear that the boy did not read, or that if he did, it was not making much of an impact.

How many children are there in the world like Jacobo? How many of our children are glued to their phones, become restless when anything becomes remotely boring? And what are we doing about it?

Jacobo was tested for hyperactivity, and not surprisingly it was confirmed. The usual treatment is Ritalin, a drug that dampens excessive neural connections in the brain (our brain has trillions of neural connections and concentrating means cutting some of them off). His parents decided not to give him the drug, despite the advice of a specialist. I did not judge them, as I'm a parent too, and you have to think hard before giving psychotropic drugs to your children.

So Jacobo continued to wreak havoc. He got into loud, childish quarrels, disturbed other students, was picked up for bad language in public. When all the students were lined up on stage to sing, he would disturb those around him so much that you could see a ripple effect in the group, like eddies of water circling from a stone dropped in a pond.

I'll come back to Jacobo. We will see what the school finally did to improve his situation. It involved mindfulness, or to be more precise, it involved something that you might want to call mindfulness, although it was actually much simpler.

THE MINDFULNESS CRAZE

Where in the world of education does one go to bring students to a state of calm, concentrated and meditative being? What are schools doing? One answer is mindfulness. Mindfulness is "a form of meditation with roots in Buddhist spiritual practices" (Anderson, Lau, Segal, and Bishop, 2007, p. 449); it is "the awareness that emerges through paying attention on purpose, in the present moment, and non-judgmentally to the unfolding experience moment by moment" (Kabat-Zinn, 2003, p. 145). Mindfulness has found numerous incarnations in school programmes across the United States and Great Britain.[2]

If more and more schools are talking about mindfulness, about the need for education to bring young people to an awareness and appreciation of the here and now, it is because we recognise that we are living in an environment that is stressful, noisy, crowded and aggressive, an environment that can easily lead young people into panic, confusion, self-doubt and fear.

CHAPTER 1

Mindfulness' pundits tell us it is a remedy to mental depression. They also claim that it helps people to think about their own thinking, to reflect on the way they think. This is what we call metacognition, a practice that improves learning through strengthening successful learning strategies, such as self-regulation.

Mark Leonard, president of the Mindfulness Exchange in the UK, claims the following:

> Mindfulness has been shown to help those suffering from depression to manage their emotions better and dwell less on negative memories and feelings… It's remarkable to see someone transformed in five weeks from an unhappy, withdrawn person who feels overburdened to someone who is receptive and upbeat and can experience pleasure in the moment. (Woods, 2014)

An increasing body of research supports this claim, although, like so much research in education and the human sciences in general, it can be questioned.[3]

VIEWS OF THE SCEPTIC AND THE CYNIC

Reports and promises about mindfulness sound too good to be true. The sceptically minded might ask how any single educational strategy could bring so much with it.

If there were an approach that could create better concentration, less hyperactivity, greater peace of mind and awareness of self and heightened levels of on-task staying power, then families and schools would have adopted it widely. Yet, mindfulness has not been so adopted. This might be because of its cost (it is commercially branded and marketed, and it implies expensive professional development for teachers) or it might be because many do not believe in it. Where mindfulness has worked, its markers of success do not go beyond non-falsifiable anecdotes, feel-good stories and results that cannot be dissociated from a host of confounding variables – which means that mindfulness may or may not be the reason schools that employ it see successful academic scores.

Will mindfulness be enough to give young people the resources they need to be fulfilled in their lives? Is there not a danger that mindfulness is something of a hyped-up, empty fad?

If one were to be less generous than even the sceptically minded, that is, a grumpy cynic, one might brand mindfulness as New Age, postmodern spirituality, the West's pathetic and half-baked attempt to rediscover religion without the core elements of faith and submission, elements that a rational, capitalist and individualistic society discards as primitive, embarrassing and inconvenient. Students are thus called upon not to pray or meditate on cosmic entities such as God or pure spirit, but rather to focus on their own bodies, to "connect" with their own thoughts and distil their thinking in self-centred moments of pseudo enlightenment. The Eastern connections lend mindfulness an exoticism and mystique that make it more appealing than church services. Thus yoga, Zen, Sophrology, meditation and mindfulness have become popular activities for those seeking to open their "chakras" and their "third eye".[4]

To present this appetizing Eastern mysticism as a solution in education raises a great many problems. First is the question of motivation. Imposing a practice on students rather than having them desire it and strive for it themselves undermines its purpose. How are teachers to ensure that the entire class is focussing on their toes or emptying their thoughts without the entire endeavour's being forced and false? And what does one do with the student who does not wish to meditate or concentrate on his or her breathing? Won't this effort reproduce the rebel of earlier years, peeking out of half-closed eyes and giggling during prayer, going through the motions while finding them ridiculous. The question of motivation is, of course, a general problem in education and can be applied to many endeavours (how to stimulate a sense of intrinsic reward in literacy and numeracy, how to encourage and animate students to do well in their subjects without the [crude] carrots of high grades and sticks of failure). And mindfulness attempts to cover a larger remit – it grapples with an approach to life itself and intimate questions of self and mind. Surely these cannot be taught through "programmes" the way cognitive domains can be, but rather will only be attained through self-driven desire.

Another problem: Is it realistic to try to transfer a cultural practice from one extensively defined context to another, quite different one? What is the point, one might ask, of getting young people to engage in mindfulness in an industrialised society that is bent on competition, profit, materialism, hedonism and individualism? Surely mindfulness belongs in a different society, one that has as its overarching principle a belief in restraint and discipline? It seems unlikely that classroom practices involving minutes of deep breathing and silence will successfully transport the rice paddies of China into the wealthy suburbs of California or the resonance of the Tibetan monk's horn into the bleak, functional office blocks of Stuttgart or the beer-swilling pubs of Northern England.

If parents, teachers and school principals really want their students to carry within them the smile of the Buddha and with it the secrets of Eastern spirituality, they should surely go much further than mindfulness and ensure that young people follow martial arts, that they read the Upanishads, that they strive for an existence that suppresses desire and seeks the Nirvana through successive reincarnations across the rack of human suffering that is the Samsara. Learners would fast, abstain, linger in silence for days, grow their hair long like Sadhus or shave it off like monks and cast aside all earthly temptations.

It is an unlikely scenario in the decadent, postmodern West. As Rudyard Kipling wrote, "East is East and West is West and never the twain shall meet".

Then again, the sceptics and the cynics won't be forging a path for future generations, and despite the fun one might poke at mindfulness, surely we wish to ensure that we are doing all we can to make young people spiritually stronger and mentally more serene in their approach to the world. Mindful Nation UK is at least proposing something, at least trying to find a solution to the void that exists.

CHAPTER 1

OTHER AVENUES FOR PEACE OF MIND

My brother taught my two children and me how to surf during one holiday in South Africa. Once we knew how to stand on the surfboard and had become used to speeding across the water with the white cusp of broken waves behind us, we started to go out to the back line and lie on the boards waiting for the next wave, with the glitter of the sun dancing on the broad back of the sea. When we did this, so far from shore, tremendous peace of mind would descend upon us.

This was in Muizenberg, near Cape Town. In the distance, edging the ocean and heading towards the eastern coast was a ring of mountains. Above in the immense sky, the odd gull would majestically circle.

Waiting for the next swell, we were at one with all around us, concentrating on the here and now, our thoughts not racing but focussed. Surely this is one effect of mindfulness. Surely the peace of mind and singleness of thought that bring peace, calm and simplicity were right here.

I suggest that elements of mindfulness should indeed be evoked in a twenty-first century education, but I think we need to take the discussion further than just mindfulness.

An education for the twenty-first century that would allow for some calm and reflection might include: moments of peace and quiet (for example, a minute's silence at the beginning of the day at home or in assemblies at school); instances in which students are brought to think about, and focus on, the simple things in life without the exercise's being contrived (for example, encouraging the observation of an animal's behaviour or the growth of a plant); outdoor education – although it need not be in the form of a "challenge" (high-adrenaline cliff-hanging, off-track skiing, bungee jumping and sky diving seem the compulsions of bored, denaturalised, over industrialised individuals, whilst climbing mountains or swimming channels seem to reflect a sorry colonial impulse to conquer and own nature), but something more modest and timeless, like a walk in the woods or a gathering around a campfire; engagement in the arts in such a way that young people are able to focus on the growth of their competences in a prolonged manner (learning an instrument, preparing for a theatrical performance or painting a detailed, large or particularly complex work); and frequent physical education in which students are able to leave their worries behind as they become engrossed in individual or group sports.

In fact, sports and the arts carry with them more psychological value than we credit them with, particularly when students in moments of pure artistic or athletic concentration and rapture can shed self-consciousness. A recent thinker on this is Mihály Csíkszentmihályi. This is how he describes what he calls "flow":

- Intense and focused concentration on what one is doing in the present moment.
- Merging of action and awareness.
- Loss of reflective self-consciousness; that is, loss of awareness of oneself as a social actor.

- A sense that one can control one's actions; that is, a sense that one can in principle deal with the situation because one knows how to respond to whatever happens next.
- Distortion of temporal experience – typically, a sense that time has passed faster than normal)
- Experience of the activity as intrinsically rewarding, such that often the end goal is just an excuse for the process (Nakamura and Csikszentmihalyi, 2002, p. 90).

Surely it is through the arts (think of the hours that go into perfecting an instrument followed by a sublime performance, or the beauty of a seamless dramatic performance) and in sports (the intensity of a sprint, the well-oiled and above-consciousness dynamics of a serve in tennis, the emotional swirl of victory or loss) that many constituents of what we might call "mindfulness" are to be found. In these concentrated, distilled, timeless moments of unity and extremity, the individual is at one with the elements and himself or herself. These moments are so pure and strong that those watching are swept up by their infectiousness. Perhaps this desire to be part of the eternal and human feeling that they create is why musical concerts and sports competitions have always attracted crowds.

Disconnect

A great many studies in radiology and neuroscience using magnetic resonance imaging have established a relationship between Internet addiction and cognitive decline.[5]

The problem is not necessarily, and certainly not entirely, linked to the intrinsic content of screen time (after all, many education apps and films are educational; and one might debate whether excessive screen time is technically addiction) but the amount of time that is spent in front of screens. Recent estimates for young people in the United States are nine hours a day (Common Sense, 2015).

One problem is that screen time takes time away from all the other things a growing person should be doing to find a healthy balance. In a day full of school, homework, revising for tests and commuting, and in which adults try to ensure that children receive enough replenishing cycles of deep sleep, little time remains to read for pleasure, to explore an instrument, to be in nature or to engage in a calm, well-developed conversation. If those precious hours are spent in front of a screen, that is time lost.

Some argue that computer gaming helps stimulate cognitive processing, particularly spatial intelligence, visual acuity and elements related to dyslexia (Eichenbaum, Bavelier, and Green, 2014; Franceschini, 2013). So one should not blame gaming for more ills than it is culpable of. I suggest that more pernicious than gaming is the idle watching of videos and trite social media sagas that rarely inform and often veer into cyberbullying. Social isolation also results from staring at a screen and not engaging with the world around you.

CHAPTER 1

The physical act of sitting hunched, research tells us, is unhealthy.[6]

In order for a healthy lifestyle to predominate in young people's lives, schools have a responsibility to monitor screen time and the physical inactivity that comes with it. Endless homework assignments that encourage online work do not help.

Parents know that if children spend too much time alone with their devices, the result is depleted attention and bad moods. Some scientific research has corroborated this effect (Romano et al., 2013). There should be clear moments at home and in school when the screens are simply folded, packed away and forgotten.

WALKING AND RUNNING

Anyone who has spent any time in primary school education appreciates that breaks are precious to children, as illustrated by the playground sounds and sights: shouting, screaming, laughing, running, chasing and excited gesticulation. Perhaps children still struggle against being conditioned into being the stationary, calm, seated (and essentially boring) office occupants so many will become. Children bolt out the door at break time and spend every second of break with intensity, a contrast with their being made to sit still, keep quiet and move only when told in stuffy, overcrowded, confined spaces for five hours a day. No wonder so many children are diagnosed with hyperactivity.

Students in general are not doing enough sports in schools. The World Health Organisation has stated the following:

In order to improve cardiorespiratory and muscular fitness, bone health, and cardiovascular and metabolic health biomarkers:

1. Children and youth aged 5–17 should accumulate at least 60 minutes of moderate- to vigorous-intensity physical activity daily.
2. Amounts of physical activity greater than 60 minutes provide additional health benefits.
3. Most of the daily physical activity should be aerobic. Vigorous-intensity activities should be incorporated, including those that strengthen muscle and bone, at least 3 times per week (WHO, 2016).

A 2013 UK study by University College London established, however, that only 63% of boys and 38% of girls were getting the recommended daily exercise (Triggle, 2013). An Irish study conducted in 2014 by the EU's Eurydice Network reported that four out of five Irish children were not getting enough exercise with, on average, Irish schoolchildren receiving an extraordinarily low 38 hours of physical education a year (instead, time was being allocated to extra maths) (McGuire, 2014). Other countries that fare poorly are Canada, the United States, Australia and Scotland (McGinn, 2014).

Where sports are taken seriously, such as in the United States or New Zealand, the zeal can be counterproductive. Excessive specialisation before adolescence, pressure from parents and injuries sustained from overly competitive and ambitious objectives lead to 70% of US young people's dropping out of sports by age 13 (Wallace, 2016). Schools and parents should ensure that while sport is vigorous, enthusiasm for it is not monomaniac, that it allows for diversity, and that it avoid the cramping effect of pressures from parents' projecting their own ambitions onto their children. The approach should be balanced.

Perhaps if our educational systems would allow for more physical activity, we might find students appreciating moments of calm more fully, and even during physical activity perhaps their thoughts would gain some tranquillity.

A particularly powerful psycho-spiritual element of sports involves the individuals' pushing themselves to their limits. Consider this quotation on running from the English actor Noel Coward:

> Running is the classical road to self-confidence, self-awareness and self-reliance. Independence is the outstanding characteristic of a runner. He learns the harsh reality of his physical and spiritual limitations when he runs. He learns that personal commitment, sacrifice and determination are his only means to betterment. (cited in Thurman, 2012, p. 113)

There is something archetypal about running and walking. The body and mind fuse in an ancient pattern of movement that embodies the pilgrimage, the quest, the search. Perhaps bipedal movement is so human, fundamental and avoidable that when it is exercised, it allows us to locate an atavistic inner harmony. Many myths and foundation stories involve pilgrimages or races: Atalanta and the great race; Pheidippides and the marathon; and the long wanderings of prophets and mystics in the desert (Moses, Jesus, John the Baptist, the Buddha, Mohammed, Saint Sebastian).

It would appear that running, walking or swimming, actions that put the body in cruising gear and allow for a gentle, pleasant amassing of thoughts and a healthy management of cognitive load, allow for better thought processing. Interestingly, two great modern Olympic champions, Michael Phelps (Wedge, 2012) and Usain Bolt (Mann, 2009) were diagnosed with hyperactivity as children, and one might see in their athletic excellence a response to the condition, allowing them to channel their thoughts into intensely experiencing the track or lane and focussing on the finish line.

Studies have established a negative correlation between physical exercise and cognitive decline (Kramer, Erickson, and Colcombe, 2006) and others a positive relationship between aerobic activities and cognitive processing (Fontana et al., 2009) and the positive effects of aerobic activity on memory.[7]

Many authors and philosophers have paid tribute to walking as a facilitator of reflective thought: Boccaccio and Chaucer have their tales told during pilgrimages, while Dante discusses the inferno with Virgil as he walks through its concentric circles. Many of Plato's dialogues take place during long walks outside the Megara, particularly in the *Phaedrus*. The relationship between travelling and literature has been consolidated in classics such as Kerouac's *On the Road* (1957) and Conrad's *Heart of Darkness* (1899). As a metaphor for life, perhaps because of the transitory

CHAPTER 1

nature of existence, the idea of a path, way, road, journey or voyage is recurrent. To move is to progress, to aspire for something else and, during this archetypal action, the mind is put at rest.

Of course, one should distinguish between the walk in the woods and the 100-meter dash, between the brisk mountain hike and the marathon, for these different types of movement elicit different types of ruminations. The walk is a ritual that allows for gentle conversation, reflection and brainstorming. Physically-challenging training, sprinting or running will bring more singular mental images, perhaps not thoughts at all but rather patterns used as markers from which the mind and body can push harder. Modern sports psychology encourages athletes to concentrate on simple recurrent images when kicking rugby penalties, serving in a tennis match or aiming for a higher bar in the pole vault.

Emile Zatopek, famous winner of the 5,000 metres, 10,000 metres and marathon at the 1952 Helsinki games, described running long distance in evocative ways, which can be accessed on the Internet. He said that running a marathon meant living a different type of life altogether, that he would run out of himself and that when he ran, his entire being was overcome by hopes and dreams. Zatopek's type of running, the type that leaves the athlete wrecked and empty, in which the body is pushed to its limit, trains the mind to home in on a few purified elements.

Zatopek, like Bolt, the Olympic athlete, represents not just the world of running, however, but more to the point for our purposes, the transcendence of self through excellence. When an individual is enthralled by the quest for a goal, when running takes on a world-class dimension characterised by thousands of hours of deliberate practice and focus (Ericsson, Krampe, and Tesch-Römer, 1993), we have a particularly impressive model of singleness of mind. Surely this type of challenge, whether in sports or some other domain, is an effective remedy for the listless mind.

Leaving world champions and examples of human achievement, we might next dwell on the modest and simple notion of the walk that allows for the mind to wander, itself a cognitive activity.

MIND WANDERING

Walking, jogging and other routine, lower-order cognitive activities allow the mind to ruminate and ideas to settle. Research points to the positive effect mind wandering can have on creative thinking and problem-solving.[8] To be clear, I'm not talking about staring aimlessly out the window, but about something routine like sketching, cleaning or walking that allows ideas to reformulate and settle.[9]

Historical anecdotes of "aha" moments that came to thinkers whilst they were involved in some other simple task include Newton's sitting under an apple tree at the Botanic Gardens in Cambridge, Archimedes' lying in his bath in Syracuse or Steve Jobs' and Mark Zuckerberg's insisting on having meetings while walking the streets of Palo Alto. Studies have drawn a correlation between "creative ideation" and walking.[10]

So while going for a walk outside might not be practical, and while not every day at school can be spent as the Scouts might use their time – pitching a tent, making a campfire or navigating the bush with a compass (although imagining such an education under the warm rays of the South American sun or in the emerald green of the Indian Ghats is pleasing), and while turning a school into an athletics academy is not often a realistic option (nor necessarily a desirable one, for while such a militaristic education might make some, it would no doubt break others), we should, surely, not be satisfied with the educational model that we have come to accept in which students spend endless hours sitting, listening, writing and shuffling from one buttock to the next to avoid pins and needles while they try to stay concentrated and wait for the bell to ring for lunch, a break or some freedom.

I would argue that outdoor education, regular field trips, well-developed extracurricular sports programmes and physical education pathways allowing for running are essential in a twenty-first century education, not only for the sake of mindfulness, but of mental and physical health too. Families, also, need to make sure that they get outdoors and go for walks so as to allow for gentle conversation and mindful thinking.

Mind wandering in the classroom can be achieved by other means, though. It is not inextricably linked to physical activity. A teacher can break up concentrated instruction and intersperse moments when the mind can gear down for a few minutes before its next spurt of concentration. Teachers should not be afraid to give students breaks.[11]

Furthermore, teachers should not be afraid to let moments of routine lower cognitive functioning prevail in the classroom, moments of "down time" for conversation, sketching, making or preparing. Parents should incorporate a similar message: overstimulating young people might create the illusion that a non-stop flow of cognitively challenging tasks is educating them in a deep, holistic sense, but the research suggests that in order to allow for ideas to recycle, some time should be given over to mind wandering.[12]

THE ARTS

While movement and off-task moments can bring peace of mind through controlled, focussed mind wandering and overall well-being, the arts allow for strong emotions on the one hand and a tranquil, unstressed mental state on the other, both potential remedies for the anxiety, lack of orientation and listlessness that plague the postmodern mind.

Historically, views on the arts have covered a wide spectrum. Plato's view was that, as a mere imitation of reality – reality itself being a distorted view of truth – art is weak, and as an appeal to irrational emotions, ultimately pernicious. Aristotle's position on art was that it could create catharsis, a purging of the individual's or group's conscience through the medium of strong emotions. This idea has not left us and is still validated by study and research, some of it going so far as to show that art is a form of therapy.[13] Tolstoy's (1898) position was that art heightens empathy. More contemporary philosophers, on the other hand, such as De Botton and Armstrong (2013), believe that art allows humans to compensate for natural weaknesses through a sublime medium. We should differentiate here between the consumption of works of art as a reader or spectator and engagement with the arts as a practising artist.

To appreciate a great work of art is to direct the mind towards something captivating and attention-shaping. This can be done in a number of ways: By a novel that one reads slowly, enthralled, the way one is pulled into Dostoevsky's dark entrails, Jane Austen's nine inches of ivory, Joyce's labyrinth of psychology or Coetzee's bleak, bizarre aesthetic. By poems one savours while appreciating a luscious, sense-filled reading, listening to the drip and ooze of Keats, the froth and mud of Heaney or the delicate conceit of Donne. By a marvellous painting that draws the spectator into its vortex of meaning and composition as one is drawn into the power of Grunewald's triptych in Colmar, Michelangelo's *Last Judgement* in the Vatican or Vermeer's *Milkmaid* in the Rijks in Amsterdam. By music that transports the listener to distant peaks and larger-than-life valleys, the way Wagner wrenches you through emotional space as if you are attached to a soaring eagle or Mozart connects each logically constructed element of harmony in a perfect palace of crystal, or Tchaikovsky draws out strong emotional climaxes in a river of brooding. All these types of art take the mind and sensibility to a higher place.

Art can also move the appreciator to a previously unknown culture, place and period. Someone who knows nothing of the Pakistani Sufi tradition will learn through the timeless incantations of Nusrat Fateh Ali Kahn; the lover of art ignorant of West African art will be transported to the deserts of Mali through Dogon masks; while Noh theatre can teach the spectator about Japanese culture. With its pedagogical and cathartic functions, art is such a potentially powerful medium that it can absorb the appreciator entirely and transport her to another place and time. This transcendent quality of art focusses not only the attention and perspective of the audience but also its emotions and values.

Parents need to take their children to appreciate great works of art, whether to art galleries, museums, musical concerts, operas, ballets, plays, films or architecture.

Most compulsory curricula across the globe contain little in the way of art history. Poland puts considerable emphasis on it, but few other examples come to mind.

Whilst the appreciation of art has its benefits, practising art puts the learner in a different set of circumstances. Concentration, challenge and singleness of purpose unite to transport the mind to a higher level of expression. Learning to align thoughts with medium, to produce a clear note, technical brushstroke or a mesmerising stage soliloquy – all encompass what some might call "mindfulness". Research has shown that the serious practice of an art has a ripple effect on concentration and on mental agility in general.[14]

It seems that artistic activity has defined humanity since its earliest traceable origins, in the form of cave paintings and instruments, as if the need to express ourselves through a medium, to reproduce the sounds, colours and images of the world around us were deep in our archetypal identity from the start. Art, whether functional, political, social, ritualistic, religious or even, as Oscar Wilde said, "for art's sake", holds a sacred place in the human psyche.

And yet, while primary schooling is punctuated by much drawing, music and theatre, these activities wane as students grow older, until they are mere options – and not frequently chosen at that – competing with so-called hard subjects, like business, mathematics and sciences. The problem is, as we all know, the relatively second-class place arts subject areas occupy in school curricula.[15]

There is no shortage of voices to advocate for the arts in schools (see, for example, Merritt, 2016), not necessarily because of the transcendent meaning that art can give to one's life, but because of the potential for the arts to stimulate competences recognised in the marketplace. However, the reality is that there is a decline in the arts worldwide when it comes to schooling, despite some efforts to incorporate some of the arts in other subjects.

No matter the amount of New Age pro-arts discourse (on creativity, entrepreneurship, confidence, problem-solving, why creativity is essential to industry, why so many industries of the future will be related to the arts in some way and so on), the deeper reasons for engaging in the arts at school are related to less popular, spiritual themes, such as those evoked in 2006 by novelist Kurt Vonnegut, who wrote to children in a US high school:

> Practice any art, music, singing, dancing, acting, drawing, painting, sculpting, poetry, fiction, essays, reportage, no matter how well or badly, not to get money and fame, but to experience becoming, to find out what's inside you, to make your soul grow. (Klein, 2014)

But in the Western world the word *soul* has little currency. Perhaps we will never achieve peace of mind or "mindfulness" if our society's goals are consistently material and practical.

And schools are not the only places students practise the arts. Parents should continue to support exposure to the arts for their children, not just to try to turn them into great artists one day, but for the development of creative, controlled and mindful thinking.

SCHOOLS AND THE ARTS

Whether sports and the arts have enough research behind them as antidotes to hyperactivity and anxiety can be discussed (researched evidence is never 100% reliable and valid, anyway), but common sense and lived experience suggest they might bring some calm to the young in the present age.

It seems difficult to imagine a school that allows for an hour or more of moderate-to-vigorous physical education per day. Even if this were possible, how likely would it be that such instruction would be delivered in a manner to enhance concentration and mind focus?

CHAPTER 1

Were the arts to play a sufficient role in the curriculum, one problem is a convention that the arts should be divided into three areas of specialisation (dramatic, musical and visual) to squeeze into the curriculum. What often happens is either a rotation in which students receive adequate instruction (for example, three hours a week) in one area but for only a third of the year, making this learning experience short-lived, or the arts allocation will be split among the three subjects, meaning that students receive something along the lines of one hour's instruction for each per week, simply not enough to consolidate any serious level of learning.

Nor can we say that by increasing sports and arts we could expect immediate results. Style and intensity of a learning experience as much as frequency will influence students' mental health and offer opportunities for peace of mind.

THREE POINTS

I reiterate three points to take into consideration: disconnect; arts and sports; mind wandering.

Disconnect

For young people to learn how to appreciate the here and now, for them to know how to disconnect from the hyperactivity-inducing world of screens, schools and parents must craft into each day moments of silence, reflection, reading (off-screen), discussion and productive social interaction. These measures might seem obvious, but with an increased exposure to screens, students' bringing hand-held devices into school, more on-line, on-screen learning in the classroom and the extraordinary surge of technology in day-to-day life, schools and parents must provide a supplement to this mode so that young people break away from screen time when at school and at home.

Arts and Sports

Human society has seen extraordinary levels of achievement through such rigorous institutions as the music conservatory and the academy. The simple idea behind these constructs has been that each individual surpass current levels of competence and productivity by means hours of training and intense instruction with a focus on concentration and unashamed excellence. For some reason, even though sports and arts coaching practices are often held up as pedagogic models, their hallmark intensity and striving for excellence feel politically incorrect in a world in which sports and arts are approached in an easy-going manner, insufficiently represented in the curriculum and treated as respite from harder, more exacting academic subjects, particularly STEM. Dumbing down teaching of the arts (turning them into a social club; not teaching instruments in the classroom but rather offering general, watered-down music appreciation) and of sports (embracing an anti-elitist, lowest-common-denominator, anti-competition ideology and thereby losing the gifted athletes in the class) holds the danger that students are not exposed to some elements of discipline, excellence and intensity – not learning skills for gaining focus and tranquillity. Serious, rigorous, high-quality sports and art should be part of any young person's life. (A note of caution is not to err on the side of obsession.)

Mind Wandering

Schools should not be afraid to let students take their time, or engage in non-demanding rituals and tasks that are simple enough and routine enough to allow the mind to process ideas while they are going on. This does not mean that learning should not be challenging. It means that times of intensity should be broken up by moments that are calmer. An overstimulated classroom or home will not allow for productive learning and calmness of spirit. The mind needs varied cadences in order to breathe and find some rhythm. To come back to the legendary Emile Zatopek, his invention of interval training (bursts of sprinting followed by jogging) reminds us that there should be variation in learning, and peace of mind. So let's not clamp down on conversations between young people, moments of controlled reflection and the simpler things that still give school its original meaning (from the ancient Greek *skholé*, meaning "leisure" and "free time"), provided that these moments are enjoyed in a balanced manner and do not take over the entire spirit of learning.

I should make clear that schools alone cannot produce more "mindful" individuals. The task must be taken on at more than one level. Parents and families need to ensure that children (and themselves) are sufficiently disconnected from the Internet, are spending quality time together doing such simple, age-old things as going for walks, listening to music in silence and drawing, and perhaps the curriculum needs to be supplemented by extracurricular sports and art activities that parents organise.

Nor can any isolated strategy be seen as *the* remedy, or panacea. A global perspective of health sees it as covering the physical, mental and moral states of an individual. The World Health Organisation says, "Ill health or disease is brought about by an imbalance, or disequilibrium, of man in his total ecological system and not only by the causative agent and pathogenic evolution" (WHO, 1978). Education in the broadest sense needs to create a balanced life, with a bit of everything.

JACOBO AGAIN

Back to the student I mentioned earlier, Jacobo. His tutor and specialists discussed him in a class review. As usual, they suggested keeping him focussed. Teachers were asked to have him sit at the front of the class and have all his lesson materials with him. He was given extra pep talks. On a "report card", his tutor signed off daily that he had behaved well that day.

These measures did little. Jacobo continued to be naughty, but in such a way that he was more or less below the radar and therefore out of trouble. But he remained

CHAPTER 1

what many would call hyperactive, often involved in disruptive behaviour. His parents, articulate, reflective and supportive people, were at their wits' end. Jacobo spent a lot of time on social media at home, but merely because his parents were not able to monitor his every Web search and computer click. He was kept off Ritalin.

But over time, Jacobo started to calm down. As he entered the senior years and started reading more serious literature, became involved in our strong arts programme and dedicated more and more time to track and field, he grew into a young man who was lively and humorous but not excitable. Although I cannot prove it scientifically, I believe strongly that the education he received at our school, one that developed the creative and physical side of each student, through time and with a slowing down of life (for instance, we placed a restriction on cell phones), helped him in the process. With healthy activities and a bit of partial patience, mountains could be moved.

CONCLUSION

It's getting late, and the setting sun cuts across the wheat field in gilded, diagonal shards of light. In the soft breeze, these lucent beams swell and sway as though alive, as though an energy or living spirit causes them to dance.

My cell phone receives a message, convulsing for a second on the oak coffee table. I'll see later who wrote. Perhaps I should turn it off altogether. But then again, I am expected to remain connected. It would not be looked upon favourably if I "could not be reached", was "difficult to get hold of" or – worse – was "not answering my e-mails".

The ancient Greeks spoke of the *eudaimonia*, meaning "the good life, a life dedicated to truth, goodness and beauty". They also spoke of *sophrosyne*, meaning "excellence of character", leading to, and coming from, associated virtues of wisdom and piety. What lies at its core? What belief, practice or strategy can bring humanity to this model, this dream? Perhaps all this talk of mindfulness, of art and sports, of tuning in and tuning out – perhaps all this is missing the point? Perhaps there is a simpler answer?

At a distance I hear the village bell sound six times. I move lazily to the glass sliding door and open it, letting the warmth, singing of cicadas and sweet scent of lavender and dried laurel pervade the room. I step out into the arms of the universe and take a deep breath, closing my eyes. When I open them again, it is all still there, the wheat swaying dreamily to the summer afternoon, the iridescent sun shimmering above and the wise silence of the world moving through every element in sight. I feel at one with my surroundings, at peace with myself and ready for a long, slow walk.

NOTES

[1] See Layard and Clark (2014). To add to this, the US National Institute of Mental Health (NIMH, 2016) reports that 46% of children between 13 and 18 are susceptible to "lifetime prevalence" – meaning they are at risk.
[2] See Cassani Davis (2015) such as the *dot b* mindfulness in schools programme (MISP, 2016).

[3] The UK-based Mindfulness All-Party Parliamentary Group (MAPPG) released a 2015 report called "Mindful Nation UK", which describes an "explosion" of interest, "more than 500 peer-reviewed scientific journal papers now being published every year" on the subject (p. 7). The paper refers to a plethora of studies, including meta-analyses (such as Zoogman, Goldberg, Hoyt, and Miller, 2014) that suggest that mindfulness enhances executive functioning (essentially problem-solving, higher-order thinking and working memory). These studies all have weaknesses in their methodological approaches to the question: Huppert and Johnson's 2010 study is a controlled trial but not randomised and attempts to measure the impact of instruction across students with multiple teachers. Diamond and Lee (2011), on the other hand, discuss studies using double-blind, randomised-control trials – so a rigorous methodology – but find little clear value added in these trials' results. The study points to tae-kwan-do, yoga and mindfulness as increasing executive functioning in students but produces the modest, tentative conclusion that "exercise alone may not be as efficacious in improving EFs [executive functioning] as exercise-plus-character-development (traditional martial arts...) or exercise-plus-mindfulness". Whilst the MAPPG allows for the sobering admission that "the current popularity of mindfulness is running ahead of the research evidence in some areas" (2015, p. 5) and in academic fashion warns that there are gaps in the research, it nonetheless enthusiastically advocates the practice throughout the report, singing its praises in the name of such feel-good twenty-first century jargon such as "emotional buoyancy" (p. 31), "coping skills" (p. 31), "social and emotional skills" (p. 30), "grit" (p. 29) and "well-being" (p. 33). It goes on to recommend that a grant of one million pounds be disseminated to schools training teachers in mindfulness (p. 8) and promotes so-called mindful parenting programmes, which apparently can "reduce parents' destructive behaviour" and "enhance their emotional availability" (p. 32).

[4] André Malraux once said that the twenty-first century would be spiritual or would not be and the idea the West might find some metaphysical response to its materialist trappings in the East has been promulgated by a great many thinkers and philosophers.

[5] Zhou et al. (2011) and Weng et al. (2013) have shown that excessive Internet surfing and gaming can lead to grey-matter shrinkage; Hong et al. (2013) and Yuan et al. (2013) found that teenage boys addicted to gaming performed poorly on a cognitive task, suggesting cortical thinning; and Dong, Devito, Du, and Cui (2012) established generally poor cognitive functioning due to Internet addiction. It should be noted that there are methodological shortcomings in these studies: Zhou et al. used a small sample (18 participants), and rather than running double-blind, randomised, controlled trials opted for matching; and Hong et al. used only 12 participants.

[6] Stamatakis, Hamer, and Dunstan (2011) sampled over 4500 Scottish participants to find (with a confidence interval of 95%) that "recreational sitting" raises the likelihood of cardiovascular disease. Mark and Janssen (2008) used a sample of over 1800 American adolescents to find – again, with a high confidence level of 95% – an increased likelihood of high blood pressure, high cholesterol and high waist circumference from high levels of screen time. We could also mention computer-vision syndrome or so-called digital eyestrain as a negative side effect of excessive screen time (AOA, 2016).

[7] Such as Lambourne and Tomporowski's 2010 metastudy.

[8] Mooneyham and Schooler (2013) reviewed the effects of mind wandering on different aspects of cognitive performance and found that whilst much has been written and studied on the pernicious effects of mind wandering on traditional cognitive domains, such as reading and aptitude tests, more recent research indicates the contrary. Singer and Antrobus (1963) opposed "fantastic, emotional, variegated, anxious, and pleasant" mind wandering (the stare-out-the-window-during-class type) to a more purposeful and focussed mind wandering that is "clearly problem-solving, objective [and] nonpersonal" (Mooneyham and Schooler, 2013, p. 14), namely, the type of daydreaming that is focussed on a subject, the type one might engage in that would involve ruminating on a single thought in various shades and hues and from different, perhaps novel, perspectives whilst involved in a non-demanding lower-order cognitive task.

[9] Seli, Risko, and Smilek (2016) point out that not all mind wandering is of the same nature or has the same effects on cognition and concentration: deliberate mind wandering as a technique to harness concentration allows for sharper results whereas common off-task daydreaming with no particular

CHAPTER 1

goal or purpose is less effective and can, of course, be counterproductive. Understanding the need for mind-wandering moments but ensuring that the conditions for these are appropriate is an informed, metacognitive approach to the question.

[10] In fact, a Stanford University study by Oppezzo and Schwartz (2014) found that walking boosts "creative ideation" with fairly strong results in four different experiments, although the authors were unable to establish whether it was the distinctly physical nature of walking that had an effect on creativity or more generally the engagement in a non-demanding routine task that allowed for productive mind wandering.

[11] In an article on mind wandering containing much discussion using prominent research findings, Szpunar, Moulton, and Schacter (2013) recommend the following pedagogic practices to ensure a mindful approach to learning that favours retention and efficacy: "interspersing periods of instruction with low-stakes quizzing", mixing up the content of lectures and "spacing study over multiple learning sessions".

[12] Mooneyham and Schooler (2013, p.15) suggest that mind wandering has the following positive effects on thinking: (1) attentional cycling (processing alternate streams of thought such as "current sensory environment, prospective planning information, remembered experiences"; (2) dishabituation (some time away from the task at hand to allow thinking to be freed from the specific, perhaps constraining confines of the task itself); (3) relief from boredom (we should not underestimate the corrosive effect of in-school boredom on thinking and being).

[13] Whilst theorists such as Aristotle, Vygotsky (1925, published 1971) and Lipps (1914) see the consumption of art as something that can heighten empathy and allow the individual to purge psycho-emotional points of tension, more recent theory and research on the act of creating art has suggested that it can have therapeutic benefits (see Malchiodi, 2008). Art as therapy has been much studied. Stuckey and Nobel (2010) investigated the relationship between different types of art and health therapy and found positive results, that the arts "decrease anxiety, stress, and mood disturbances" but admitted that the results are not strong enough to generalise with confidence.

[14] In a 2009 summit on neuroeducation at Johns Hopkins University, over 300 researchers agreed that there were "'tight correlations' between arts training and improvements in cognition, attention, and learning" (Rich and Goldberg, 2009, p. 3). Hallam (2010) has shown how active engagement with music improves cognition:

> Research on Western classical musicians has shown that long years of active engagement with particular musical activities are associated with an increase in neuronal representation specific for the processing of the tones of the musical scale, the largest cortical representations found in musicians playing instruments for the longest periods of time. (p. 270)

Her study also establishes fairly confident correlations between self-esteem, social and personal development and active music learning (p. 278).

[15] The Warwick Commission came up with the following statistics for the UK in 2014:

> There are…worrying trends towards a decrease in participation by children in most cultural activities…: between the years 2008/9 and 2013/14, the proportion of 5–10 year olds who engaged in dance activities dropped from 43.1% to 30.4%; participation in music activities dropped from 55.3% to 37.2%; participation in theatre and drama activities dropped from 47.1% to 32.1%; arts and crafts activities dropped from 80% participation to 75.7%.

> The only significant increase in participation was in the area of film or video activities, which grew from 49% to 71.1%, confirming that digital technologies offer a potential for enhancing participation and developing new ideas and forms of personal cultural expression that ought to be capitalised upon. (Warwick Commission, 2015, p. 34)

In the United States, a 2012 survey issued to over 1000 randomly assigned public school teachers by the Farkass Dufett Reasearch Group and the Common Core saw 51% of interviewed teachers report that they saw a decline in the arts as curriculum becomes increasingly narrowed towards mathematics and the sciences (Common Core, 2012). A 2008 survey showed that between 1982 and 2008, the percentage of African Americans and Hispanics between 18 and 24 who reported having received an arts education had dropped dramatically from around 50% to around 27% (Rabkin and Hedberg, 2011, p. 16).

REFERENCES

Anderson, N. D., Lau, M. A., Segal, Z. V., & Bishop, S. R. (2007). Mindfulness-based stress reduction and attentional control. *Clinical Psychology and Psychotherapy, 14*, 449–463. doi:10.1002/cpp.544

AOA [American Optometric Association] (2016). *Computer vision syndrome.* http://www.aoa.org/patients-and-public/caring-for-your-vision/protecting-your-vision/computer-vision-syndrome?sso=y

Biegel, G. M., Brown, K. W., Shapiro, S. L., & Schubert, C. M. (2009). Mindfulness-based stress reduction for the treatment of adolescent psychiatric outpatients: A randomized clinical trial. *Journal of Consulting and Clinical Psychology, 77*, 855–866.

Cassani-Davis, J. (2015, August 31). When mindfulness meets the classroom. *The Atlantic.* http://www.theatlantic.com/education/archive/2015/08/mindfulness-education-schools-meditation/402469/

Common Core (2012). *Learning less: Public school teachers describe a narrowing curriculum.* http://greatminds.net/maps/documents/reports/CommonCore-FDR-CompleteFindings-111208.pdf

Common Sense Media (2015). *Landmark report: U.S. teens use an average of nine hours of media per day, tweens use six hours.* San Francisco, CA: Common Sense Media. https://www.commonsensemedia.org/about-us/news/press-releases/landmark-report-us-teens-use-an-average-of-nine-hours-of-media-per-day

De Botton, A., & Armstrong, J. (2013). *Art as therapy.* London: Phaidon.

Diamond, A., & Lee, K. (2011). Interventions shown to aid executive function development in children 4 to 12 years old. *Science, 333*(6045), 959–964.

Dong, G., Devito, E. D., Du, X., & Cui, Z. (2012). Impaired inhibitory control in 'internet addiction disorder': A functional magnetic resonance imaging study. *Psychiatry Research, 203*(2–3), 153–158. doi:10.1016/j.pscychresns.2012.02.001

Eichenbaum, A. E., Bavelier, D., & Green, C. S. (2014). Video games: Play that can do serious good. *American Journal of Play, 7*, 50–72.

Ericsson, K. A., Krampe, R. T., & Tesch-Römer, C. (1993). The role of deliberate practice in the acquisition of expert performance. *Psychological Review, 100*(3), 363–406. http://projects.ict.usc.edu/itw/gel/EricssonDeliberatePracticePR93.pdf

Flook, L., Smalley, S. L., Kitil, M. J., Galla, B. M., Kaiser-Greenland, S., Locke. J., Ishijima, E., & Kasari, C. (2010). Effects of mindful awareness practices on executive functions in elementary school children. *Journal of Applied School Psychology, 26*(1), 70–95.

Fontana, F. E., Mazzardo, O., Mokgothu, C., Furtado, O., & Gallagher, J. D. (2009). Influence of exercise intensity on the decision-making performance of experienced and inexperienced soccer players. *Journal of Sport & Exercise Psychology, 31*(2), 135–151.

Franceschini, S., Gori, S., Ruffino, M., Viola, S., Molteni, M., & Facoetti, A. (2013). Action video games make dyslexic children read better. *Current Biology, 23*, 462–66.

Hallam, S. (2010). The power of music: Its impact on the intellectual, social and personal development of children and young people. *International Journal of Music Education, 28*(3), 269–289. http://ijm.sagepub.com/content/28/3/269.full.pdf+html

Hong, S.-B., Zalesky, A., Cocchi, L., Fornito, A., Choi, E. J., Kim, H.-H., Suh, J.-E., Kim, C.-D., Kim, J.-W., & Yi, S.-H. (2013). Decreased functional brain connectivity in adolescents with Internet addiction. *PLoS ONE, 8*(2), e57831. doi:10.1371/journal.pone.0057831

Huppert, F. A., & Johnson, D. M. (2010). A controlled trial of mindfulness training in schools: The importance of practice for an impact on wellbeing. *The Journal of Positive Psychology, 5*(4), 264–274.

Kabat-Zinn, J. (2003). Mindfulness-based interventions in context: Past, present, and future. *Clinical Psychology: Science and Practice, 10*(2), 144–156.

Klein, R. (2014). Kurt Vonnegut once sent this amazing letter to a high school. *Huffington Post.* http://www.huffingtonpost.com/2014/03/14/kurt-vonnegut-xavier-letter_n_4964532.html

CHAPTER 1

Kramer, A. F., Erickson, K. I., & Colcombe, S. J. (2006). Exercise, cognition, and the aging brain. *Journal of Applied Physiology, 101*, 1237–1242. doi:10.1152/japplphysiol.00500.2006

Lambourne, K., & Tomporowski, P. (2010). The effect of exercise-induced arousal on cognitive task performance: A meta-regression analysis. *Brain Research, 1341*, 12–24. doi:10.1016/j.brainres.2010.03.091

Layard, R., & Clark, D. (2014). *Thrive: The power of evidence-based psychological therapies*. London: Penguin Books.

Lipps, T. (1914). *Aesthetik: Psychologie des Schoenen und der Kunst: Grundlegung der Ästhetik* (Vol. 1). Leipzig/Hamburg: Voss.

Malchiodi, C. (2008). Drawing on the effort-driven rewards circuit to chase the blues away. *Psychology Today*. https://www.psychologytoday.com/blog/arts-and-health/200808/drawing-the-effort-driven-rewards-circuit-chase-the-blues-away

Mann, L. (2009). What makes Usain Bolt tick? *BBC*. http://news.bbc.co.uk/sport2/hi/athletics/8049584.stm

MAPPG [Mindfulness All-Party Parliamentary Group] (2015). *Mindful nation UK*. http://www.oxfordmindfulness.org/wp-content/uploads/mindfulness-appg-report_mindful-nation-uk_oct2015-002.pdf

Mark, A. E., & Janssen, I. (2008). Relationship between screen time and metabolic syndrome in adolescents. *Journal of Public Health, 30*(2), 153–160. doi:10.1093/pubmed/fdn022

McGinn, D. (2014). Why kids over 5 aren't doing enough physically. *The Globe and Mail*. http://www.theglobeandmail.com/life/health-and-fitness/health/why-kids-over-5-arent-doing-enough-physically/article18770171/

McGuire, P. (2014). PE in schools: Are we all doing enough? *The Irish Times*. http://www.irishtimes.com/life-and-style/health-family/pe-in-schools-are-we-all-doing-enough-1.1907614

Merritt, S. (2016). Squeezing out arts for more 'useful' subjects will impoverish us all. *The Guardian*. https://www.theguardian.com/commentisfree/2016/jun/25/squeezing-out-arts-for-commercially-useful-subjects-will-make-our-culture-poorer

MISP [Mindfulness in Schools Project] (2016). What is .b curriculum. https://mindfulnessinschools.org/what-is-b/

Mooneyham, B. W., & Schooler, J. W. (2013). The costs and benefits of mind-wandering: A review. *Canadian Journal of Experimental Psychology, 67*(1), 11–18.

Nakamura, J., & Ciskszentmihayli, M. (2002). The concept of flow. In S. J. Lopez & R. Snyder (Eds.), *The Oxford handbook of positive psychology*. Oxford: Oxford University Press.

NIMH [National Institute of Mental Health] (2016). Statistics. https://www.nimh.nih.gov/health/statistics/index.shtml

Oppezzo, M., & Schwartz, D. L. (2014). Give your ideas some legs: The positive effect of walking on creative thinking. *Journal of Experimental Psychology: Learning, Memory, and Cognition, 40*(4), 1142–1152.

Rabkin, N., & Hebgerg, E. C. (2011). *Arts education in America: What the declines mean for arts participation*. Washington, DC: National Endowment for the Arts. https://www.arts.gov/sites/default/files/2008-SPPA-ArtsLearning.pdf

Rich, B. R., & Goldberg, J. (Eds.) (2009). *Neuroeducation: Learning, arts and the brain: Findings and challenges for educators and researchers from the 2009 Johns Hopkins University summit*. New York, NY: Dana Press. http://steam-notstem.com/wp-content/uploads/2010/11/Neuroeducation.pdf

Romano, M., Osborne, L. A., Truzoli, R., & Reed, P. (2013). Differential psychological impact of internet exposure on internet addicts. *PLoS ONE, 8*(2), e55162. doi:10.1371/journal.pone.0055162

Sanger, K. L., & Dorjee, D. (2015). Mindfulness training for adolescents: A neurodevelopmental perspective on investigating modifications in attention and emotion regulation using event-related brain potentials. *Cognitive, Affective, & Behavioral Neuroscience, 15*(3), 696–711.

Seli, P., Risko, E. F., & Smilek, D. (2016). On the necessity of distinguishing between unintentional and intentional mind wandering. *Psychological Science, 27*(5), 685–691.

Singer, J. L., & Antrobus, J. S. (1963). A factor-analytic study of daydreaming and conceptually- related cognitive and personality variables [Monograph Supplement 3-V17]. *Perceptual and Motor Skills, 17*, 187–209. doi:10.2466/pms.1963.17.1.187

Stamatakis, E., Hamer, M., & Dunstan, D. W. (2011). Screen-based entertainment time, all-cause mortality, and cardiovascular events: Population-based study with ongoing mortality and hospital events follow-up. *Journal of the American College of Cardiology, 57*(3), 292–299. doi:10.1016/j.jacc.2010.05.065

Stuckey, H. L., & Nobel, J. (2010). The connection between art, healing, and public health: A review of current literature. *American Journal of Public Health, 100*(2), 254–263. http://doi.org/10.2105/AJPH.2008.156497

Szpunar, K. K., Moulton, S. T., & Schacter, D. L. (2013). Mind wandering and education: From the classroom to online learning. *Frontiers in Psychology, 4*, 495. http://doi.org/10.3389/fpsyg.2013.00495 https://www.ncbi.nlm.nih.gov/pmc/articles/PMC3730052/

Thurman, R. L. (2012). *One more step – The 638 best quotes for the runner: Motivation for the next step*. Bloomington, IN: iUniverse.

Tolstoy, L. (1898). *What is art?* London: Bloomsbury.

Triggle, N. (2013). Children need more exercise: Especially girls, study says. *BBC*. http://www.bbc.com/news/health-23778945

Vygotsky, L. S. (1925/1971). *The psychology of art*. Cambridge, MA: MIT Press. http://www.marxists.org/archive/vygotsky/works/1925/index.htm

Wallace, K. (2016). How to make your kid hate sports without really trying. *CNN*. http://edition.cnn.com/2016/01/21/health/kids-youth-sports-parents/

Warwick Commission (2015). *Enriching Britain: Culture, creativity and growth*. Warwick: University of Warwick. http://www2.warwick.ac.uk/research/warwickcommission/futureculture/finalreport/warwick_commission_final_report.pdf

Wedge, S. (2012). From ADHD kid to Olympic gold medalist. *Psychology Today*. https://www.psychologytoday.com/blog/suffer-the-children/201209/adhd-kid-olympic-gold-medalist

Weng, C.-B., Ruo-Bing, Q., Xian-Ming, F., Bin, L., Xiao-Peng, H., Chao-Shi, N., & Ye-Han, W. (2013). Gray matter and white matter abnormalities in online game addiction. *European Journal of Radiology, 82*(8), 1308–1312. doi:10.1016/j.ejrad.2013.01.031

WHO [World Health Organisation] (1978). *Traditional medicine: Proposed programme budget for the financial period 1981*. Geneva: WHO.

WHO (2016). *Global strategy on diet, physical activity and health*. Geneva: WHO. http://www.who.int/dietphysicalactivity/factsheet_young_people/en/

Woods, J. (2014). Why does the government want to teach mindfulness in schools? *The Telegraph*. http://www.telegraph.co.uk/lifestyle/wellbeing/10694775/Why-does-the-Government-want-to-teach-mindfulness-in-schools.html

Yuan, K., Cheng, P., Dong, T., Bi, Y., Xing, L., Yu, D., Zhao, L., Dong, M., von Deneen, K. M., Liu, Y., Qin, W., & Tian, J. (2013). Cortical thickness abnormalities in late adolescence with online gaming addiction. *PLoS ONE, 8*(1), e53055. doi:10.1371/journal.pone.0053055

Zhou, Y., Fu-Chun, L., Ya-Song, D., Ling-di, Q., Zhi-Min, Z., Jian-Rong, X., & Hao, L. (2011). Gray matter abnormalities in internet addiction: A voxel-based morphometry study. *European Journal of Radiology, 79*(1), 92–95. doi:10.1016/j.ejrad.2009.10.025

Zoogman, S., Goldberg, S. B., Hoyt, W. T., & Miller, L. (2014). Mindfulness interventions with youth: A meta-analysis. *Mindfulness, 6*(2), 290–302.

CHAPTER 2

SINGULARITY

I'm in a workshop on education. The presenter, a pock-marked, silver-haired Australian academic, wearing an oversized grey suit and a tie of brown and orange squares interwoven with an early 1990s computerised motif, stammers his way through his presentation of his research, his books and his vision, pointing the PowerPoint clicker's red laser dot shakily at the screen, where his tables and diagrams gently and barely perceptibly buzz in their pixelated materialisation.

Participants photograph each screen with their iPhones, Samsung Galaxies or iPads. At one point he says that the presentation will be shared with us via Dropbox. People ignore the message and continue to photograph the presentation slides. A third of the audience are not really listening, frowns of concentration directed onto the pale light emanating from phones hidden in their laps or under the table. Four who sit next to one another display quasi-identical postures and almost the exact same expressions, as if answering e-mails brings about a universal body language and expression; as if for a moment they are absorbed by something bigger than them, some spirit or universal biological mechanism.

To my left, a bald, middle-aged, pink man in a green polo-neck shirt plays Sudoku on his phone with embarrassing ostentation. He squints in concentration as he deliberately presses keys. To my right, a young woman in black with translucent pale skin, cropped red hair, a green tattoo of a Mobius knot under her left studded ear and thick plastic-rimmed designer spectacles, works on her own PowerPoint presentation on her laptop. Every once in a while, she shifts her gaze to the speaker, as if to absorb a bite of information. Then she returns to her own work. She must be "multitasking".

The presenter drones on, "The jobs of the future do not yet exist, and many that currently exist will become automated". "In a post-industrial, technologically advanced economy", he tells us, "we have to teach competences that cannot be outsourced to machines". "As knowledge can be accessed by anyone off the Internet, how much do we have to actually know?" Around the room I see a different category of people: those not taking photos or sending e-mails but typing fast on their devices. They seem to be rushing to note each of the speaker's words before the slide disappears. "By 2030", he says; "by 2045", "by 2050", "the next generation", "our generation", "our parents' generation". He talks of Z and X generations, of digital natives and so on. He tells us that computers are catching up with human beings, that they already have superior processing power and that they will soon be

© JOINTLY BY IBE-UNESCO AND KONINKLIJKE BRILL NV, LEIDEN, 2018
DOI:10.1163/9789004381032_002

CHAPTER 2

able to simulate non-algorithmic functions such as inference-drawing, guesswork, synthesising and analysing. "Prostate cancer diagnosis is more reliable with artificial intelligence", he says. "Automated cars have far fewer accidents than do humans". He shows a slide with a giant human brain next to a computer. The audience seems unperturbed, each wedded to a device.

I ask myself what the participants will do with all this information. Will they store their notes on their desktops and read them later? Or will they save them in folders that will later be stored in other folders and eventually deleted? And what about the photographs? Will they be archived and read again? Or left there until one day the memory of the machine is at capacity and they have to be deleted? Then again, if it is all in the cloud, will that day of maximum memory ever come? Or is the cloud infinite? Will the cloud ever burst into an endless shower of cyber shrapnel, a torrent of words, numbers, graphics, logos, sounds that cascade out of the ether and litter the earth with broken, useless data? Or, even more disturbing, perhaps it will all be "lost", disappear as though sucked into a black hole or whisked off to a remote, unnavigable part of the universe?

As I have these idle thoughts, I take notes on a Google spreadsheet to which another colleague is adding notes at the same time. His notes are different in tenor and style to mine. I'm not sure I agree with the way he is synthesising the information, and I wonder what he thinks of my notes. We are trying to create a collective statement. We are trying to collaborate, because we are told that collaboration is an important twenty-first century skill. In fact, the presenter says something about collaborative problem-solving as I have the thought; or maybe he said it first and then I had the thought. We will later share this spreadsheet with other colleagues back at work, assuming, of course, they will read it. Perhaps they will download it onto their devices and read it later. Or perhaps they will star the e-mail I send with the link to the notes and forget to read it. They might also delete the e-mail without reading it at all. It occurs to me that the presentation we are watching seems to be made up almost entirely of screenshots and images copied from the Web, almost as if we were merely running to keep up with the spinning of a giant treadmill coming from the Web and going back into it, without any of our own ideas actually driving the process – pushed along by the terrifying energy flowing out of a vast collective swamp of information belonging to everyone and no one. For a second, in my mind's eye I see a caged hamster aimlessly racing on a wheel, and as I have this thought, I imagine that what triggered it was the pitter-patter of fingers on keyboards all around me, which resembled the soft sound of hamsters' paw steps.

I look about me once more. Only one man, an elderly professorial type, whose thick grey beard contrasts with his olive skin, seems to be listening without any device. He takes notes on a piece of paper, "ums" and "ahs", winces a little as though judging the information he hears and sees.

Just before the coffee break the presenter shows a slide filled with website URLs, links to YouTube videos and technology-provider logos. He is "sharing resources" with us. The person on my right reduces her own PowerPoint and googles one of the

SINGULARITY

"resources". The web page she arrives at is a brightly-coloured smorgasbord of graphs, statistics in giant, childish font, video insets, futurist quotes and links to other websites. Perhaps those websites contain links to other websites, and those to others still. Are we in Borges' circular ruins? Or perhaps this is merely one representation of the endlessly cyclical and associative nature of knowledge in general. Perhaps this is what happens in a library when conducting old-fashioned, "pre-X-generation" research anyway: references pointing to other references, pointing to others and so on.

At the coffee break, many participants whip out their phones and fuss over their screens, presumably browsing through text messages and e-mails. I notice three people standing in a circle, each looking at their screens, not communicating with each other. Once I've checked to see if any e-mails have arrived, I have a cup of insipid coffee and find myself in conversation with a colleague, who shows me a web page breaking the news that Bob Dylan has just been awarded the Nobel Prize for literature. We discuss whether he should have won it. I defend the choice but cannot remember the exact turns of phrase in songs I think are good, such as "Hey, Mr. Tambourine Man", "Gates of Eden" or "It's All Right Ma, I'm Only Bleeding", so I Google them and read them off my screen. Someone states a bold fact about past Nobel Prize winners, including a claim that Tolstoy never won it. I'm not convinced; so I Google that too, while he chatters with mouthfuls of croissant. It appears he is right. At the end of the conversation, I shuffle off to another part of the conference venue to a coffee machine I'd noticed. I slot my coin in, and out whirrs a capsule for me to place in the machine's chrome-lipped mouth. Once the capsule has been crunched and the hot water has run through it into my cup, I savour the strong brew, reflecting on how much better it tastes than the human efforts at filtered coffee. I notice soft music in the background, a song the words of which are "Round like a circle in a spiral, like a wheel within a wheel/Never ending or beginning on an ever spinning reel".[1]

Back in the conference room, the presenter shows us his last slide. It's the crowning glory of the presentation, its apogee, a culmination of his examples of new technologies and their relevance for education, made up of a succession of images animated to appear from nowhere onto the screen, one by one. What appears are: a desktop computer, a laptop computer, an iPad, a Chromebook, an interactive whiteboard, a Legamaster board, an Apple TV, a cell phone, an iPhone, an iPod, Google Glasses, an Apple watch, newly designed prostheses, a series of robots, a 3D printer, a drone, Google cardboard, apps (about 25 education apps – they appear in one cluster), a digital genome, a self-driving car, a hair clip that allows deaf people to feel sounds, a child wearing a virtual reality headset and more.

What does this explosion of technological applications really signify for education?

MEANING OF "SINGULARITY"

The Hungarian born John von Neumann was one of the most brilliant mathematicians and logically intelligent people the planet has known. At six he could mentally divide and multiply two eight-digit numbers (Henderson, 2007) and was so dazzling that

CHAPTER 2

when his teacher, the famous mathematician Gábor Szegő, met the then 15-year-old von Neumann, he wept in awe (Glimm et al., 1990). He was famous for memorising large texts, including telephone directory pages, at a single reading. A professor at Princeton at the same time as Einstein, von Neumann simultaneously worked on ergodic theory (behaviour of mathematical models over time), worked on high-powered algebraic properties, invented a new type of geometry, established axioms for quantum mechanics, invented game theory and used mathematics to describe explosions and fluids.

When dying of cancer at 53, from his hospital bed he wrote the unfinished and posthumously published *The Computer and the Brain* (1958), in which he drew on the old idea that a brain was like a computer and that because of this, a computer could eventually simulate and perhaps even exceed the computational complexity of a human brain. It was von Neumann who coined the word *singularity:* "the ever accelerating progress of technology … gives the appearance of approaching some essential singularity in the history of the race beyond which human affairs, as we know them, could not continue" (Schneider, 2009, p. 204). What von Neumann meant by *singularity* was that moment in time when technology would be so advanced in its ability to carry out human operations as to create a dramatic and irreversible change for human beings, who would have to adapt significantly to accommodate it. Singularity would change the very morphology of human life and could even threaten it.

In a sense, at the outset the very idea of a computer is an attempt to create artificial intelligence. The word comes from the Latin *computare*, meaning "to calculate". Calculation is an early human cognitive trait that that sets Homo sapiens apart from other mammals and characterises our ability for abstract thought. To create a machine that does this instead of a human being is a way of mechanising a thought process. The first rudimentary attempt at this, in Sumeria in 2700 BC, was the abacus – a simple counting machine.

The first sophisticated attempt at a plan for a modern computer, capable of complex, multifaceted calculations, was drawn up by the British scientist and inventor Charles Babbage in the 1830s. The idea was that human thought, to a large extent, is based on binary code (each human thought, utterance or action will essentially be governed by an either-or premise). Therefore, to copy human thought, a system of cards with punched holes that could be overlaid on each other in a number of configurations so as to give different outputs, akin to logical conclusions, was designed by Babbage as what he called a "Difference Engine" and then, more ambitiously, an "Analytical Engine" (Bromley, 1982). This approach was picked up about hundred years later by the famous cryptologist Alan Turing, alongside von Neumann. Since then, as is well known, computers can simulate certain human operations to an increasingly impressive extent: today you can speak to your GPS, have your Fitbit tell you how much you should walk to keep fit, send automated messages to others and so on.

There is a science fiction fantasy and fear that one day artificial intelligence will outperform and displace human intelligence.[2] For this to happen, however, a threshold would have to be passed whereby a machine would no longer be a piece of metal and plastic that could only perform through the computing of a human-written and implanted software, but would actually become recursively self-improving and autonomous, animated by a type of personality or soul. This development presupposes two fundamental points: first, that human intelligence – in its deep, spiritual and not merely mathematical sense – can be simulated and transcended by software; and second, that computers could somehow take on a life of their own. I will now respond to these two questions: Can human intelligence be simulated? And can computers take on a life of their own?

CAN HUMAN INTELLIGENCE BE SIMULATED?

Sasha

My most intelligent student ever I will call Sasha (not her real name). She was a 16-year-old Russian with long brown hair, soft features and eyes that, of course, seemed to hold within them the complexity and enigma of human intelligence. I say "of course" not only because of the Biblical adage that the eyes are the window of the soul, but also because I believe that highly intelligent people have a special vivacity in their eyes, as if the ocular portal into their brains were part of their brilliance. In any case, everyone who has struck me as intellectually gifted has a curious sparkle in their eyes. Sasha was no exception; her eyes were like vortices into the galaxy.[3]

In those days, I was an English teacher. The class was discussing Shakespeare's *Hamlet,* a play that attracts bright students. Sasha remained quiet during most of the discussion, which involved the usual platitudes about Hamlet's being suicidal, suffering from an Oedipus complex, suffering from procrastination and so on. When it seemed that everyone had said what needed to be said, Sasha murmured in an off-hand way that Hamlet was like Madame Bovary, everything and nothing, a mirror for anyone to gaze into and find their darkest dream or noblest poet. She went on to say that he was at once cruel and childish, brave and cowardly, passionate and stand-offish – in sum an expression of all of humanity's extremes.

How easily and fluently such mature and creative ideas came to her! She was light years ahead of the others, me included. What about her made her so brilliant? Put another way, were her reflections nothing more than polished, extremely logical assertions that a well-programmed machine might produce? Or was it conceivable that she had read a huge amount and was therefore able to reach into a repertoire of references that made creative connections seem all the more impressive when in fact they were the result of extreme bookishness? Or was there something else, something more mysterious and uniquely human about her type of intelligence?

I'll come back to Sasha's story later in this chapter.

CHAPTER 2

Human Intelligence

We must first establish what human intelligence is. Theories of intelligence essentially date to the turn of the twentieth century. Since then, psychologists have agreed that the mind's functionality can be broken down into three or four fundamental parts: creative, analytic (or intellectual), practical (or applied, including social intelligence) and psychomotor.[4]

Intelligence can be broken down into subcomponents. Some say there are multiple types of intelligence, but ultimately the word defines a mechanism whereby the individual can absorb information, process it and do so whilst adapting, redirecting, morphing and growing according to the pressures of context.[5] Fundamentally, therefore, intelligence is adaptation to the environment.

In that case, for a piece of software to be truly intelligent, it would have to be programmed to adapt to different environments the way that humans know how to behave in different climates and under different circumstances.[6]

Artificial Intelligence

Artificial intelligence describes a machine-based pattern-recognition functionality that allows non-human devices to perform higher-order human tasks, such as interpretation of complex data, natural language recognition and production, and complex-task delivery, such as driving a car and playing games. A further and essential difference between artificial intelligence and simple computer programming is that the former entails what is called "machine learning", in other words, a process whereby software gathers data on past operations and synthesises and establishes patterns from the data to make predictions about future applications. This is the premise behind the search engine, which is based on the seemingly human mental domains of association and comparison.

So if we are to consider these functions alongside human intelligence, we see that in some areas (and only in some – the point needs to be stressed), software can effectively enable lower-order functions of knowing and understanding and even some higher-order thinking skills such as synthesis and inference-drawing. We should not, however, lose sight of the fact that the only possible premise for this type of computation is probabilistic and strictly data-driven. It does not derive from metaphysical aspects that, at least for the time being, seem uniquely human (emotions, belief systems, motivation, ethics, judgement, aesthetics, subjectivity, culture, existential decision-making).

An open letter expressing concern about the potential of artificial intelligence, written by dozens of academics across the globe, gives a precise definition of artificial intelligence, its constituency and applications:

> The adoption of probabilistic and decision-theoretic representations and statistical learning methods has led to a large degree of integration and

cross-fertilization among AI, machine learning, statistics, control theory, neuroscience, and other fields. The establishment of shared theoretical frameworks, combined with the availability of data and processing power, has yielded remarkable successes in various component tasks such as speech recognition, image classification, autonomous vehicles, machine translation, legged locomotion, and question-answering systems. (Future of Life, 2016)

Is Human Intelligence Algorithmic?

Before exploring the extent to which software might ape, reproduce or even transcend human thinking, we should ask ourselves whether human thinking is by nature akin to software. This is a fundamental point to clarify, since so much in the discussion about singularity builds upon it.

To what extent can we say that the human brain is like a computer, taking intelligence theory into account? The American computer engineer, author and futurologist Ray Kurzweil, whose 1999 book, *The Age of Spiritual Machines,* predicts that by 2045 computers will have the emotional and intellectual capacity of humans, describes human brains as complex machines working on elaborate algorithmic pathways.[7] If you break down information-processing in the human brain to the bare mechanics of electrochemical transfer, you will find a similar process of binary code, cabling and signal reception to that at work in a microprocessor.

However, to break down the information processing of a neuron this way does not take into account the fact that synaptic responses tend to activate many different nerve fibres at once: they are far more multivariate than Kurzweil suggests.

Other thinkers have referred to human thought using analogies to artificial intelligence. For example, the best-selling author Yuval Harari in his tongue-in-cheek *Homo Deus: A Brief History of Tomorrow* (2015), describes human beings as carbon algorithms.[8] The academic Steven Pinker describes thinking as mathematical combinatorial programs in the mind.[9]

In the 1950s, the cryptologist Alan Turing explained how the brain was like an onion with various layers of the same matter and that it was not by looking at it or the way it functions that we would find the mind.[10] This suggests that the mind's essence might not exist as such, but rather it lies in the invisible, multiple relationships between each stratum. Turing is pointing out that if we attempt to describe the mind as a series of mechanical processes, although we might be able to model each one fairly clearly, this exercise will not lead us to a deep understanding of what the mind is.

To describe human beings as carbon algorithms, mental processes as onion skins or thinking as programmatic is justified to a certain extent by experience. Decision-making will go along a path of "do-do not" binaries, and one could map some types of thinking using a tree diagram; but as we all know intuitively and empirically, decisions are not always taken this way: they can be delivered in "fast" (emotional and biased) or "slow" (logical) ways.[11]

Furthermore, even if we remain in the sphere of logical thinking, where one might argue things work a little as they do in a computer, mental binary processes are often interrupted or short-circuited by leaps in thinking that involve guesses and inferences. Humans regularly leapfrog chains in a sequence.

I would argue that whereas baseline cognitive functions involve mechanical processes (such as encountering, storing and retrieving information) that can be described algorithmically, the higher neocortical functions of evaluation, creativity, multifaceted interpretation and abstract thought are not only too multivariate to be described through machine analogies but also too intertwined with cultural, emotional, ethical and belief-related elements to be described as simple algorithms governed by binary code. This analysis suggests that higher functions cannot be automated.

The troublesome dimension of the comparison between human and artificial intelligence is that in some spheres of thought, artificial intelligence can actually operate at a high level. A high-powered algorithm could certainly synthesise information or analyse it when a statistically likely prediction is involved, something that software can do quite comfortably in such fields as finance and health. However, artificial intelligence can only so operate if the variables at work are stable and programmable. Wherever there is paradoxical or ambiguous information, artificial intelligence falls down. For example, in dealing with simple or complex mathematical calculations or finding the right solution to an algorithmic problem, artificial intelligence will be easily superior to human intelligence, whereas in others arenas, involving culture, context, emotions, meaning, intentions and values, such as commenting on the emotional impact of a piece of Shakespeare or the ethical pros and cons of a politician's speech, artificial intelligence will not be able to cope, since the variables at work are too many and too subtle to be programmed.

This is why Sasha, the brilliant Russian literature student, could not be duplicated or improved-upon or made obsolete by an algorithm.

For the less futurologically inclined, the generative spirit of the mind, its inner recesses of belief, emotion and spirituality, seem impossible to automate.[12]

CAN COMPUTERS TAKE ON A LIFE OF THEIR OWN?

Exponential Growth

One argument for eventual automation and recursive self-improvement by machines is that technological growth is exponential and loads onto itself, so the more sophisticated programmes are, the closer we will get to a stage at which they start to programme other programmes, capitalising on the evolution of software sophistication and standing on each other's giant-like shoulders, so to speak. This will lead us to a networked society where there is "the Internet of things" or a "smart world" in which just about everything is automated and can communicate with itself using Swarm intelligence. There are already examples of systems that are almost entirely automated, such as those marketed by the company Libelium (2016).

In fact, most natural growth cycles are exponential, as Kurzweil explains:

> The evolution of DNA took a billion years to form. The evolutionary system fed on that to bring about the Cambrian revolution (where plant and animal life on earth started). That took place over 10 million years – so 100 times faster. A few hundred thousand years later, Homo sapiens (the first technology-using species) evolved. It took him only tens of thousands of years to harness fire, stone tools and the wheel. (Kurzweil, 2016b)

What is important to grasp in this statement is not just the exponential curve that it describes, but also the fact that this growth rate comes about because at each step, information loads onto that which preceded it, improving and correcting itself twofold. This scenario is what implies that computing muscle will eventually become human in its power. At its steepest incline of exponential growth, dramatic breakthroughs will occur every decade, taking technology to places we cannot yet conceive of.[13]

Human beings struggle to understand (or deal with) exponential curves, because our consciousness, built fundamentally on empirical perception, experiences the world day to day in a seemingly linear fashion. This is part of why, despite graphs and curves showing us the future of artificial intelligence, many continue to live in denial that singularity is coming exponentially closer. The truth is that while we can conceptualise arithmetic growth by envisaging, for example, one to 30 steps, imagining that growth in an exponential system would, by the thirtieth step, take us to over one billion, is, for a human brain, mind-boggling and counter-intuitive.[14]

The model of exponential growth in the world of technology was posited by the businessman Gordon Moore (1929–), who showed in a 1965 paper that the transistors in a microchip would double in number every year. This phenomenon partly explains the fast decrease in size of retailed computers from the large, cumbersome boxes that they first were to the cell phones of today and nanotechnology of the present and near future.

Machine Learning

It is true that in recent years, extraordinary examples of machine learning give the impression of increasing algorithmic autonomy, as Harari (2015, pp. 321–322) discusses:

- 1996. The computer Deep Blue defeats Gary Kasparov at chess.
- 2002. The Oakland Athletics baseball team pioneers, with impressive results, algorithm-based talent spotting (now a widespread practice).
- 2011. David Cope's programme Annie produces music and haikus indistinguishable from humans' work. The IBM computer Watson beats human world experts at Jeopardy!

- 2014. The Hong Kong company Deep Knowledge Ventures appoint an algorithm called "VITAL" to its board of directors.
- 2015. DeepMind learns to play 49 classic Atari games by itself (with the only information available to it "pixels on a screen and the idea that it had to get a high score").

Harari goes far, insisting that the near future will mark the end of individualism and liberalism because more reliable machine-learning will be able to take better decisions and guide humans better than humans could guide themselves; that we will live in an era of techno-humanism (p. 366) populated by upgraded superhumans (p. 346). The authors Nick Bostrom (2014) and Max More (2013) and the company Google demonstrate a similar futurologistic appetite, predicting a world in which algorithms will govern society and take decisions while upgraded humans will possess quasi-limitless technology-enhanced thinking and prolonged living capacity.

When and How Does Machine Autonomy Happen?

Were we to use exponential logic to reflect on the way technology has grown in the past half century, especially in medicine and communication, and then to forecast the next 50 years, the conceptual leap is greatest where we would need to jump into the idea of programmes taking on programming power and becoming, therefore, self-propagating.

Crucially, however, none of these voices (Kurzweil, Harari, Bostrom, More or Google) can explain when exactly the world will cross the threshold after which algorithms will operate entirely of their own accord, that point at which a computer will programme another computer without having been programmed by a person in the first place. The dilemma is that a force outside of a process must give birth to the process. Nowhere on earth can we see in complex organisms self-induced inception or spontaneous generation of complex, decision-making entities. Intelligence is born from some other source, and in the case of computer programming, that other source must be human. If the other source is an intelligent machine, then that machine will need to have been switched on by someone, and so on.

Put simply, an algorithm, software or a machine can operate only if a human being pushes the button for this to happen. So ultimately, the idea that machines might take over the world of their own accord remains in the realm of popular science fiction, like *Terminator: The Rise of Machines* (2003), but science fiction does not point out that a human living outside the realm of machines must be the agent to start the process. This principle does not mean that algorithms cannot self-improve.

Anyone who has used Google Translate over the past 15 years will tell you how dramatic the recursive improvement has been. Google Translate improves by analysing entire sentences and configuring translated versions by sentence rather than by word, a process called "neural machine translation" (Nieva, 2016).

POINTS MADE THUS FAR

To summarise my answers to the two questions fundamental to the premise of the discussion on singularity:

- Human intelligence can only be simulated by machines in certain logical, quantitative fields and at a low level of cognitive architecture and therefore cannot take over all of thought. Machine-brain analogies are only partially accurate.
- Machine autonomy's threatening human beings by its own decision-making power appears to be more fantasy than reality, as a threshold exists that seems impossible to pass, namely the appearance of spontaneous decision-making capacity without any outside force having galvanised it.

However, neither hypothesis should be entirely written off. Algorithms duplicate human processes more and more. And there is a growing belief that the seeming unlikelihood of spontaneous machine decision-making might be reversed when one considers the exponential growth and unimaginable future of computing power and potential software application.

EDUCATIONAL RESPONSES

We must ensure that their education equips students to thrive in a world approaching singularity (whether we actually get to singularity or not) so that they are not left dazed in the wake of rampant changes in technology. Resisting technology or banning it outright (some voices suggest this) would make students the future fodder, rather than the drivers, of technological change. Consequences of our not equipping students has ramifications for economic parity as well as for workplace skills, since we could well find ourselves in a world in which a tiny elite controls the algorithms and a vast majority are mere consumers of Internet and programme-driven painters of reality.

Many elements deserve consideration in the composing of an educational response to the growth of technology. I have grouped them into three areas. Each area will be developed in more detail, but first, here is a summary of each:

- For students to drive and control change in an ethical fashion and to be able to share the economic profit to be made from technological advances, an emphasis on forward-looking STEM learning must feature strongly in schools. STEM education must focus on potential consequences of computer programming, with attention to human and environmental dimensions. I call this *ethical, consequential STEM.*
- Students need to understand the role of technology in each of the subject areas that they approach: They need to know how scientific research using probes, virtual laboratories and pattern detection has changed the scientific method. How computer-generated data-mining and statistics are massively important real-world applications of mathematics. How the social sciences are refined and sometimes rewritten because of statistical banks, automated search processes, carbon testing, magnetic resonance imaging, positron electron tomography and computer-driven

algorithms. How technology is used in sports coaching and fitness and health analyses. How language learning has been, and will be, affected. And how technology has revolutionised the arts. I call this *integrated technology*.
- Since we cannot avoid the power of algorithms to gather information and "know" huge amounts of data (Watson developed its long-term memory by reading everything on Wikipedia), and since machine-learning does threaten many basic and even higher-order thinking domains, in order to harness our originality as a species and not send people out into the world with a skill set that will make them outsourceable as soon as they arrive at the marketplace, we must enable deeper learning in those domains that cannot be automated, such as character, resilience, curiosity, emotional intelligence, compassion, courage, creativity, entrepreneurship, innovation, divergent thinking, risk-taking, wisdom, philosophical thought, active listening, ethical humanity, deep questioning, intercultural competence, understanding and reducing prejudice, grappling with culture, multiliterateness, and open-mindedness. I call this *post-singularity higher-order thinking and being*.

At home, parents can support any of these ideas in their approach to technology and uniquely human interactions.

I shall now look into each of these three elements with examples of classroom, curriculum and school reform that should be enacted for meaningful, powerful impact.

ETHICAL, CONSEQUENTIAL STEM

STEM, as we know, stands for Science, Technology, Engineering and Mathematics. But STEM should not simply be the insurance that students are studying mathematics, science, engineering and technology alongside one another. One needs to conceptualise the interplay between these facets of science in order to understand how STEM can be a powerful, integrated way of learning. Students should learn relevant scientific and mathematical content through project-based learning that uses technology and the design principles of engineering. We would need to add to this model the consequences and ethics of STEM work.

Schools need to establish assessment criteria for STEM work that focus not only on technical skill or cognitive competence but also on attitudes, to ensure that students are made aware of the importance of thinking collaboratively, ethically and responsibly as they engage in STEM.[15]

The Dangers of Programming Software with Potentially Powerful Applications

When it comes to the specific dynamics of programming, algorithms that imply powerful applications, such as machine-learning itself, require certain types of caution and foregrounding. "If, then" coding language should thus not be entered into a system without sophisticated reflection on how exactly the software will respond, given that the reaction to the command will be literal and will not be able to relativise, contextualise, suspend or alter the command unless the programme somehow allows for these operations.

Concretely, if an algorithm is given a primitive command such as "keep children away from the swimming pool", firstly the definitions of *keep away, children* and *swimming pool* would have to be programmed rigorously and with care, taking into account especially the possible misapplications that could arise from the interpretation of the definitions (this would require extensive discussion, reflection and prototyping). Secondly, the project designers would have to think about what would happen in the unlikely event of a fire or some other such destabilising event that might drive children to the swimming pool. The programme would ideally want them to stay in the shallow end, stay afloat on something or be rescued by an adult already in the pool. The challenge for the future is thinking through all the variables: the unpredictable, volatile, complex, ambiguous, uncertain and paradoxical situations that human beings would be able to interpret but algorithms would not understand.[16]

INTEGRATED TECHNOLOGY

Technology Integration as a Paradigm Shaper

An extraordinary thing about STEM is the extent to which it has pervaded all fields of research and development. The scientific method proposed by humanist figures such

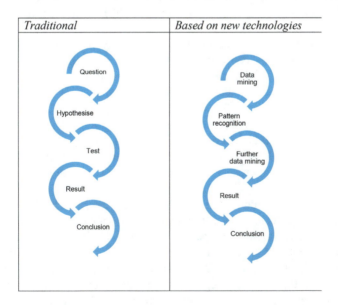

Figure 1. The scientific method, pre- and post-twenty-first century

CHAPTER 2

as the Renaissance philosopher Francis Bacon or the nineteenth century scientist Claude Bernard, whereby questions were asked before hypotheses were developed and tested, needs to be rethought in an age in which probes, computational geometry, satellite imagery and geographic information systems are gathering massive amounts of data.

Modern science means that the ability to discern patterns is possibly more fundamental than hypothesis testing.

On the other hand, computational power has allowed for more reliable and accurate data-mining in the humanities, as Thomas Piketty describes in his book *Capital in the Twenty-First Century* (2013). Piketty takes Kuznet's method of tax declaration analysis to deeper and far-reaching levels, producing a series of curves that tell a refined, accurate story of wealth distribution across many countries.

Subjects such as biology and psychology have undergone something of a Copernican revolution because of studies in both molecular biology (particularly genomics) and neurology, fields enhanced and made possible by powerful visualising technology (powerful cameras, positron emission topography and magnetic resonance imaging). We now conceptualise human biology differently than we did for much of the twentieth century.

Software for musical composition and production has allowed "garage" musicians to reach high levels of output without their having to rely on large companies or professionals for technical platforms for studio work or distribution. Samples available in music production software have been drawn from the best instruments and microphones, while the intensity of a note can be modulated digitally to create a sound that not only simulates a real performance by human musicians but in many regards is superior to it.

As concerns the visual arts, the levels of quality possible to obtain through common commercial devices such as cell phones has increased artistic production and general standards of film and photography considerably. In another vein, new technologies have accelerated improvement in the quality of art restoration. The sumptuous 2016 restoration of Vasari's *Last Supper* (1543) in Florence used state-of-the-art electronic scans and control boxes regulating internal humidity. One might argue that new technologies have opened up and democratised access to the arts. This trend is part of a deeper historical pattern whereby technological innovation has tended to make information, technical exploitation and autonomy more available to the masses.

Therefore, when teaching different subject areas, teachers should be mindful to approach the use of technology conceptually. They should explain the relationship between past technologies and past historical, scientific, artistic or linguistic developments, not just treat technology as a synonym for computers. Previous examples of technology might include sharp instruments, fire, the wheel, the printing press, electricity, the steam engine, medicine, space travel. Teachers should consider STEM a paradigmatic lever that can open a central way to explain many aspects – although not all – of historical development.

At home, to get children's minds thinking about technology in a healthy, critical manner, good dinnertime conversation would be on the eventual human and environmental consequences of such important scientific developments as stem-cell research, genetically modified crops, alternative energy sources and artificial intelligence.

STEM across Disciplines

Schools should not treat STEM as relating only to the sciences and mathematics. It can be used in interdisciplinary projects, for artwork and many types of research. Rather than having students sit through each class with an open laptop (quite possibly hiding an e-mail conversation or game) and harbouring the illusion that this is making them technologically literate, schools should weave into teaching and curriculum high-powered technology that will enhance productivity whilst stimulating creative thinking, collaborative problem-solving and critical thinking.

Whenever engaged in these uses of technology, students should be asked to think about how they are using the principles of engineering in their design and in what ways technology is advancing the quality of their work. Such impetus toward metacognition will allow for meaningful reflection on the value of STEM.

POST-SINGULARITY HIGHER-ORDER THINKING

Since the age of singularity threatens not only routine labour, but many white collar jobs, too, Harari (2015, p. 315), perhaps guilty of some exaggeration, warns that algorithms will soon be seen as more reliable than human lawyers, doctors and life-coaches, and so educational practice needs to put much emphasis on higher-order thinking such as analysis, synthesis, evaluation and creativity. One might add those non-outsourceable dimensions of human behaviour: ethics and values.

We have seen how a number of strictly cognitive higher-order operations can be simulated, and perhaps even improved-upon, by algorithms, especially those that deal with logico-mathematical intelligence involving multivariate analysis, deduction and statistically-based predictions based on hard data. This does not mean that schools will no longer promote these skills, but rather that the skills should be developed alongside what algorithms can already do. By learning alongside powerful software instead of spending time on what software can do already, students' logical higher-order thinking can be channelled towards practical and creative applications of information or towards modifying creative scenarios according to varied hypothetical contexts.[17]

A word of caution, though: young people still need to learn and develop a strong basis of academic knowledge in order to activate these higher-order thinking skills. They still will need to read long, detailed and well-written texts, learn historical facts and master many concepts.[18]

If parents are being told by spin doctors that all that matters are soft skills and that children need not know much in the twenty-first century, they should be wary.

CHAPTER 2

While a software programme might allow us to access large amounts of information without having to learn it off by heart, thus reducing psychic energy and cognitive load and thereby freeing up humans to engage in more creative tasks, the problem will be the limitations on what humans can do if they are not carrying information in their minds in the first place. What will be the basis of decision-making, analysis and creation if the raw materials of such processes (information bites, facts, perspectives) are contained in a physically separate vessel? How will we build pictures of the world and come to conclusions? The only way this could work would be for pre-programmed knowledge to be loaded into our minds, as is the case in the 1999 science fiction film *The Matrix*. This possibility seems far-fetched, although Kurzweil's thesis on computer-brain interfaces does not exclude it.

On the other hand, because automatable thinking skills are reaching higher on the rungs of cognitive architecture, with software capable of driving stock market decisions, medical analyses or legal outcomes, schools need to focus on facets of being that are dispositional, teaching not only social intelligence, but also ethical decision-making, entrepreneurship and innovation. Most schools will claim to do so on their websites, but how many have the courage to inject into their actual curriculum, formal assessment and timetabling the learning experiences that will allow these competences to flourish? Most national curricula are made up of academic subjects and physical education, high-stakes examination preparation, content testing and a strong culture of grade status, but few deliberately and openly assess character or take students off timetable to work on character.

At one school where I worked, we ensured that students were taken off timetable for "community and character" days. They engaged in trust building, self-awareness exercises, team building and entrepreneurship. Students self-assessed their intercultural competence, innovation and entrepreneurship as they engaged in service learning projects throughout the school year.

Note how these competences are non-automatable, elements of human behaviour that no algorithm could reproduce, but that will always be necessary, especially in a time when restorative, regenerative, socially beneficial and environmentally sound actions are needed to save the planet. By their developing character, students will know how to use STEM in ethical ways.

Confidence and STEM

Confidence is a character-related facet of human attitude that plays a vital role in learning, social impact and happiness. Confidence should be considered a higher-order, uniquely human phenomenon. With regard to building confidence, it should be said that many students fear mathematics and the sciences; they are seen as difficult, and they cause students to baulk.

How many parents see their children suffering from maths anxiety or find their children saying things like "I'm not good at maths" or "I was never good at science"?

It is well known that girls feature less in STEM learning than boys for a variety of reasons, including male role models and teachers, and societal pressure for boys to become engineers and physicists rather than girls.[19] Research tells us that girls are not necessarily less competent in STEM, but less socially inclined or indeed less pressured to follow STEM careers.[20]

In order to give girls and boys the confidence to tackle STEM, schools should ensure staffing diversity (including gender diversity) in department head and teaching positions, break down the fear factor and build student belief in themselves when it comes to STEM. There are examples of programmes that do build such confidence.[21]

Sasha

What happened to Sasha, my bright Russian student of literature? Interestingly, she went to Cambridge not to study literature or the humanities, but to study medicine. This is arguably the field most outsourced by new technologies, and yet students still queue to gain admission to medical school.

Sasha would never be seen with a smartphone; in fact, I am not even sure that she had one. However, she always had a book in her hand, whether Mark Twain, Thomas Mann, Fyodor Dostoevsky or Jane Austen. How well did this passion for literature help her in the admissions examination?

After her admissions interview, I asked what the college don had asked her. It was the famous trolley problem: if you have the means to switch a train hurtling towards a family tied to the rails so that it takes another path but hits a man, what do you do? Sasha had responded:

> I said that there was no right answer, that it was a higher-order moral imperative that involved a trade-off between utilitarianism and absolutism, whether it was better to act for a greater good but to instrumentalise a life in order to do that, or better to stand by a more fatalistic principle of never taking someone's life under any circumstances. A little like Raskolnikov's dilemma in *Crime and Punishment*.

Which algorithm could produce that? I wondered.

Sasha today is a successful surgeon.

CONCLUSION

The room is now stuffy from the two-hour presentation. Our speaker has developed a film of sweat over his face, and I have developed a headache that I imagine comes from the Wi-Fi signals running through the room. My eyes are tiring, too, from so many screens (the PPT, my cell phone and my laptop). We are now in the discussion part of the presentation. I notice that many participants fold away their devices and for the first time seem interested. A nondescript, middle-aged man

CHAPTER 2

clears his throat: "The relationship we have with machines is now an unavoidable educational question. Teachers continue to have students handwrite notes, learn by heart information that can be gleaned instantaneously from the Internet, do things that computers do; and we need to move beyond that". Another responds, "Don't we need to store information in our minds and consolidate lower-order thinking in order to launch into another, more creative and abstract space?". "I think the question is a different one", says another. "It's how can we learn alongside computers".

The woman on my right, the one with the tattoo under her ear, speaks with a high-pitched metallic voice: "Have you heard of IBM's million-neuron TrueNorth chip? It eats up only 70 milliwatts of energy and is able to perform 46 billion synaptic operations every second".[22]

As she rattles on, I wonder if it is true. I think back on Kurzweil, who speaks of a transhumanism whereby, like the cognitive revolution that took place about 70,000 years ago with development of the neocortex in Homo sapiens' brain, human beings are now – and will be increasingly in the near future –able to use cloud-based knowledge networks as an extension of abstract thought, thereby extending creative, evaluative and analytical thought processes beyond neurobiological capacity. Furthermore, with the advent of nanotechnology, access to the cloud, until now requiring typing into machines, will happen seamlessly as neurons communicate with nano computers in our bloodstream. This "connection with neocortical hierarchies in the cloud" will mean accessing information is quicker and could even mean accessing pre-loaded knowledge. Kurzweil predicts that this will happen in 2045, claiming that the brain's neurotransmitter power operates at 10 to the 14th while some computers are already able to perform at that level or higher.[23]

I no longer follow the thought but allow my eyes to rest on a couple I see walking and holding hands in the park outside the conference room window. They stop to hug each other. I imagine this is a symbol of the ultimate resistance to singularity, the last outpost of uniquely human sensibility: our sentience and corporeality, our ability to enjoy life physically and emotionally along with all the shocks that the flesh is heir to.

It is the end of the discussion. The presenter thanks us and directs his remote control at the projector. A message flashes on the screen: "Are you sure you wish to switch off?" He clicks the mouse-like device, and the light of the screen folds in on itself swiftly and silently.

NOTES

[1] "The Windmills of Your Mind" (Bergman and Bergman, 1968).
[2] Expounded by such authors as Isaac Asimov (1950), Arthur C. Clarke (1968) and Hans Moravec (1999).
[3] In fact, scientific research confirms the idea that the eye tells you something about personality. See Ludden (2015).
[4] The foundational psychologist Charles Spearman established a general theory of intelligence in 1904, in which he proposed that mechanical, verbal, spatial and numerical facets of human thought

all share a group of common characteristics (this general intelligence, fundamentally mathematical and verbal, has dominated intelligence quotient testing for decades); more recent thinkers have seen multiple elements in intelligence, from Robert Sternberg's triarchic theory of intelligence (1985), which includes analytical, creative and practical elements, to Howard Gardner's theory of multiple intelligences (2006), which includes verbal-linguistic, mathematical-logical, musical, visual-spatial, kinaesthetic, interpersonal, naturalist and existential elements. So we see that theories of intelligence have evolved from those positing a single type (general intelligence) to a more pluralistic model that tries to account for the full gamut of human behaviours, domains and capacities.

5   Sternberg (1985) says that intelligence is the ability to survive in a particular environment, whereas Piaget described it as equilibration (meaning a constant assimilation of new information into a conceptual framework).

6   Hierarchies of intelligence ranging from the Swiss psychologist Jean Piaget's model of cognitive development (1950) to Bloom's 1954 and 2001 taxonomy (Anderson and Krathwohl, 2001) or Biggs and Collis' SOLO (the Structured Observation of Learning Outcomes) taxonomy (1982), all establish a baseline level (factual knowledge absorption, recall of single facts or information bites, literal understanding and nothing more than information reorganising), a higher level (involving collecting facts into clusters and making some new meaning out of them, dealing with multiple strands of information simultaneously, applying information to different contexts and seeing more symbolic elements of information) and a highest form – something that is concentrated in the neocortex of the brain (which involves degrees of abstraction, figurative meaning, the ability to evaluate information and create new elements from it).

7   "We are spiritual machines [working with] 300 modules that recognise patterns, each of those modules has 100 neurons, each of those neurons have ion channels [these are gates that control the flow of molecules across cell membranes], dendrites [neural projections that enhance electrochemical transfer] and axons [nerve fibers]" (Kurzweil, 2016a).

8   In Harari's words:

> Organisms are algorithms. Every animal – including Homo sapiens – is an assemblage of organic algorithms shaped by natural selection ... Algorithmic calculations are not affected by the materials ... Hence there is no reason to think that organic algorithms can do things that non-organic algorithms will never be able to replicate or surpass. As long as the calculations remain valid, what does it matter whether the algorithms are manifested in carbon or silicon? (p. 319)

9   In describing the development of cognitive psychology, Pinker points out that "an infinite range of behaviour can be generated by finite combinatorial programs in the mind" (2003, p. 36). Here we have two notions in one: the infinite and the finite, but bound by a linear relationship that sees thinking as programmatic and combinatorial. This vision attempts to explain human unpredictability through mathematical modelling.

10 Alan Turing, on the subject of whether a machine could ever think, wrote the following:

> The "skin-of-an-onion" analogy is also helpful. In considering the functions of the mind or the brain we find certain operations which we can explain in purely mechanical terms. This we say does not correspond to the real mind: it is a sort of skin which we must strip off if we are to find the real mind. But then in what remains we find a further skin to be stripped off, and so on. Proceeding in this way do we ever come to the "real" mind, or do we eventually come to the skin which has nothing in it? In the latter case the whole mind is mechanical". (Turing, 1950, p. 452)

11 As Daniel Kahneman (2011) points out.

12 Turing concluded that "the original question, 'Can machines think?' I believe to be too meaningless to deserve discussion" (Turing, 1950, p. 450).

13 Unfortunately, similarly exponential statistics show the demise of the planet as destructive capacity loads onto itself too. This topic is discussed in the chapter on sustainability.

CHAPTER 2

[14] A well-known game that illustrates the counter-intuitive conceptualisation of exponential growth is the so-called wheat and chessboard problem (Pappas, 1989, p. 17).

[15] Most assessment criteria or standards for STEM learning focus on conceptual understanding, technical application and scientific or mathematical knowledge. For example, the American Next Generation Science Standards (NGSS, 2013) explain that "every NGSS standard has three dimensions: disciplinary core ideas (content), scientific and engineering practices, and cross-cutting concepts" (p. 1).

[16] Russell, Dewey, and Tegmark explain how this problem might arise:

> 'If the environment satisfies assumptions ϕ then behavior satisfies requirements ψ.' There are two ways in which a verified agent can, nonetheless, fail to be a beneficial agent in actuality: first, the environmental assumption ϕ is false in the real world, leading to behavior that violates the requirements ψ; second, the system may satisfy the formal requirement ψ but still behave in ways that we find highly undesirable in practice. It may be the case that this undesirability is a consequence of satisfying ψ when ϕ is violated; that is, had ϕ held the undesirability would not have been manifested; or it may be the case that the requirement ψ is erroneous in itself. (Russell, Dewey, and Tegmark, 2015, p. 108)

[17] For example, a school can set things up so that geography students, instead of going outside and counting the number of cars that pass along a road, can access this information – or similar information – through a quick computer search and then spend more time guessing and debating what the traffic flow might be like under different conditions (good or bad weather, weekend or week, with more or fewer public transport links covering the same route, with more or fewer schools and businesses in the vicinity).

Thus, educating for higher-order thinking should be considered in the context of the computational power, design acceleration and automation that STEM can produce. Many processes involved in project development and learning itself can be automated at the foot of Bloom's taxonomy. For example, students can accelerate lower-order routines in research by using search engines to access references and key information quickly so as to spend more time and psychic energy on synthesising; hand-plotting graphs does not seem necessary in an age of graph-plotting software that teaches computing skills, releasing more time for mathematical reasoning; data-gathering for subjects like geography and the sciences can be automated and drawn up swiftly, allowing more time for pattern detection and analysis, while general knowledge and understanding in a number of subjects can be tested through random item selecting software.

[18] For a more detailed analysis on the necessity to teach baseline knowledge before teaching accessing skills, see Hirsch (2006).

[19] The American National Center for Education Statistics showed in 2015 that, in 2011–2012, popular master's degrees taken by men were "Electrical/Electronics/Communications Engineering, Computer Science, Mechanical Engineering, Computer and Information Sciences, [whereas] most graduate degrees taken by women leaned more towards education, nursing, social work and counselling" (Marks, 2015).

[20] Interestingly, a 2016 National Assessment of Educational Progress (NAEP) test in technology and engineering the United States showed that "girls averaged 151 points (out of a possible 300), three points higher than for boys. Measured another way, 45 percent of females met or exceeded the proficient level, compared with 42 percent of males" (Richmond, 2016).

[21] An example of STEM-related character building is the mathematical resilience programme that uses Carol Dweck's growth mindset model (2012) as a premise for inspiring students to go further and with less fear in maths as they move from over-sheltered learned helplessness to conceptual mastery through confidence-building (Goodall and Johnston-Wilder, 2015).

[22] About TrueNorth:

> Unlike the prevailing von Neumann architecture – but like the brain – TrueNorth has a parallel, distributed, modular, scalable, fault-tolerant, flexible architecture that integrates computation,

communication, and memory and has no clock. It is fair to say that TrueNorth completely redefines what is now possible in the field of brain-inspired computers, in terms of size, architecture, efficiency, scalability, and chip design techniques. (Modha, 2016)

[23] Proponents of singularity and transhumanism (Kurzweil, 1999, 2005; Vinge, 1993; More, 2013) are convinced that this revolution will take place, whereas debunkers, such as Harvard's Steven Pinker and MIT's Noam Chomsky, argue that we are nowhere near such a revolution.

REFERENCES

Anderson, L. W., & Krathwohl, D. R. (2001). *A taxonomy for learning, teaching and assessing: A revision of Bloom's taxonomy of educational objectives.* New York, NY: Longman.
Asimov, I. (1950). *I, robot.* New York, NY: Gnome Press.
Biggs, J. B., & Collis, K. F. (1982). *Evaluating the quality of learning: The SOLO taxonomy (structure of the observed learning outcome).* New York, NY: Academic Press.
Bostrom, N. (2014). *Superintelligence: Paths, dangers, strategies.* Oxford: Oxford University Press.
Bromley, A. G. (1982). Charles Babbage's analytical engine, 1838. *IEEE Annals of the History of Computing, 4*(3), 197–217. doi:10.1109/mahc.1982.10028
Clarke, A. C. (1968). *2001: A space odyssey.* London: Hutchinson.
Dweck, C. S. (2012). *Mindset: How you can fulfill your potential.* London: Constable & Robinson.
Edutopia (2015). Website. https://www.edutopia.org
Future of Life (2016). An open letter: Research priorities for robust and beneficial artificial intelligence. http://futureoflife.org/ai-open-letter/
Gardner, H. (2006). *Multiple intelligences: New horizons in theory and practice.* Cambridge, MA: Basic Books.
Glimm, J., Impagliazzo, J., & Singer, I. M. (1990). The legacy of John von Neumann. *American Mathematical Society Symposium, 50,* 334. http://dx.doi.org/10.1090/pspum/050
Goodall, J., & Johnston-Wilder, S. (2015). Overcoming mathematical helplessness and developing mathematical resilience in parents: An illustrative case study. *Creative Education, 6,* 526–535. http://dx.doi.org/10.4236/ce.2015.65052
Harari, V. N. (2015). *Homo deus: A brief history of tomorrow.* London: Harvill Secker.
Henderson, H. (2007). *Mathematics: Powerful patterns into nature and society.* New York, NY: Chelsea House.
Hirsch, E. D. (2006). *The knowledge deficit: Closing the shocking education gap for American children.* New York, NY: Houghton Mifflin.
ISG [International School of Geneva] (2017). *Character reports: La Grande Boissière community handbook.* Geneva: ISG.
Kahneman, D. (2011). *Thinking fast and slow.* New York, NY: Farrar, Straus & Giroux.
Kurzweil, R. (1999). *The age of spiritual machines: When computers exceed human intelligence.* New York, NY: Penguin.
Kurzweil, R. (2005). *The singularity is near: When humans transcend biology.* New York, NY: Penguin.
Kurzweil, R. (2016a). *2029: Singularity year, Neil deGrasse Tyson & Ray Kurzweil* (YouTube interview). https://www.youtube.com/watch?v=EyFYFjESkWU
Kurzweil, R. (2016b). *Singularity is near: The 2016 documentary* (YouTube, published 25 May by Enigmas of the Universe). https://www.youtube.com/watch?v=7P7ee5TF7LA
Lewis, C. S. (1964). *On being human: Poems.* New York, NY: Harcourt Brace.
Libelium (2016). Website. http://www.libelium.com
Ludden, D. L. (2015). Your eyes really are the window to your soul. *Psychology Today.* https://www.psychologytoday.com/blog/talking-apes/201512/your-eyes-really-are-the-window-your-soul
Macrae, N. (1992). *John von Neumann: The scientific genius who pioneered the modern computer, game theory, nuclear deterrence, and much more.* New York, NY: Pantheon Press.
Marks, G. (2015). The real reason most women don't go into tech. *Forbes.* https://www.forbes.com/sites/quickerbettertech/2015/03/16/the-real-reason-most-women-dont-go-into-tech/#5cc9e1e46d7a

CHAPTER 2

Mars Education (2016). *NGSS STEM lesson plans.* https://marsed.mars.asu.edu/stem-lesson-plans

Modha, D. S. (2016). *Introducing a brain-inspired computer: TrueNorth's neurons to revolutionize system architecture.* http://www.research.ibm.com/articles/brain-chip.shtml

Moore, G. (1964). The future of integrated electronics. *Fairchild Semiconductor* (Internal publication).

Moravec, H. (1999). *Robot.* Oxford: Oxford University Press.

More, M., & Vita-More, N. (Eds.) (2013). *The transhumanist reader: Classical and contemporary essays on the science, technology, and philosophy of the human future.* Oxford: Wiley-Blackwell.

NGSS [Next Generation Science Standards] (2013). *The Next Generation Science Standards: Executive summary.* http://www.nextgenscience.org/sites/default/files/Final%20Release%20NGSS%20Front%20Matter%20-%206.17.13%20Update_0.pdf

Nieva, R. (2016, November 15). Google Translate just got a lot smarter. *C/net.* https://www.cnet.com/news/google-translate-machine-learning-neural-networks/

Pappas, T. (1989). *The joy of mathematics.* San Carlos, CA: Wide World/Tetra.

Piaget, J. (1947/1950). *The psychology of intelligence.* London: Routledge & Kegan Paul.

Piketty, T. (2013). *Capital in the twenty-first century.* New York, NY: Belknap.

Pinker, S. (2003). *The blank slate.* New York, NY: Penguin.

Richmond, E. (2016). The complex data on girls in STEM. *The Atlantic.* https://www.theatlantic.com/education/archive/2016/05/data-girls-stem/483255/

Russell, S., Dewey, D., & Tegmark, M. (2015). Research priorities for robust and beneficial artificial intelligence. *AI Magazine.* http://futureoflife.org/data/documents/research_priorities.pdf

Schneider, S. (Ed.) (2009). *Science fiction and philosophy: From time travel to superintelligence.* Oxford: Wiley-Blackwell.

Shapiro, B. (2015). *How to clone a mammoth.* Princeton, NJ: Princeton University Press.

Sternberg, R. J. (1985). *Beyond IQ: A triarchic theory of intelligence.* Cambridge: Cambridge University Press.

Turing, A. M. (1950). Computing machinery and intelligence. *Mind, 49,* 433–460.

United Nations (2016). *Sustainable development goals.* http://www.un.org/sustainabledevelopment/sustainable-development-goals/

Vinge, V. (1993). *The coming technological singularity: How to survive in the post-human era.* https://edoras.sdsu.edu/~vinge/misc/singularity.html

CHAPTER 3

TERRORISM

I've been writing at the kitchen table for the last few hours. It's close to one in the morning. My children and wife are asleep, and it's high time I turned in. We've had a busy day enjoying the good weather of southwest France and the colourful celebration of the 14th of July in the local village. I start to clear the decks, tend to the dishwasher, and switch off the lights. As I look over my cherubic sleeping children, for a few seconds my being is overcome with that primal feeling of the family adult protecting his cubs. The world outside is dark, but all is warm and safe inside, and I'm under the impression – or is it an illusion? – that this safety comes from me, the parent, the leader of the pack and the protector of the clan. In the lounge, the television is still on. From a distance I notice written along the bottom of the screen an emergency message scrolling across a red band.

That familiar but morally ambiguous feeling comprising a mix of expectation, anxiety, voyeurism and excitement floods over me as I move closer. "Dozens dead at Nice", I see. I sit down and spend the next 30 minutes watching the sound bites repeat. A lunatic, it would appear, has driven his truck through a crowd, killing many children.

The next day at the breakfast table, I keep the information with me. I do not want to spoil the lazy holiday feel, especially for my children, who are learning to grow up with the dark shadow of a terrorist threat, something I do not want. A few hours later, when the children are in the garden, I tell my wife. The response is as it has been on past occasions: weariness combined with sadness, as if to say, "Yet again".

The victim count rises: at least 40, more like 60, closer to 80. It stops the next day at 84. Twenty days later, an eighty-fifth victim throws in the towel. By then, more attacks have hit Europe: a 19-year-old opened fire in a German McDonald's; a priest had his throat cut in a church in Rouen, France; and police officers were attacked with machetes in Belgium. Bomb blasts killed hundreds in Afghanistan and Pakistan. What I do not yet know is that this time next year, similar attacks will have taken place in Germany, the UK and Spain.

The newspapers are full of the Nice attack, international messages of solidarity circulate, we see photographs of the killer by the beach, with his friends, smiling at the camera with a commonplace, "Mr. Nobody" gaze. The habitual phrases are used. On the one hand, a cluster of adjectives describe the victims – "people", "women and children", "European citizens", "fellow citizens", "families" who represent "our values", "freedom" and "innocence". On the other hand is the world of the killers, and here the adjectives range from "extremists", "fundamentalists", "jihadists"

© JOINTLY BY IBE-UNESCO AND KONINKLIJKE BRILL NV, LEIDEN, 2018
DOI:10.1163/9789004381032_003

and "radicals" to the strong nouns that describe acts of "barbarity", "cowardice", "hatred", "horror" and, of course, "terror". And then there is the response from the authorities, hard language: "We will continue to fight". "No concessions". "Increase attacks on terrorist strongholds". On the ground meanwhile, it's "maximum security" and a "state of emergency".

9/11 ONWARDS

Of course human society has lived with terrorism for at least as long as events have been recorded. Groups such as the IRA, the Red Brigades, Intifada and the Taliban have marked modern history. Some governments have been, and can be, described as "terrorist states". Attacks on unfortunate, defenceless people are nothing new and will probably never stop.

However, at least from the perspective of the so-called Western world, the rise of Al Qaida, the Islamic State and affiliated groups such as Boko Haram is changing the face of modern politics. Many feel that the world is veering into chaos, a type of third world war, and statistics show that terrorism is ravaging populations more than ever before.[1]

I remember vividly, as so many of us do, the 9/11 twin towers attacks. I was teaching in a boarding school in India. Teachers and students spent what felt like hours staring at the television while CNN broadcast the images that would turn the page of the history books. A colleague, a history teacher, said ominously, "This will change the world".

Others in a more polemical vein, pointed out that this was a post-historical, or at least postcolonial, symbol: monoliths of power had been disturbed, and the decadent, cushioned Western world was getting a taste of its own medicine, learning what it means to live under a shower of bombs and oppression, suffering the way so many had suffered under violent Western foreign policy – for decades, even centuries.

For sure, 9/11 did change the world, as since that day international security protocols, the feeling of not being entirely safe and, of course, the attacks themselves, have caused society to steadily morph into a mistrustful, polarised, paranoid place. Modern terrorism has propelled xenophobic discourse into the mainstream and permitted many leaders to stoop to resorting to language and legislation of essentialism, stereotyping, prejudice and war.

Where fundamentalists have taken power and proclaimed an Islamic State, as is the case in parts of the Middle East and West Africa, humanity has been subdued into a barren, unhappy state of affairs, without freedom of speech, without freedom of choice and – surely one of the worst things anyone could propose – with no music.

Terrorism and its effects confront the world of education with considerable challenges that can be summed up as three questions, which I will attempt to address:

WHAT IS IT THAT DRIVES PEOPLE TO BECOME TERRORISTS AND HOW CAN EDUCATION PREVENT OR REDUCE IT?

Salif

Salif (not his real name) used to call himself Lucky. This was in Johannesburg in the late 1990s. Lucky wore dreadlocks, thick, black-rimmed spectacles like a 1960s American professor and colourful ethnic shirts. We would play pool at a club we called Tandoor, and over beers, a cigarette dangling from his mouth, he would reinvent Africa, gesticulating broadly as he talked about historical figures such as Markus Garvey, Kwame Nkruma, Joshua Nkomo and Robert Sobukwe. Like all African revolutionaries – or would-be revolutionaries – he would read the classics, such as Lenin's *Imperialism, the Highest Stage of Capitalism,* Franz Fanon's *The Wretched of the Earth,* Cheikh Anta Diop's *Black Africa: The Economic and Cultural Basis for a Federated State* and Steve Biko's *I Write What I Like.*

I liked Lucky because he was an intellectual with passion and with a splash of radicalism that he would toss into the pot every now and then. Above all, he was a young man growing up with convictions and a dream. He wanted to change things.

I lost sight of Lucky for a number of years, mainly because I had left South Africa to study in the south of France and came back only intermittently. But during one summer holiday in South Africa, I rented a room in a house with a group of students in Johannesburg, and it turned out Lucky was one of them.

We recognised each other straight away, but Lucky was standoffish and severe, unwilling to shake my hand. He had grown a thin beard and wore a taqiyah. He had converted to the Nation of Islam, swore by Luis Farrakhan and called himself Salif. He would comment judgementally on the fact that we were drinking beer, would express disgust when a roommate ate ham with his breakfast eggs and would break away from house conversations or activities and go to his room to pray.

I admire Islam as a powerful religion. I love to lose myself in the Sufi voice of Nusrat Fateh Ali Kahn, as he sings Surahs from the Koran. I look up to the great Muslim scholars of the past, Al Gazali, Avarroes and Avicenna. And I have been deeply affected by the dignity and purpose of Islamic culture I experienced during travels through Egypt, Jordan and India. However, I have never liked sectarianism or fundamentalism, whether Christian, Jewish or Muslim. There is, I find, something selfish, sociopathic and disturbing when someone enters into the solipsistic black box of radical faith. Those around such people but who do not share their dogmatic opinions feel rejected, judged and even scorned.

On one evening, as we sat in a circle in Salif's room, he tried to indoctrinate us into the path he was taking, telling us that the white race had been invented by an ancient black scientist called Yakub, who, over 6000 years ago, lived on the island of Patmos and bred out the blackness of his slaves by progressively mating them with lighter-skinned people until white people, who incidentally were "devils", Salif told us, were created. He added that the Negroid Olmec heads in the Yucatan were statues of Yakub. At that point I said I was tired and shuffled off.

CHAPTER 3

It was the worst cock-and-bull rubbish I had ever heard. The scary part was that Lucky, or should I say Salif, was an intelligent young man. What on earth had happened for him to have been drawn into this garbage? And why would anyone want to sit and listen to such drivel? For sure, he did not seem to be heading anywhere positive.

Simplistic Ideas

The typical response to terrorism is that it comes from anarchical societies in which ignorance, extreme hardship and poverty, along with low levels of education, are rife, creating a toxic stew of desperation and extremism. This picture can be contrasted with that of the well-educated, middle-class moderate who lives in a society structured by laws and regulations. The belief emerges that with education, as well as with the creation of a society more equitable socio-economically and under law, humans will be less prone to engage in extremism. After all, terrorist actions are misanthropic, violent and monstrous to the point where it is difficult to imagine that the person behind them could possibly come from a decent, balanced background, have sat in classes on mathematics and history and could share the fears, aspirations and musings of other run-of-the-mill middle-class people.

This vision of bearded, wild-eyed, desperate madmen, screaming incantations and carrying machine guns and bombs on the one hand and on the other, well-groomed functionaries in spectacles and suits, with well-combed hair, fretting silently about their jobs, is part of a causal, liberal and rational view of human behaviour that is related to constructs such as Maslow's hierarchy of needs and capitalist, classical liberal economics. The idea – stemming from Renaissance humanism – is that an education in the humanities, coupled with some level of status in society and conjugated with a social contract (essentially, laws ensuring moderate behaviour), would be enough to keep human beings rational and peaceful.

So it goes that many still carry the colonial, Renaissance idea of a hierarchy running from savagery to enlightenment, with instruction and socialisation representing the rungs of the ladder that allows the person to lift himself or herself from the abyss of animal passions to the pure plains of abstract thought and reason. This was the thinking behind missionary schools and many of the fathers of modern education (Plato, Aristotle, Erasmus, Kant and Locke).

This contrast of violence with peace, chaos with order and frenzy with moderation is nothing new. Ancient Greek archetypes of violence and cruelty are mostly associated with monstrosity and extreme imbalances, whereas those of peace and moderation are associated with rulers, mentors, philosophers and wise men. The idea appears in Greek mythology, in which the rational balance of the world that Zeus upholds after the clash of the Titans is threatened by deformed creatures from the underworld (Gorgons, the Hydra, the Hekatonkheires and Furies), which are put in their place by heroes representing the cardinal values of truth, beauty and goodness (such as Bellerophon, Perseus, and Jason).

A More Troubling Picture

Even the Greeks realised, however, that this dichotomy was not enough to explain cruelty and madness; so tragic heroes such as Herakles, Odysseus and Achilles, endowed with godly powers, are beguiled by their so-called *pharmakos* or tragic flaw and abandon themselves to deeds of horror (Herakles' killing of his own children in an act of rage; Achilles' brutal savaging of Hector's body as revenge for Patroclus' death; and Odysseus' unnecessarily gruesome hanging of his maids in the surprisingly brutal final chapter of Homer's otherwise soothing *Odyssey*). Here we are presented with a less rational and more troublesome picture, as if to say that an inexplicable primal darkness or madness (the Greeks called it *bia*) can turn just about anyone into a bestial, bloodthirsty creature. We should not forget how well educated and princely these heroes were: Herakles was taught music by Linos, the son of Apollo (whom he killed); Achilles was mentored by the great Centaur Chiron; while Odysseus, famous for his intelligence and wiliness, was described as "of the nimble wits".

Perhaps the greatest failure of the Western humanist project, the historical event that was to undo any oversimplified notion of a division between madness and sanity, was the Holocaust. The German heritage and tradition of a fine education, emblematised by excellence in the arts, philosophy and literature, was devastated by some of the worst human behaviour known to humanity.

The Holocaust cast a shadow over the unfalsifiable and comforting theory that an education is enough to civilise people. It ushered in modern existentialism, with its radical idea that there is effectively no human nature, no human essence, and only a physical existence that will be defined and shaped by choice in a meaningless world. The educational paradigm of ancient Greece, Rome, the Middle Ages, the Renaissance and the Enlightenment, so grounded in reason as a guiding principle, was challenged to the core, and educational reform after the World War II, especially in the wave of thinking that swept over Europe and America after May 1968, sought patterns in subjectivity, immanence, meaning-making and constructivism, as if to say that civilisation had to be carved out of nothing, that human identity could not be nourished through discipline and the *artes liberales,* but had to be cobbled together through a painful process of questioning, doubt and choice.

Nonetheless, there is still, I believe, a basic assumption that education can reduce violent behaviour, that it will lead to less extremism. This position is based on the following premises:

- That terrorists come from undereducated backgrounds.
- That the way people are brought up will determine the social decisions they take later on in life.
- That the brainwashing discourses pushing individuals to become terrorists are a form of education or schooling and produce terrorist acts.

I believe that each of these three points can be deconstructed. Firstly, one of the most shocking revelations about the recent spate of terrorist attacks is that the perpetrators are often from middle-class backgrounds.[2] The question goes beyond education in the Western sense but touches on terrorist education too: where there is terrorism, there is a highly developed educational network.[3]

Secondly, the idea that it is the education that we provide that will determine how people react later on is, of course, true, but it needs to be nuanced. Research shows that that transformative trauma often leads to the awakening of the violent approach that characterises terrorists.[4] In other words, some event out of school, such as the death of a close relative, seems to trigger radical behaviour later on. The question, therefore, is not so much how an education can prevent someone from becoming radical per se but more how to anticipate the shocks and wounds that might trigger a violent response, how to teach young people to respond to difficult situations in their lives.

Many terrorists became radical in their thinking while in prison, which leads me to my third point, that if it is an educational experience that pushes individuals to become terrorists, then we are talking about a special type of education that takes place in a shorter burst of time than classical schooling. It often involves the role of a strong individual mentor or guru who indoctrinates not children but young adults. So the education that we provide young people should be strong enough – if indeed it is through a school education that we can hope for the cognitive and attitudinal shaping that will allow this – to protect students from encounters they will have later on with charismatic individuals who might lead them astray, or worse.

What to Do?

Education for less prejudice (Hughes, 2017), peace and conflict studies (Webel and Galtung, 2007) and peace education (Burns and Aspelagh, 2013) point to the following essential approaches to create less extremism in individuals and groups.

Educating for peace explicitly, as a value and superordinate goal. Educating for peace involves taking education beyond subjects and disciplines and making clear that the values of peace and dialogue are important to the school. These should be woven into the curriculum through the teaching of the humanities and literature. They should be transparent in the ethos of the school through the behaviours that the school acknowledges and celebrates. An ongoing discussion with students about the value of peace in society should be implemented. To "peace", one could add "empathy", in other words, an educational programme that allows students to reflect critically on other people, their positions and approaches.[5]

Education for peace has to model its values by avoiding violent language and behaviour at all cost while communicating to students in a critical, reflective manner why peace is a vital social goal. History textbooks contain too much over-simplified patriotism, glorification of conquest and war. The way they present revolutions, battles and military strategy is not going to create a more peaceful world: their subliminal messages are veneration of sacrifice, might-is-right ideas, retribution and destruction. This is not to say that the traditional nation-building narrative of history is a direct catalyst for terrorism, but it is an educational discourse centred on an acceptance of violence rather than peace as a mediator, which is a problematic starting point.

Needless to say, this is not something that is the exclusive remit of the classroom. Parents should value peace openly and clearly in their households through the discussions they hold, the rules they implement and the type of social models they venerate.

Teaching and modelling dialogue, mediation and negotiation skills. Allowing students a chance to air their views is a constructive step towards moderate, nuanced decision-making. It breaks the gridlock of alienation that is strengthened unhealthily by isolation and lack of exchange with others.[6] It also allows for pent-up frustration and anger to be vented and shed. Many acts of violence in schools, such as high school shootings in the United States, have been perpetrated by frustrated individuals who before taking action used social media to deliver a monologue, as if it were a subliminal cry for help or a reaching out for dialogue. These angry young people clearly had not had their views listened to and also challenged in discussions. Classrooms based on carefully structured talk and dialogue tend to be more constructive and, ultimately, more positive learning environments (Alexander, 2006).

Whenever conflict arises, dialogue should be opened and the skills of listening, trying to understand and seeking solutions should be exercised.[7] A dialogic, interactive classroom environment should be a place where students are confident to say what they feel. In the twenty-first century, dialogue is related to social media. For this reason, and especially because so much propaganda and recruitment come through these organs, schools must in all cases have some idea of the type of social media activity that young people are engaging in. The school can get this information in different ways according to the school's context and needs (parent information sessions, workshops with students, discussion groups, careful monitoring) but should at every step involve the central pillar of discussion, for it is through discussion that potentially dangerous decisions will be unearthed and can be treated.

It is especially important that young people feel confident to speak openly about their experiences, fears and beliefs at home. A healthy twenty-first century home is not a place where families exchange only single-word sentences, everyone is glued to their screens and no one actually knows what young people are doing on their phones.

Teaching democracy and human rights as intrinsic truths. Peace education theory emphasises the learning of human rights and democracy for less violence and extremism. The essential idea is that humans are ends unto themselves and not merely means to an end[8] and that their views should be taken into consideration wherever possible.

CHAPTER 3

Teaching young people about the Universal Declaration of Human Rights (United Nations, 1948) and some of the models of democracy in the world, such as direct democracy in Switzerland, representational democracy in the United States and the UK and Islamic democracy in Iran, allows them to internalise democratic principles and respect the entity and volition of other people consistently and knowledgeably.[9]

Of course, some will argue that rights and democratic principles represent deeply Western styles of thinking and that one needs to be careful not to turn classrooms into arenas of Western propaganda. These arguments may have merit if human rights and democracy are presented as uniquely Western constructs, but they need not be. Different philosophies emphasising humanity and caring for other people such as *Ubuntu* (shared humanity) in Southern Africa, the notion of *Téranga* (extreme hospitality) in Senegal, the Islamic concept of *Adab* (courtesy and respect) or the Confucian virtue of *Ren* (altruism) can be taught and celebrated.

Ensuring a context-specific approach. Given that terrorism has specific contextual trappings in each of its multiple expressions, the education system must not adopt a standardised response but must design responses on the ground according to local circumstances. The wave of attacks rippling through France is not the same as what is happening in Iraq or Nigeria, the United States or Pakistan, even if the thread of jihadism running through all of these attacks has a similar morphology.

Children growing up in Muslim countries need to be taught to appreciate the humane, peaceful side of Islam and Sufism, so that the tenets of the religion are not hijacked by hardliners. Concerning France – and here the situation is complex because of the tradition of secular education in which religious symbols are not allowed in schools – questions of faith should not be brushed aside or swept under the carpet, as this practice creates a polarised community and allows for religious messages to be appropriated and diverted away from the stage of centralised meaning-making.

In countries in which a conflict is going on related to terrorist activity, such as Israel, Syria or Iraq, exchange programmes between children from different groups should be activated to ensure that the fear and stereotypes that grow in isolated groups can be dispelled and given context.[10]

Finally, I would add this fifth point to those above.

Offering spiritual transcendence through education. Surely one of the issues that is leading young people to radicalisation, most especially in the Western world, is a vacuum in their lives, a spiritual emptiness that leads them to seek meaning and the transcendent in mysticism. The post-industrial, technocratic global order, based on materialism, self-interest and practicality, leaves individuals without spiritually transcendent values to which they can aspire or through which they can better themselves.

Perhaps this vacuum is why young people living in middle-class Western suburbia, when faced with deep challenges, do not always have the inner moral compass or resilience to steer the ship through the storm but instead fall under the sway of demagogic false prophets. Human beings need something larger than themselves to cling onto, some idea, principle, being, philosophy or religion that supplements rational thought and sates the hunger we all have for a transcendent dimension in life.

Some might disagree, seeing this view as mumbo jumbo and arguing that we can get by with practical goals, logic and empirical truths. I would argue, however, that this argument is naïve, as every deep intellectual pursuit has some element of the transcendent in it, whether a universal truth, a sublime correspondence of ideas, fame or fortune. We would like to think that by working with science or arguing for political resolve to social problems, we are far from religion, but as Nietzsche wrote in his poetic, provocative but brilliant *Twilight of the Idols* (1889) once man has killed God, he merely resurrects him in the transcendentalist beliefs of scientism, patriotism and ideology.

We know that human beings are attracted to irrationality: the mystic, the unfathomable, the sublime and even the contradictory. At the core of this inquiry is soteriology, in other words, the doctrine of salvation. Human beings, when faced with death, need to be comforted by a philosophy that will help them learn to die. The twenty-first century Western world, in the wake of the 1905 French law separating the church and the state, is seeing the collapse of an atheistic, rational model of society, neither mystical nor spiritual enough to motivate and bind people.

Without their necessarily becoming religious entities, schools, families and community centres must offer young people avenues to explore the deep questions of life (How do I live? What do I believe in? How do I face death? What is my relationship with the cosmos?). Teaching philosophy is thus crucial, so that students are put into contact with the historical narratives that take on these questions through philosophies such as Stoicism, existentialism, Confucianism and the great world religions. The type of teaching that is needed here is not purely didactic and informative (a course on the philosophers per se, for example) but one that actually makes students ask big questions and seek the relevance of philosophy in their lives – as a response to the various perceptual and moral dilemmas they will face.

I believe that philosophical conversations around the dinner table are vital pedagogic moments, even if they do not take place under the guidance of a trained teacher. The act of discussion, exploring values and belief systems, allows for a healthy and secure exchange that secures the foundation of a good spiritual life.

HOW SHOULD THE EDUCATION WE DESIGN FOR YOUNG PEOPLE PRESENT THE PHENOMENON OF TERRORISM HISTORICALLY, POLITICALLY AND PHILOSOPHICALLY?

The challenge of terrorism goes well beyond the question of how to educate young people to be less extremist and more moderate in their thinking, in other words, educating from the perspective of prevention. An added challenge is educating from the perspective of the victims or potential victims. Here we are faced with the difficulty of avoiding the temptation to fall into a trap of oversimplification, raw emotion and stereotypes. The presentation of terrorism to young people needs to be done with extreme care.

CHAPTER 3

Resources abound and should be used.[11] They tend to have in common detailed historical coverage of the factors surrounding terrorism. Without knowledge and understanding of the sociopolitical context of conflict, young people will unlikely develop informed, balanced opinions. Using these same resources, on the other hand involves a risk: they tend to demonstrate pronounced ideological sway, either excessively nationalistic or excessively anti-establishment. A problem related to teaching students about terrorism is the danger of falling into propagandising.

One man's propaganda is another man's truth, some might say, as national history programmes can be viewed as extremely propagandistic, especially when scrutinised critically using a lens of postcolonial theory. Edward Said (1993), who critically explored Western expansionism on the one hand and the West's representation of the East on the other; Abdul JanMohamed (1985), who critiqued the phenomenon of colonisation, and Frantz Fanon (1963), who discussed the distribution of political and economic wealth in the world, have done so with much scrutiny. These postcolonial theorists were attempting to deconstruct the Western hegemonic view of world history, told essentially from the victor's point of view, so as to give readers instead the vantage point of the oppressed and marginalised, the colonised and enslaved.

In the 1960s, 1970s and 1980s, this rethinking of history was part of a movement in consciousness-raising, but in the twenty-first century, it is needed to help us understand the thoughts and actions of anti-Western movements. Indeed, the teacher of history has to grapple with the dynamics of racism and imperialism in the context of the modern world so as to offer students some understanding of the thinking behind many terrorist manoeuvres, no matter how violent and inhumane they may be. After all, our understanding extremists' positions does not mean we endorse them, and it can only be a good thing, leading us away from grotesquely simplistic binary conclusions: barbarity versus civilisation, terror versus freedom.

I have already complained about a lack of sufficiently critical postcolonial theory in the teaching of history in many school systems (Hughes, 2009, 2014, 2017). I argue that what predominates is still a largely nineteenth century model of glorification and one-sidedness: Columbus discovered America, Rhodes drew a line from Cape to Cairo and Turkey was the sick man of Europe. Nor are things getting much better. In 2005, the French law on colonialism actually stipulated that schools should teach the positive values of colonialism. Many troublesome historical facts, such as the Cameroonian underground resistance to French colonisation,[12] the lives of resistance figures and African leaders such as Thomas Sankara and Patrice Lumumba, the creation of the princely states leading to modern-day conflict in Kashmir, and the Balfour Declaration leading to the creation of Israel by the British – none are analysed sufficiently in the classroom to leave students with any inkling of the fault lines that lie beneath contemporary tensions.

Most history courses still centre on European and Western history: ancient Egypt, Greece and Rome; the Middle Ages; the French and American revolutions; the Weimar Republic; both World Wars; the Cold War and the rise of single party states in Europe predominate. They depict a world that leaves the subaltern and the colonised sidelined, in the shadows. Such a unidimensional approach leaves students gasping at terrorist attacks as if they had materialised out of nowhere, or had burst forth from of an enraged group of madmen standing outside of history.

As controversial and difficult as it might be for them to say so, schools and academic institutions in general should not be afraid to make clear that the motives behind terrorist actions are not uniquely fanatical; they are also strategic, political and financial, stemming from a global imbalance, resource scarcity, behind-the-scenes political shenanigans and a long and considerable history of violence and suppression in which Europe has dominated the scene and to which Europe has supplied a latent causality. Perhaps problematic historical figures such as Pissarro, De Gaulle and Churchill need to be eased off their pedestals and presented as something a little less convenient than larger-than-life heroes. And the plight of the colonised needs to be brought to the surface more frankly.[13]

The analysis needs to touch on history that is more recent too, including the creation of the Taliban during the Afghan civil war, multiple American oil and arms deals, American foreign policy in general in the Middle East and neocolonial French dominance in West Africa. Knowing about these political issues (just some of many) helps one understand the current situation.[14]

More than shifting the centre of the narrative of history, any learning about terrorism should be as dialogic as possible, allowing young scholars opportunities to build meaning together and reflect on different interpretations of the facts whilst respecting each other. Academic, content-based knowledge of the reasons leading to an act of terrorism (if, of course, these can be given, since some cases, such as the Nice attack, involve seemingly isolated, mentally disturbed individuals and cannot be easily tied to any political motive) will not be enough: there must be active reflection involving student agency, personal testimonies and the sharing of ideas.[15]

Parents, mentors, families and all those who help shape an educational discourse away from the classroom clearly play an essential role in the way that perspectives on history and geopolitics form. If we wish our children to grow up as moderate, informed people, then we need to avoid emotionally charged, simplistic or propaganda-fed views of the world from developing unabated.

HOW DO SCHOOLS PREPARE YOUNG PEOPLE PSYCHOLOGICALLY AND SPIRITUALLY FOR A WORLD IN WHICH TERRORISM EXISTS?

Unfortunately, educational institutions are directly affected by terrorism more and more.[16] This leaves schools with the challenge of preparing themselves for potential attacks and knowing how to work with students in the aftermath of attacks.

Security

First there is the question of school security. It goes without saying that bomb-alert and intruder-alert practices, fire drills, first aid training and general safety awareness campaigns have to be strengthened in schools. Students need to know what to do quickly and calmly in the event of an attack, and much experience and research tells us that certain behaviours (lockdown, dispersing, lying low) are highly effective, while recent attacks in Europe have shown us how responding with streetwise knowhow, seeking out effective hiding places, using cell phones judiciously and thinking laterally in the heat of the moment have saved people's lives.

When interviewed by the BBC on survival strategies during attacks, survival psychologist John Leach gave the following advice:

- React quickly and do not wait for others to take the lead (typically, a minority take the initiative to save themselves or others, whilst most are dumbstruck and do not react).
- Make yourself a smaller target (keep out of sight and seek cover).
- Get as far away as possible.
- Help other people (Ruz, 2015).

A terrorist attack calls on higher-order, creative and on-your-feet thinking. Students must abide by certain protocols that the institution has agreed on and practised but also be ready to take initiative and adapt according to the situation, since each attack will be different and the dynamics will involve unforeseen circumstances and variables.

School security needs to be reinforced as much as possible, but this can be difficult for financial and philosophical reasons. Creating a bunker with armed security guards is not the wish of most schools. So reinforcing the badging of visitors, routine identity checks, surveillance cameras, keeping an open, fluid discussion in the community about any unusual movements or sightings and keeping a good relationship with the local authorities so that any contact with the police at the time of an attack will lead to the quickest possible response – are all sensible measures.

Trauma and Counselling

All those who try to pick up the pieces after an attack (school, teacher, mentor, counsellor, family, friend) have to try to not only to ensure that students discuss and share thoughts about terrorism but also do everything they can to prevent the victims from falling into deep anxiety. This obligation puts teachers and mentors in the role of psychologists and therapists and requires certain techniques and strategies. Fortunately, some have developed basic guidelines based on case studies and research.[17] However, schools need to use their psychologists, counsellors and nurses effectively in such circumstances, as they are the specialists, with the most relevant knowledge.[18]

A Spiritual Response

Preparing young people for a world of terrorism is not only a psychological challenge but a spiritual one too, as individuals need to show exceptional strength, forgiveness and positivity in overcoming such trauma. Studies show that spiritual approaches are more remedial than others in the healing process.[19]

History also has shown the importance of religious structures in helping victims of oppression survive morally: the role of the South African Council of Churches under Desmond Tutu in the 1980s was not only a resistance movement to apartheid but also a system that allowed for healing and forgiveness; the Sandinista liberation theology in Nicaragua gave the poor hope and determination in the 1960s and 1970s; and the role of Negro spirituals and religious belief in the African American resistance to slavery and to the trampling of civil rights in the nineteenth and twentieth centuries are all examples of how spirituality allows communities to face extreme adversity.

This is not to say that schools should take on religious responses to terrorism but rather that, since terrorism is an abhorrent phenomenon, which defies logical constructs of decency, curtailment of conflict, rules and fairness (from the point of view of the victims, of course), then a response based on logic or on the dry and technical world of psychological therapy might not be enough to strengthen students sufficiently as they try to reckon with something that defies understanding. As sad as it is to say, for true healing to take place the requirements may be an element of fatalism, a belief that adversity exists to test and strengthen and an acceptance that is needed. Such spiritual (as opposed to rational) responses can be forged through various classroom experiences, such as the teaching of philosophy, one-on-one coaching with mentors and student discussion groups.

Salif

What became of Salif, my friend who took a strange turn towards fundamentalism? Did he change his ways?

Truth be told, I do not know what happened to Salif. He disappeared, and to this day I have no idea where he is or what he does. I have confidence that common sense and a good grounding brought him back to his senses, that the dead-end towards which he was headed was simply a phase. But possibly he went even deeper into his philosophy of hate and destruction.

I hope he did not. I was young at the time and did not know how to respond. Had I met him today in such a state of mind, I would done everything in my power to turn him away from the darkness. I'm sure there was something beneath it all that was haunting him, some pain that he could not let go. I'll never know.

CONCLUSION

As I finish my last sentence, the Nice attack feels far enough behind us – at least for those who lived through it from the safe distance of a television screen – for the world to be focussing on other things that smack of normality like the Rio Olympics. However, just the other day, the death toll increased once more, to 86, as another person succumbed to wounds incurred in the attack. And every day, if one looks

CHAPTER 3

enough, one will find some news of an attack, an act of hatred, even if not featured prominently in the media because it is in a place off the media's beaten track, such as the north of Cameroon or Nigeria.

And as I reread this draft one summer later, the newspapers are full of reports of a car attack in Barcelona, which killed 13, and later in the year, another in Barcelona, in which a truck driven into a crowd killed 130. The violence continues.

My children found out about the Nice attack without my telling them. A neighbour brought it up in a discussion. Perhaps I was wrong to keep it from them in the first place, since it is not by hiding the world from young people that we will make it a better place. Then again, they are still young and innocent, and the horror of the terrorist attack seems too much for them to absorb and too weighty to carry on their shoulders. That is a debate to be had: to what extent school should be a place that prepares young people for the world and to what extent it should do the opposite and protect them from it. I'm not sure any of us have the definitive answer, but presumably it lies in balance.

An image that I could not hide from them, a different one, was of a young child, dazed and bloodied, caked in cordite, hoisted from the ruins of a bombing in the Syrian war. The image does not generate any comments: no one knows what to say. It defies any reliance on nice speeches and platitudes. It is a monstrous auto-signifier; it tells its own story of darkness and extreme cruelty. The boy's name, we are told, is Omran.

The image goes against the substance of education. For what kind of person could do that to another person, let alone a child? And since we are dealing with education, what went so wrong in someone's education, in our collective education as human beings, for such an act to be committed? As the question crystallises in my mind, I realise, with despair, that the image leaves me with so much we are trying to control through education: raw anger, heated outrage, overwhelming, unprocessed pity and fear.

Whether education can truly cure us of such bestiality is difficult to hypothesise or to measure, but it remains a dream and for now is something we must believe. Let us do everything we can in our schools, with our students or our own children, with ourselves and with political leaders (for no one is impervious to an education) to settle our disputes in non-violent ways.

What I am implying is nothing short of a revolution in educational practice, discourse and content. We need to present, as models of success, peace and dialogue, not imperialism and violence – which essentially means rewriting the history books. We need to ensure that we are doing more than narrowing the curriculum to academic subjects and find the time to engage in open discussion on the issues that are plaguing humanity every day – have the courage to forget about examinations and league tables once in a while. We need to create a climate in which emotion and hatred can be put aside and dialogue and peace predominate, despite images and news bulletins portraying despicable inhumanity.

Finally, if there is in the human mind a predisposition – or perhaps a thirst – for spirituality, then education must occupy that space. We must offer young people opportunities not only to learn philosophy, but also to "do" philosophy, for themselves and for the people they will become when faced by adversity and difficulty later on. This doing of philosophy – grappling with big questions and reflecting on the self – should bring young people spirituality in the name of life and not in the name of death.

NOTES

1. "Since the beginning of the 21st century, there has been over a nine-fold increase in the number of deaths from terrorism, rising from 3,329 in 2000 to 32,685 in 2014" (Global Terrorism Index, 2015, p. 2).
2. A classified MI5 document produced in 2011 pointed out that more than 60 percent of "British terror suspects" were from "middle-class backgrounds and those who become suicide bombers are often highly educated" (Taher, 2011). This surprising reality has also been reported and examined by Krueger (2008) and Bergen (2015).
3. This phenomenon has been explored by Forest (2006), who discusses the strategic and tactical approach employed by terrorists, including the pedagogy of training camps, virtual reality and social media. Olidort and Sheff (2016) discuss Islamic State textbooks and how some of them engage in a "sophisticated reshaping of the classical Islamic curriculum, such as by interspersing letters from jihadist ideologues with chapters on medieval Arab poetry, or listing the Islamic State as the final stage in the history of Islamic governments".
4. The MI5 report explained this sequence, too.
5. I have shown in my book on prejudice (Hughes, 2017) how empathy can be developed at different levels, via case studies and the arts at a basic level and at a higher level via direct personal contact with other people through field trips and exchange programmes.
6. Allport's contact hypothesis (Allport, 1954; Pettigrew and Tropp, 2008), involving people of different backgrounds coming into contact with each other in non-threatening, group-based projects, is social psychology's most studied theory on the subject of reducing prejudice and animosity. Important parts of the endeavour are group discussion, and a baseline understanding that the goals of the institution presiding over proceedings are related to peace, living together and a celebration of diversity – meaning that students have to be aware of the ground rules in discussions and that the ground rules should be respectful and positive.
7. Programmes such as Matthew Lipman's Philosophy for Children (2003), which calls for extended reflective discussion in class during which students are able to take ownership not only of the development of the discussion but also of the subject matter of the discussion, ensure that students get a chance to express themselves, listen to each other and argue for or against positions. Similarly, structured debating strengthens critical thinking and models (for young people) the idea that it is through sharing of ideas and grappling with ideological positions that we can arrive at suitable conclusions, as opposed to through violence.
8. This is effectively Emmanuel Kant's categorical imperative.
9. For a masterly account of the history of democracy, see A. C. Grayling's *Democracy and its Crisis* (2017).
10. Brockhoff, Krieger, and Meierrieks (2015) point out how socioeconomic variables allow us to cluster countries in analysing the relationship between higher education and terrorism, the results' showing specific trends:

    > For the group of poorly developed countries (often located in Latin America, Asia, or Sub-Saharan Africa), we find that variables reflecting lower education (primary education, literacy rate) are associated with more terrorism, while higher education (university enrollment) does not play a role… For the group of countries in which conditions are more favorable, we find no positive association between lower education and terrorism. Instead, we find a negative (terrorism-reducing) and statistically significant effect of higher education (university enrollment) on domestic terrorism. (Brockhoff, Krieger, and Meierrieks, 2015)

    Elu and Price (2015) discuss the specific variables leading to terrorism in Africa, explaining how existential "other worldly" elements of religious ideology are important factors; Malik's *Madrasas in*

CHAPTER 3

South Asia (2008) deconstructs some of the oversimplifications embedded in Western understanding as to Islamic education in Pakistan and India; while Webb (2012) explores teaching sociopolitical themes that are contentious and are related to terrorism in the Middle East, primarily by using Middle Eastern literature as a gateway into the historical and collective psyche of place. Webb explores ways that delicate issues such as the Iraq War can be taught and understood in the classroom.

[11] Resources for teaching students about terrorism proliferate on the Web. These include Frontline's "Roots of Terrorism" teachers' guide (Frontline, 2016), emphasising political and historical reasons for Jihadism, anti-Semitism and nationalism; the Zinn Education Project (2016), which discusses the semantics and symbolism of representation in political discourses about terrorism (Zinn Education Project, 2016) and the US Department of State's curriculum guide on terrorism (Office of the Historian, 2016), which takes a more official, diplomatic approach to the question by exploring US foreign policy and international relations from the US point of view.

[12] Cameroon was liberated on paper but merely became part of "La France Afrique" in a neocolonial pseudo transfer of power (see Beti, 2006).

[13] An example of a text that offers an alternative view of American history, although not without having suffered some criticism for its degree of factual accuracy, is Howard Zinn's *A People's History of the United States* (1980) which offers a Marxist, postcolonial viewpoint of mainstream events but also gives prominence to previously underdiscussed class struggles of the nineteenth century. A more contemporary iteration of the debate over revisiting history is in the discussion over whether statues of confederates should remain part of mainstream American historical iconography, a debate that raged throughout the United States in 2017.

[14] Derek Gregory's *The Colonial Present* (2004) explains the historical relationship between British colonialism in the Middle East, American foreign policy and contemporary political tensions.

[15] Duckworth (2014), following the ideas of Zinn (1980) and having conducted qualitative and quantitative research, concludes that the oral tradition should be used in teaching about terrorism, notably the case of 9/11. This approach involves seeking personal testimonies and stories so as to make events seem closer and more tangible for students than they would appear in a removed, academic, third-person narrative.

By bringing a direct, experiential narrative into the discussion of terrorism, schools also encourage students to share their own feelings, fears and positions, thereby breaking the silence and ensuring a dialogue of mediation. The United States Institute of Peace (2001) has developed a teaching guide with a continued focus on language, discussion and sharing of ideas. According to the guide, students are asked to define terms, grapple with difficult questions and share viewpoints. This social constructivist pedagogical response to terrorism is aligned with Vygotsky's notion of learning, in which language plays a vital role in taking ideas to a higher plane of conceptualisation and meaning is built through speech production, listening and response (1987).

[16] The University of Maryland's Global Terrorism Database has shown that attacks on educational institutions have risen from roughly 70 per year during the 1980s and 1990s to well over 300 per anum from 2012 on (GTD, 2016).

[17] The University of Virginia (2015) has issued guidelines for teachers on what to do with students who have been affected directly by terrorism. These include the following:

Take time to talk about a terrorist attack; review what has happened; help students express their feelings about the tragedy. Express anger in an appropriate manner. Talk about constructive responses. Be thoughtful and planful and not opportunistic. Remember that you are a source of safety and security for children in school. Remember that children will pick up what you are anxious about.

[18] For a detailed account of the psychological and biomedical ramifications of trauma related to war and terrorism, see Ochberg (1987).

A number of cognitive therapy models have been developed and tested for catering to post-stress trauma. For example, Ehlers et al. (2005) ran a randomized controlled trial (with a waitlist condition) on 28 participants, to find significant improvement in those who were subjected to a model involving careful long-term follow-up and a deeper understanding of personal history. Silver et al. (2005) found positive results from post 9/11 patients who followed EMDR therapy (eye movement desensitisation and reprocessing – a therapy in which participants recount traumatic events, while following the finger movement of a specialist). Josman et al. (2006) surveyed the use of computer-generated virtual reality scenarios as a means of helping Israeli patients reconstitute the past and process emotionally traumatic events.

What these models have in common is the need for victims of terrorism to retrace and reconstruct events while discussing them so as not to occult them and let them fulminate at the subconscious level. As with so much else related to education for less terrorism, dialogue and discussion, taking experiences and thoughts to the level of socialisation and exchange, are paramount.

The American Academy of Child and Adolescent Psychiatry (2015) has issued similar guidelines to those of the University of Virginia, with much focus on careful listening and answering young people's questions but without putting pressure on them to discuss issues they are not ready to take on board. A common recommendation in both of these sets of guidelines is to be discerning about exposing students to violent film footage.

[19] Meisenhelder and Marcum (2009), having surveyed over 1000 subjects (all of them Presbyterians), came to the conclusion that positive spiritual coping mechanisms were more effective than other methods in helping people deal with post-terrorism trauma. Farkas and Hutchison-Hall (2008) discuss how the spiritual response to 9/11 in the United States was extremely strong and an appropriate forum for the types of existential questions that were unearthed by the trauma.

REFERENCES

AACAP [American Academy of Child and Psychiatry] (2015). *Terrorism and war: How to talk to children.* Washington, DC: AACAP. http://www.aacap.org/AACAP/Families_and_Youth/Facts_for_Families/FFF-Guide/Talking-To-Children-About-Terrorism-And-War-087.aspx

Alexander, R. (2006). *Towards dialogic teaching: Rethinking classroom talk* (3rd ed.). Cambridge: Dialogos.

Allport, G. (1954). *The nature of prejudice.* Cambridge, MA: Addison-Wesley.

Bergen, P. (2015, February 27). 'Jihadi John': The bourgeois terrorist. *CNN.* http://edition.cnn.com/2015/02/19/opinion/bergen-terrorism-root-causes/

Beti, M. (2006). *La France contre l'Afrique.* Paris: La Découverte.

Brockhoff, S., Krieger, T., & Meierrieks, D. (2014). Great expectations and hard times: The (nontrivial) impact of education on domestic terrorism. *Journal of Conflict Resolution, 59,* 1186–1215. doi:10.1177/0022002713520589

Brockhoff, S., Krieger, T., & Meierrieks, D. (2015). *More education = less terrorism? Studying the complex relationship between terrorism and education.* https://politicalviolenceataglance.org/2015/12/04/more-education-less-terrorism-studying-the-complex-relationship-between-terrorism-and-education/

Burns, R. J., & Aspeslagh, R. (Eds.) (2013). *Three decades of peace education around the world: An anthology.* New York, NY: Routledge.

Duckworth, C. (2014). *9/11 and collective memory in US classrooms: Teaching about terror.* London: Routledge.

Ehlers, A., Clark, D. M., Hackmann, A., McManus, F., & Fennell, M. (2005). Cognitive therapy for post-traumatic stress disorder: Development and evaluation. *Behaviour Research and Therapy, 43*(4), 413–431.

Elu, J., & Price, J. (2015). Causes and consequences of terrorism in Africa. In C. Monga & J. Yifu Lin (Eds.), *The Oxford handbook of Africa and economics: Context and concepts.* Oxford: Oxford University Press.

Fanon, F. (1963). *The wretched of the earth.* New York, NY: Grove Press.

Farkas, Z. D., & Hutchison-Hall, J. (2008). Religious care in coping with terrorism. *Journal of Aggression, Maltreatment & Trauma, 10*(1–2), 565–576.

Frontline (2016). *Roots of terrorism teachers guide.* http://www.pbs.org/wgbh/pages/frontline/teach/terror/

Global Terrorism Index (2015). *Quantifying peace and its benefits.* Sydney, New York, NY & Mexico City: Institute for Economics and Peace. http://economicsandpeace.org/wp-content/uploads/2015/11/Global-Terrorism-Index-2015.pdf

CHAPTER 3

GTD [Global Terrorism Database] (2016). *Global terrorism database*. College Park, MD: University of Maryland. https://www.start.umd.edu/gtd/

Grayling, A. C. (2017). *Democracy and its crisis*. London: Oneworld.

Gregory, D. (2004). *The colonial present*. Oxford: Blackwell.

Hughes, C. (2009). International education and the International Baccalaureate diploma programme: A view from the perspective of postcolonial thought. *Journal of Research in International Education, 8*(2), 123–141.

Hughes, C. (2014). How can international education help reduce students' prejudice? *Prospects, 44*(3), 395–410.

Hughes, C. (2017). *Understanding prejudice and education: The challenge for future generations*. London: Routledge.

JanMohamed, A. (1985). The economy of manichean allegory: The function of racial difference in colonialist literature. *Critical Inquiry, 12*, 59–87.

Josman, N., Somer, E., Reisberg, A., Weiss, P. L. T., Garcia-Palacios, A., & Hoffman, H. (2006). BusWorld: Designing a virtual environment for post-traumatic stress disorder in Israel: A protocol. *CyberPsychology & Behavior, 9*(2), 241–244. doi:10.1089/cpb.2006.9.241

Krueger, A. B. (2008). *What makes a terrorist: Economics and the roots of terrorism*. Princeton, NJ: Princeton University Press.

Lipman, M. (2003). *Thinking in education* (2nd ed.). Cambridge: Cambridge University Press.

Malik, J. (Ed.) (2008). *Madrasas in South Asia: Teaching terror?* London: Routledge.

Meisenhelder, J. B., & Marcum, J. P. (2009). Terrorism, post-traumatic stress, coping strategies, and spiritual outcomes. *Journal of Religion and Health, 48*, 46. doi:10.1007/s10943-008-9192-z

Ochberg, F. (1987). *Post-traumatic therapy and victims of violence*. New York, NY: Brunner/Mazel.

Office of the Historian, US Department of State (2016). *Introduction to curriculum packet on "Terrorism: A war without borders"*. https://history.state.gov/education/modules/terrorism-intro

Olidort, J., & Sheff, J. (2016). *Teaching terror: The Islamic State's textbooks, guidance literature, and indoctrination methods*. Washington, DC: Washington Institute. http://www.washingtoninstitute.org/policy-analysis/view/teaching-terror-the-islamic-states-textbooks-guidance-literature-and-indoct

Pettigrew, T. F., & Tropp, L. R. (2008). How does intergroup contact reduce prejudice? Meta-analytic tests of three mediators. *European Journal of Social Psychology, 38*, 922–934.

Ruz, C. (2015). What should you do in an attack? *BBC*. http://www.bbc.com/news/magazine-34844518

Said, E. (1993). *Culture and imperialism*. New York, NY: Vintage Books.

Silver, S. M., Rogers, S., Knipe, J., & Colelli, G. (2005). EMDR therapy following the 9/11 terrorist attacks: A community-based intervention project in New York City. *International Journal of Stress Management, 12*(1), 29–42. http://dx.doi.org/10.1037/1072-5245.12.1.29

Steiner, G. (1967). *Language and silence: Essays 1958–1966*. London: Faber.

Taher, A. (2011, October 15). The middle-class terrorists: More than 60pc of suspects are well educated and from comfortable backgrounds, Says secret M15 file. *Daily Mail*. http://www.dailymail.co.uk/news/article-2049646/The-middle-class-terrorists-More-60pc-suspects-educated-comfortable-backgrounds-says-secret-M15-file.html

United Nations (1948). *Universal declaration of human rights*. http://www.un.org/en/universal-declaration-human-rights/

United States Institute of Peace (2001). *Teaching guide on international terrorism: Definitions, causes, and responses*. http://www.usip.org/sites/default/files/terrorism.pdf

University of Virginia (2015). *Talking to children about terrorism*. http://curry.virginia.edu/research/projects/threat-assessment/talking-to-children-about-terrorism

Vygotsky, L. S. (1987). Lectures on psychology. In R. Rieber & A. Carton (Eds.), *The collected works of L. S. Vygotsky*. New York, NY: Plenum.

Webb, A. (2012). *Teaching the literature of today's Middle East*. London: Routledge.

Webel, C., & Galtung, J. (2007). *Handbook of peace and conflict studies*. London: Routledge.

Zinn Education Project (2016). Whose "terrorism"? http://zinnedproject.org/materials/whose-terrorism/

Zinn, H. (1980). *A people's history of the United States*. New York, NY: Harper & Row.

CHAPTER 4

SUSTAINABILITY

INTRODUCTION

It's Saturday afternoon, which means I'm doing the shopping with my family. No other point in the week leaves time for it, and as much as I would rather be walking by the seaside or reading a book in a sunlit café, it must be done. During the week, work is so all-encompassing that chores such as this must be done hastily in a narrow corridor of weekend time, one that we unfortunately share with thousands of other shoppers.

Usually we shop at an organic food outlet, with its brown paper bags, locally produced crops, pale, dreadlocked till managers and slow, trim, peaceful shoppers in hiking boots and loose Asian clothes, who shuffle meditatively from gluten-free maize waffles to lactose-free yoghurts.

But today allowed no time for that; so we have settled for a gargantuan shopping centre, assaulted by frozen meat, plastic, imported sad-looking tropical fruits, endless shelves of refined and industrially produced products. The shoppers here are less glamorous. They waddle shamelessly from shelves of gigantic packets of crisps to those of jumbo discounted toilet rolls to displays of electric-blue laundry softener. In the background, of course, is a radio programme's inane babble, interspersed with pop songs about broken romance or love at first sight, incongruous as you try to nudge past a purple-wigged, thick-set, floral-draped grandmother deliberating as to which packet of white sugar to buy.

Shopping here is a potent mix of denial, guilt and greed, and as I hoist packets of chemically enhanced food from shelves, our trolley fills up with a brightly coloured heap of single-use plastic that will not be recycled, that will sit, insolent and ugly, on the earth's surface as part of our trail of pollution. The food itself will pass aggressively through our digestive tracts and then join the tonnes of human waste, the aftermath of this unhealthy expression of consumerism, through the labyrinth of drainpipes to the ocean.

One has to wonder how much of what we mechanically grab and toss into the shopping trolley is actually necessary. It is as if we are pawns in some scheme, taken over by a compulsive, unthinking consumerist Geist, propelled by imaginary hunger, a sense of false provision.

And once we have loaded the fridge at home, we will yet again surprise ourselves at the impressive pace at which we make our way through the produce, and fill rubbish bags with double, triple and quadruple our own weight with that of the detritus our household expels daily.

© JOINTLY BY IBE-UNESCO AND KONINKLIJKE BRILL NV, LEIDEN, 2018
DOI:10.1163/9789004381032_004

CHAPTER 4

If truth be told – and I have a feeling that we all feel this way, me and every other shopper morosely ploughing through the sorry business of shopping – what I'm doing disgusts me. It does not feel natural to buy so much food.

Yet, this is just part of routine human activity that all contributes to the planet's steady, painful demise. We spend hours in traffic jams, emitting carbon monoxide into the atmosphere. We burn endless amounts of electricity on a host of household tasks – including switching light bulbs on and off hundreds of times a week – only a fraction of which are necessary for our survival. We chew up reams of paper in photocopies at work. We use air conditioning when it gets too hot. We turn on heating when it gets too cold. We accelerate the extraction of heavy metals as we buy, use and then discard our handheld devices, looking always for the latest model. Our activity is a blind lurch towards a future we are not thinking about.

As I write this, Cape Town approaches "day zero", when there will be no more tap water. It's having the worst drought in South Africa in 200 years. How do we face such a catastrophe? Those with borehole water continue to water their swimming pools and lawns, but this is not the right approach, for such behaviour will ultimately drain not only the water table under the earth's surface, but also the phreatic levels beneath the water table. The threat of drought forces us all to rethink the wasteful manner in which we use water, up to 400 litres per day per person. We have to rethink showering, dishwashing and toilet flushing.

In the early twenty-first century, 60 years after the post-World War II boom in consumerism and 200 years after the Industrial Revolution, we have become so wasteful and our behaviour so unsustainable, that it seems difficult to imagine life any other way.

And when one does decide to turn one's back on such a lifestyle, to stop driving everywhere, to eat less meat, to live frugally and ecologically, to settle for the life of a nineteenth century pilgrim, transcendentalist philosopher or hippie, one finds oneself swimming against a powerful ideological current of gigantic, remorseless and pitilessly normalised consumerism, a lone rebel fighting a lost cause.

Bafia

My wife comes from a village in central Cameroon called Bafia. We travel there from time to time and walk through the forest and bush, our eyes roaming the misty palm fronds that speckle the horizon in hues of pale green and grey.

It is beautiful. A special plant there, a type of fern, shrinks when you touch it, as if it were a living person responding to contact. The earth is a rich red, and the tallest trees loom high, stretching their thorny canopy to the heavens. Like ancestors from a prehistoric age, they look down on you silently.

But my wife tells me that Bafia is nothing like it was when she was a child. Then, it was lush rainforest, difficult to access. The inhabitants travelling to and from Bafia took a ferry to get across the river. The bush was alive with monkey sounds and bird calls. Her grandfather told of buffaloes roaming the savannah. Today the country boasts not a single wild buffalo. Children know of such animals from folk legends, as symbols.

Then a highway was built between Yaoundé (the capital) and Bafia. This is what we call "progress", allowing people to travel by car to and from the village. But this artery into the heart of the land was used to bleed it of its wealth. Foreign logging companies, some of them illegal, have destroyed 15% of the country's forests and related biodiversity in the space of 25-odd years. When one drives along the road, it seems that every fourth vehicle is a truck taking logs to the city to export to Europe. Those felled trees, hundreds of years old, will be used to adorn the dashboards and glove compartments of luxury cars. If your car is decorated with teak, think of that next time you run your hand across its smooth, stripy surface. That was once a mighty tree, standing over greenery as far as the eye could see in one of the planet's former lungs.[1]

The White Rhino

As a child in South Africa, I would always look forward to the opportunity to travel into the Kruger National Park. Here the land radiates the primeval heat of the very origins of life. I did not know that in those days anyone who was not white was not allowed in the park. Apartheid managed to keep the heart of Africa away from Africans, the ultimate insult.

Whilst it was rare to see leopard or lion, you would be sure to spot white rhinos. These majestic creatures would shuffle across the dry heartland and monitor you, surreptitiously, through small dark eyes on either side of a dinosaur-like face.

Not long ago, I took my children to the Kruger Park. It was an incredible experience as we cut through the bush, spotting four of the "big five": enthralled by the towering elephant prodding the land with padded feet; by the majestic gait of the male lion with its dazzling mane; by the brooding power of the black buffalo; and by the spotted beauty of the sleeping leopard, curled under an acacia, flicking its ear from time to time, its coat a deep gold.

We saw one rhinoceros, but it had been poached. Carrion birds circled above, and as the 4 × 4 slowly approached, we saw the mighty creature under a swarm of scavengers, including vultures and wild dogs. Poachers had sawed its horn off. Rhino horns are worth more than gold. Poachers come in and out of the park at will, and three are poached a day (Save the Rhino, 2017).

How do we undo this nightmare? What do we need to do to restore the planet's animals and trees?

THE CATASTROPHE OF THE ENVIRONMENT: WHAT RESEARCH TELLS US

What do we know of the state of the planet? Evidence is less and less easy to discount or contradict, and sources are manifold. Few can seriously pretend that we are not destroying the planet at a galloping pace through an entirely unsustainable lifestyle.

CHAPTER 4

The Anthropocene Paradigm

The idea here, quite simply, is that for the first time in the 4.5 billion years of the planet's existence, "human activities now rival the great forces of nature in driving changes to the Earth System" (Gaffney and Steffen, 2017, p. 1). Human-caused forces such as "rates of change of biodiversity, atmospheric chemistry, marine biogeochemistry and land-use change" (ibid., p. 3) are having such a marked impact on the state of the planet that they can be considered part of a new planetary era, once in which human activity has an effect comparable to the elements themselves. What is known as the "Great Acceleration" is seen to have taken place from roughly the 1950s, when technology and capitalism coalesced into an unprecedented force for change.[2]

As we know, the consequences of a rise in temperature are potentially devastating. Warming has a series of appalling knock-on effects, including the melting of glaciers and ice caps, which in turn leads to rising sea levels and seasonal changes that cause premature blossoming and less productive natural yields.[3]

Impact on Animals

Studies show that our planet's animals are under attack[4] and that up until now the impact of human activity on animals has been massively underreported.

Human Behaviour Cannot Be Sustained by the World's Resources

Over 80% of the world's population lives in countries running ecological deficits (meaning that they use more biocapacity than their country offers). Human activity produces carbon dioxide emissions at a rate of 60% greater than the planet can absorb and regenerate from. This is known as an ecological overshoot (Global Footprint Network, 2017).

Pollution

The World Wildlife Foundation estimates that world pollution increased 400 times between 1930 and 2000, while the use of pesticides and fertilizers has increased 26-fold in the past 50 years (WWF, 2017). These contaminants have contributed to a world in which 1.1 billion people do not have access to clean water and 2.4 billion do not have access to adequate sanitation.

The International Energy Agency claimed that in 2017 the extent of climate change due to carbon dioxide emissions has become unsafe (Harvey, 2011).

Concentrations of rubbish have become particular toxic, famous examples being the Agbogbloshie 20-acre dumping ground of electronic waste in Ghana (Minter, 2016) and the Great Pacific Garbage Patch in which a massive accumulation of microplastics and non-biodegradable detritus is concentrated (National Geographic, 2017).

Many countries dumped radioactive waste in the ocean until the Basel and London Conventions banned the practice in 1993,[5] while the harm done to the ocean in the form of oil spills and waste dumping is extreme.

Even in space, a growing collection of rubbish is drifting in the ether, often colliding with itself, perforating the solar panels or chassis of satellites or breaking against asteroids.[6] Much of the junk in space is related to satellite activity or the leftovers of collision of objects in space.

Deforestation

Experts tell us that the world originally comprised 16 million square kilometres of rainforests, but today only 6.2 million square kilometres remain (Nature Conservancy, 2015). This dramatic depletion, caused mainly by heavy farming, has various deleterious effects on the environment, ranging from global warming caused by excesses of carbon dioxide released in the process (IPCC, 2007) to distorted water cycle patterns created by excess run-off of precipitation (Raven and Berg, 2006) and a decline in biodiversity.

Deforestation has been a well-known environmental problem for decades, and despite increasing awareness of its consequences, any meaningful advances to stop it are rendered ineffective by the excessive agricultural practice that traumatises the planet's lungs (namely, the Amazon rainforests and the Congo basin).

Marine Biodiversity

Since the Industrial Revolution in the nineteenth century, marine biodiversity has suffered enormous losses.[7] A great many coral reefs are either extinct or dying, while heavy commercial traffic crosses the oceans and unsustainable fishing continues. Various estimates claim that there will be few, or even no fish in the oceans in the next half century. The fishing industry has not been seriously curtailed by this forecast.

Fracking

Fracking – technically, hydraulic fracturing – is a method of extracting oil and gas from shale rock. This technique is practised widely in the United States and other parts of the world. It is controversial because of the colossal amounts of water the process wastes, the potentially harmful chemicals it injects into the shale rock and the fact that the process can pollute the water table.

This method of oil and gas extraction is the subject of debates, as many governments fully support it and argue that it is a much-needed alternative to the Middle East-dominated oil industry on which so much energy production relies. Environmentalists claim that fracking can have long-term disastrous consequences for the environment and human health.

CHAPTER 4

The Threat of Nuclear Holocaust

Although the threat of nuclear holocaust was seen as at its highest during the Cold War, notably during the Cuban Missile Crisis in 1962, the threat has not disappeared in the twenty-first century. According to Noam Chomsky (2016), it is technically speaking, greater than ever, because powerful nuclear weapons still proliferate and are in the hands of increasingly irresponsible leaders.[8] With the rise of fundamentalist jihadism, furthermore, the possibility of nuclear warheads falling into the hands of terrorists who seek to destroy as many lives as possible is not negligible.

Chomsky points out that a glance at recent world history indicates that the United States government, which used atomic warfare in Japan to end World War II in the Pacific, has been close to redeploying it on a number of occasions, not only during the infamous Cuban Missile Crisis.

A Ticking Time Bomb

The list goes on. It is becoming common knowledge that by predicted cited dates (often around 2050), marine biodiversity will be dramatically lessened, the number of species on earth will dramatically decline and not only the majority of the planet's animals, but human beings too will experience more difficult living conditions. The environment is a ticking time bomb. Without a dramatic response, the forecast is bleak.

HUMAN RESPONSES

Responses to the environmental crisis can be divided into three. At one extremity are activists, non-governmental organisations such as the World Wildlife Foundation and Greenpeace, alongside militants whose aim is to put the spotlight on environmental travesties and mobilise public opinion.

At the other end of the spectrum are multinationals, corporations, governments and lobbyists who do not want to see any change in the way that the planet's resources are being used. Their arguments range from outright denial to economic pragmatism.[9]

Between the extremes are consumers who give little thought to the problem or who might be concerned but not necessarily enough to do anything significant.

To be clear, this middle ground spans a number of behaviours. Those closer to the activists and awareness-raising agents will make conscientious decisions about their consumption and aim to respect the environment (people who purchase organic products, refuse to eat meat, avoid excessive use of carbon monoxide-emitting transport, fit out their houses and organisations with renewable energies). Those closer to the anti-environmentalists make little or no effort to respect the environment, throwing rubbish away in mixed heaps, consuming colossal amounts of water, fuel, non-renewable energies and so on.

What can an education for the twenty-first century do to reduce environmentally unsustainable behaviour? That is the question. What should we be teaching young people in order for them to make a difference in the world so that the future of the planet is not compromised?

All Is Not Lost

First, to reverse the fate of the planet is entirely possible, even despite the rampant demographic growth that humanity is witnessing: the prospect of improving the future of the planet markedly is realistic and attainable.[10] Holding onto this optimism is important, since one is tempted to give in quickly to the seemingly irrepressible power of nation states and large corporations that use up the planet's resources without showing any signs of relinquishing such practice because of protests by "small men". It is also easy to shrug one's shoulders and explain that the world's population makes improving the fate of the planet impossible. This mindset will not help create a more sustainable future.

The second big idea to grasp is that the deeper approach to a sustainable future for the planet is more about ideas than about action, at least in the first educational instance. This is not to say that an education for sustainability should not involve action – of course it should. It is to say, rather, that the roots of long-lasting environment-oriented behaviours are ideological and philosophical. I say this because quite often schools will conduct fund-raising activities, tree-planting initiatives, protest marches and special activity days dedicated to environmentalism. These are laudable exercises but will not necessarily shift a young person's mindset and make her feel outraged enough to commit to behaviour that is purposefully and permanently environmentalist. One can easily end up with a number of field days, each having some impact, but none striking the deep chord that is needed to distinguish a superficial education from a lasting, powerful one.

Schools and families can easily desensitise young people to a number of good causes if they involve them in too many trivial activities.[11] True revolution starts first and foremost in the minds and hearts of people. Then, once people embrace and internalise the key message or concept, powerful and authentic action will take place.

Educational experiences should, therefore, give young people the information, exposure and emotionally related stimuli that will cause deep-seated reactions within their moral frameworks, so that they take ownership of the learning process and make a difference as citizens.[12]

So in which areas can we aim to shift mindsets and influence values? I suggest five.

Understanding the Dynamics of a Consumer Society

The first thing to get young people to understand is that they live in a society built on consumer values in which the average person, because of market forces, is encouraged to buy and use products at a rapid rate. Consumerism implies that the route to happiness and fulfilment involves being able to afford any number of products and actualising that potential by buying them and using them extensively (or not: extreme consumerism creates a particularly perverse effect, whereby people purchase goods to hoard or display and not actually use). The mode of behaviour of the consumerist Western person – regular trips to shops, large weekly expenditures, high levels of plastic wastage and energy consumption – has been so normalised that to stand back and look at it with fresh eyes, as a peasant from the Middle Ages or a hunter gatherer in East Africa might, is difficult. Were we able to adopt such a perspective, we would no doubt see that this normalised behaviour is in fact compulsive and unnatural.

Consumerism indoctrination starts early. Young people preoccupy themselves with the brand of clothes or shoes they wear, the model of electronic device they have or the car that their parents drive. Of course, this phenomenon presents itself in more or less subtle ways and should not be generalised too easily. Most parents would no doubt deny that their children were growing up to be rampant materialists. However, young people experience much peer pressure to conform to a mode of living that entails some element of consumerism. The lyrics of much popular music, especially rap, promote crass materialism. Corporations that control children's entertainment tend to influence young people, via aggressive publicity campaigns, to consume or plead with their parents to consume.

Having students discuss this type of materialism and peer pressure is helpful, as it unearths tensions and identifies influences, bringing students to an awareness of the dynamics of consumerism that act on them informally through their social circles. It should be noted that seemingly trivial details, such as the type of clothes students wear or the gadgets and objects they carry, are important to them, and student-centred discussion probing them can yield rich, critical reflection.

For adults the situation is not much better. What used to be called the American Dream but what is now a type of universal middle-class doctrine, whereby a couple own a house, own a car, take their children on exciting holidays and live in material comfort, remains the objective of billions of people across the planet. Interestingly, popular revolts against this vision of society included the social revolutions after World War II that created Communist regimes in Asia and Eastern Europe, and also the hippie movement and iconic Parisian student revolt of May 1968 in the West. This honeymoon appears to have ended, however, perhaps with the fall of the Berlin Wall in 1989, and today it appears that the majority of the planet's population lives under the ideological sway of capitalist material consumerism.

Studying these historic counter-movements is healthy for young people, as it not only strengthens their knowledge of history but also suggests ideological contrasts to the monopolistic character of the consumer capitalism in which we find ourselves. Students need to know that large-scale revolts against consumerism have occurred, and against capitalism in general. Marx and Engels' short, visionary and highly relevant *Communist Manifesto* (1848) is a helpful text for students to know and read.

More contemporary alternative models also exist, such as the idea of degrowth, which originated in the 1970s in France and pointed out that many counter-models to unsustainable economic growth still proposed reinvestments in other types of growth and did not grapple with the concept that real change must involve a much more radical positioning in terms of societal goals – that human beings have to want less.[13] A surprising source for this alternative voice is Pope Francis' 2015 Encyclical *Laudato Si'*, in which he writes, "The time has come to accept degrowth". The encyclical is a strong, poetic song of praise for nature and an exhortation to humanity to change its ways concerning the environment.

As long as we believe that it is in purchasing material goods or giving immediate release to passions of ownership, consumption and appetite that we will be happier people, a sustainable future for the planet seems unlikely.

A number of critics of consumer society, such as Herman and Chomsky (1988), Cohen (2012) and Baudrillard (1970), point out that, some time after World War II and a surge in commercial activity, services became the new major human economic activity, and an entire class of consumers was created; from then on it had to be maintained in order for economic activity to be sustained. Because of this economic context in which we find ourselves, we end up spending much time shopping, consuming, throwing away old models to purchase new ones and essentially succumbing to the pressure that advertising puts on us to carry on consuming.

Algorithms embedded in search engines analyse our behaviour on the Web and create consumer profiles of us, based on statistically likely tastes and our potential future purchases. Advertisers then target us with subtle campaigns, drawing us in to the need to consume further. If we do not pay too much overt attention to the phenomenon, it deceives us into seeing it as the lure of a natural process, as if the things we would like to consume appear before us conveniently or the advertising campaigns we stumble across happen to speak to our interests. However, the process is a contrived one, and we need intellectual discernment and distance to understand it.

This is not a small point. Schools and parents must make clear to young people that consumerism is not a natural state of affairs. It is the product of a mode of production that requires individuals and groups to behave in a consumerist fashion. If tomorrow we all decided to curtail our spending, grow our own crops and sustain our own needs, industries would collapse and something of a financial recession would result. Recession might not be the aim of a future society, but young people must be taught to think about consumerism with some agency and critical thinking.

In order to fully understand the extent of the materialist paradigm, young people should be exposed to some of the literature and films that address the matter in a critical light.[14]

Teaching the history of consumerism as a form of economics and suggesting that the fragile ideological premise on which it is based is a belief system will help empower young people to liberate their minds from a mindless consumerism and from a lack of interest in, or, more perniciously, a blind acceptance of, the way things are, as if such a state of affairs were natural and could be no other way.

CHAPTER 4

Educational discourse needs to not only deconstruct consumerism in terms of its being a purely financial design, but it should also spotlight the general effect on human behaviour of the entertainment industry and superficial, hedonistic advertising campaigning (which characterises so much of modern media). As Marcuse and the so-called Vienna School of cultural Marxists pointed out, popular culture takes on the role that religion does in Marx's vision of social control; it becomes an opiate of the people and lulls them into a state of apathy and fecklessness, makes them passively receptive. Multibillion-dollar industries such as football and basketball leagues, television programmes (particularly sitcoms and fictional series), time- and energy-sapping social media platforms – all take us away from action and thus prevent revolution. It is, as Herman and Chomsky say, a case of manufacturing consent.

Countervailing voices now also proliferate on the Web and are quick to castigate multinational corporations for non-environmentally-sustainable practices and to suggest alternative pathways. Anti-globalisation movements represent a new approach to questions of sustainability.

Indeed, one might argue that social media platforms such as YouTube and Facebook serve, or at least can serve, the pro-sustainability purpose by stimulating awareness and provoking a critical response to issues of environmental degradation and social injustice. The social networks enabled by social media proved to be important in political uprisings such as the so-called Arab Spring of 2011 (a number of pro-democracy and anti-government protests that took place across the Middle East). Similarly, they proved important in the uncovering of a number of environmental crises: alternative narratives and whistleblowing posts featured on Twitter and Facebook during the Deep Water Horizon oil spill (an oil tanker exploded in 2010 off the Gulf of Mexico); Greenpeace used YouTube to highlight anti-environmental practices by Shell Oil in the Artic and during the 2015 drought in California, citizens used Instagram and Twitter to share information about the drought with each other (Dosemagen, 2017).

This intensive use of social media poses a certain danger; namely, it gives users the illusion of social activism when, in reality, any form of actual praxis will have been substituted for by statements of outrage, acts of protest by proxy or a type of armchair revolutionary activity consisting of reading posts and forwarding or "liking" them.[15]

So part of educating about consumerism is educating about the media and how they can displace genuine thought and action. Schools and educational institutions must put time into teaching young people how media work and how they affect human action.

Learning to Love Nature

An essential step towards a sustainable mindset involves the emotional and spiritual response we have to nature itself. Looking upon nature logically and dispassionately as an abstract entity that is the victim of heinous human behaviour and needs to be "fixed" is not enough to anchor a profound and lasting desire to care for, and protect, our natural surroundings.

One reason the world is in its present predicament is a centuries-long history of having pillaged and plundered with an aim of subduing nature to human will and enslaving it in the service of the economic and industrial activity of modern Homo economicus. The nineteenth century approach to nature, as something bestial and aggressive, even when the romantics sugared this view with notions of charm and innocence, has propelled northern European and Western cultures – which we can now consider a worldwide paradigm – far into a totally unsustainable relationship with nature. This cultural framework regards nature as a human backyard or, worse, refuse pile, and animals as either dangerous beasts or pitiable halfwits.

The treatment of animals is a telling example of this *Weltanshauung* (world view). The quantity of animals that die in abattoirs every day and the comparative thoughtlessness with which most people go about eating meat are symptoms of a deep-seated cultural approach which says that the natural world is put before men and women to serve them and to be exploited by them. In Genesis 1:26, for instance, God declares that man shall "have dominion over the fish of the sea, and over the fowl of the air, and over the cattle, and over all of the earth, and over every creeping thing that creepeth upon the earth". This approach might have understandably gone some distance in the early twentieth century, when little was studied and known about the extent of the ecological footprint that meat eating creates, but in the early twenty-first century, to carry on eating vast quantities of industrially prepared meat, as if such behaviour were normal or acceptable, requires a selfish, self-centred, head-in-the-sand approach.

Our treatment of animals (as pets on the one hand and as food on the other) represents a contradictory, unstable relationship. A number of powerful contemporary writings,[16] along with more established older writings by famous vegetarians such as Pythagoras, the Buddha, Plutarch and Percy Bysshe Shelley, or animal rights advocates such as Jeremy Bentham, can be used to awaken a consciousness in students of how we treat animals with cruelty, self-centredness and hypocrisy. This is surely a necessary first step in their altering their behaviour in the direction of a more sustainable modus operandi.

What these texts show us, and what the overwhelming majority of human behaviour to animals – outside of India – is missing, much like what is missing in the oceans that we pollute and the forests that we cut down, is love and respect. Without loving nature, we will never truly set out to save it.

Possibly one reason we do not deeply love nature is that society has tamed it to a point of unrecognisability, that in a sense it is no longer nature but rather the human-trodden remnant of nature, something that inspires less passion.

Consider the typical urbanised European rural landscape. Much of the natural layout has been chopped up into agricultural parcels. Geometric fields, paths and fences decorate the setting, with neat roads criss-crossing the whole. Human settlements are in the form of houses that depend on electricity, plumbing, concrete and bricks, while the gardens consist of mowed lawn, pruned trees, tended patches and potted flowers. Insects are killed, wild animals (if there are any left, which is unlikely) reviled and plants trained and pruned to human desires. This landscape hardly reflects a love of nature and is not the type of environment that will allow young people to grow up with such a love.

Of course some children will grow up on farms; others might find themselves in the rare pockets of unspoiled nature that have survived in Europe such as the fjords of Norway, the forests of Poland and the mountains of Montenegro; others will grow up with parents who make considerable efforts to venerate and love nature. But on the whole, agricultural activity in the Western world is less and less a primary source of income. Urban sprawl has edged out the rough, authentic voice of nature, relegating it into the outer peripheries. Some children grow up never seeing wild animals, and some will not even be familiar with farm animals, such as ducks and cows.[17] Nature for these generations is unfamiliar, the consequence of an historical process that began with the Middle Ages and has intensified ever since. Where unspoiled nature remains, it will be in pockets of land marketed as reserves or parks, existing – or so it would seem – for the entertainment of tourists and weekenders.

Now consider the typical African rural landscape. Vast expanses of desert, savannah or jungle spread across the land, with few incursions of human settlement.[18] Where signs of human activity do exist, they are either small traditional settlements, villages with small pockets of subsistence farming that quickly give way to the bush, the occasional outpost or, unfortunately – at least from an environmental perspective – some form of mechanised agriculture, with symmetric groves of palm oil trees, maize fields or sugar cane.

But big farms are the exception. The majority of the African landscape is of prehistoric beauty, inhabited by wild animals and teeming with the powerful energy nature provides. Such a setting encourages respect for nature and veneration for the millennia that have gone into carving its rock formations, sweeping its virgin coastline and nurturing its vast, ancient trees. When children play in the garden, they know that a poisonous snake or spider might be lurking under a rock or in the grass, that they might come upon a chameleon in the trees or a tortoise in the thicket. These simple experiences give the young person an inkling of how precious, awe-inspiring and beautiful nature is and, I would argue, push them to love nature more.[19]

The situation is complex and paradoxical, however, for many of the highly motivated nature lovers are European, or at least Western: it is often European- or North American-based non-governmental organisations, such as the World Wildlife Fund, Friends of the Earth or Greenpeace, that protest about pollution and petition against the treatment of endangered species.[20]

And on the other hand, littering in Africa, lack of seriously enforced legislation to protect flora and fauna, widespread illegal poaching of endangered species, a strong so-called developing-world discourse in favour of industrialisation and what appears to be a general lack of common awareness about the environment in many African countries – all these seem to suggest that Africa cares little for nature. However, this is the case only in some countries, as a number of African nations have taken the lead on banning plastics, in particular Rwanda.[21]

I would suggest that this state of affairs has to do with modern political and economic history. On the one hand, from the Industrial Revolution onwards, the European tradition of venerating nature has been forsaken (though it has caused a counter-perspective to surge in modern environmentalist circles). The dominant paradigm is, and has been for over two centuries, technological growth with the underlying message that nature is a type of endless resource serving the exploitative greed of humans. The African colonial experience has changed a society with the deepest respect for nature (animism, voodoo, shamanism, a life without artificial industrialised products, respectful and extremely small-scale agriculture), into one that emphasises urbanisation, social mobility, so-called Western values and, at root, a conversion from traditional religious naturalism to an imported Christian and Muslim religious structure that essentially sidelines, and even makes taboo, all things natural (a cliché would be the distaste with which an urbanised, Western-educated African will typically view traditional practices in the countryside with its superstition and strains of witchcraft).[22]

The point is more what the archetypes of Africa and Europe send us as educational messages about nature. I would suggest that the African landscape and traditions, no matter how battered and transformed by colonisation, give us more of an answer as to how we can develop a love of nature in our students than do the asphalted and urbanised landscapes of the West. Schools and families should aim to get young people into direct contact with unspoiled nature as early as possible through field trips, regular outdoor excursions, exposure to literature about the beauties of nature and guest speakers who spark a sensitivity for nature within young people.[23]

Studying Indigenous Knowledge Systems

If I may extend of the idea of loving nature, an additional undertaking can be to study those human societies that have modelled their cultural practice on a deep respect for nature. These indigenous knowledge systems can open the eyes of young people to models of sustainability through a reverence for nature. Anthropologists and ethnographers have identified a number of common traits that present themselves in indigenous knowledge systems (a belief in the spirit world, ancestor worship, strict initiatory rights, cyclical time and – relevant to this chapter – reverence for nature). This last element of indigenous philosophy should be investigated and appreciated more generally in curriculum, instruction and simply the way we bring up children.

In indigenous knowledge systems, such as that of the Aborigines, the Khoi San or the Yanomami, strikingly, nature is appreciated as an ecosystem with finite resources that are to be respected and not exploited. The approach can vary from a mystical one, whereby nature is conceived as a deity that should not be irked for fear of

CHAPTER 4

reprisal in any number of strong natural expressions such as drought, hail or violent, crop-ravaging storms, to nature's being seen as a living person with needs and a defined character.

The underlying pattern is the view that human beings and nature are related to one another in mutual respect and interconnectedness. Human beings are not beyond or above nature; they are inextricably part of it.[24]

Education systems around the world should communicate this idea of rapport between humans and nature, not just as a series of case studies of certain groups' beliefs and practices, but as a philosophy to consider and adopt in a world in which natural resources are treated with such disrespect and lack of foresight.[25]

Separate from this specific purpose, the study of indigenous knowledge systems is a crucial part of humanity's cultural transmission. The United Nations Convention on Biological Diversity states that humans should "respect, preserve, and maintain knowledge, innovations and practices of indigenous and local communities embodying traditional lifestyles relevant for the conservation and sustainable use of biological diversity" (United Nations, 1992).

Thinking and Acting Locally

Further to loving nature and understanding indigenous approaches to nature, schools, educational institutions, parents and cultural organisations need to model and develop the idea of respecting first and foremost the immediate, local environment because the environment in the twenty-first century has come to represent an abstract, worldwide notion that has planetary causes displacing local ones. For example, the media has brought our attention, rightly, to animals threatened by extinction around the globe, pollution in the oceans and in the air and overall environmental predictions about planet as a whole. They place before us a worldwide stage so large and far-reaching that one hardly knows where to start.

The concept of the environment as a finite global problem is relatively recent. For millennia, human beings lived, and were only aware of, finite spaces – hence traditional knowledge systems' veneration for highly localised natural entities such as certain trees, mountains or areas. Not until the Renaissance and Mercator's maps were the parameters of planet earth calculated with accuracy. This new understanding then led to a period of European expansionism, which regarded space as an ever-accommodating entity into which industry and economic gain could grow. No one reflected on the eventual limits or consequences of such expansion. Early colonialism consisted mainly of European settlers invading space with this mindset – that nature is to be owned and dominated – while natives saw sacred natural elements of their lifestyle destroyed. This collective mentality marked the Enlightenment, the Industrial Revolution and the first half of the twentieth century.[26]

Not until the invention of the atom bomb did anyone seriously entertain the idea of the earth's vulnerability. But from then on, human beings became responsible not just for their neighbourhoods, but also for the entire world. We felt suddenly possessed of the omnipotent, godlike capability of destroying the entire ecosystem. The new awareness and responsibilities brought along with them the international organisations with which we are familiar today, such as the United Nations, World Health Organisation and World Wildlife Fund. Most pollution and environmentally unsustainable practices take place, however, on a local scale. We litter in our own streets, use excessive amounts of electricity and water in our homes and go about separating waste – or not – locally. Schools, educational institutions and families need to ensure that students are engaged in such local projects as litter pick-up and cleaning local natural resources (such as lakes and parks). They need to model environmentally sustainable practices, such as using public transport or traveling to and from work by foot or bicycle, ensuring that waste is separated, monitoring and controlling electricity use and empowering students to set up task forces to further engage the entire student body in mindful, environmentally sustainable behaviours at a local level.

A simple starting point is the school itself. Every member of the community should take pride in their place of work and wish to keep it clean. Litter pick-ups and a consistent effort to keep educational sites well kept should be a norm. Management should keep a close eye on unnecessary paper and plastic consumption, encouraging teachers to avoid mass photocopying. In the school cafeteria, students should be made conscious of the value of healthy food and the environmental sustainability of local produce: a simple choice of victuals and products that are local rather than exotic, organic rather than industrial, can make a difference. No-meat days with information made available to students illustrate why eating less meat or no meat is better for the planet and for a person's health.

Needless to say, modelling environmentally friendly behaviour with a positive effect on the local community should take place in every household. Parents need to be careful about the wasteful consumerism they model for their children and strive to curtail it in favour of a more balanced approach to life.

If young people are going to have their awareness raised about the plight of animals that are threatened by extinction, it would be useful to direct their attention to local fauna and flora rather than exotic, distant species that represent a noble cause further afield. These more immediate, authentic connections will help them ground and direct their actions towards a visible, localised impact that they can take in and appreciate.

Modelling and Teaching Regenerative Systems

What needs to be taught is an entirely new approach to systems and processes. We need to move from the linear, waste-intensive model of the nineteenth and twentieth centuries towards a model of regenerative, cyclical development based on clean technology.

Consequently, objects should be used for longer, fixed rather than discarded, recycled and reassembled in imaginative ways. Consumption needs to be mindful and scaled back; the insatiable appetite created by a consumerist culture needs to be curbed with self-discipline and wisdom.

Constituencies should share resources. Neighbours need to pool tools and be prepared to circulate the things they own. Indeed, this mentality of sharing and re-using needs to start early on so that young people are habituated to it. School culture is still premised on individualism and a zero-sum, competitive approach. It assesses children mainly individually, ranks them according to grade, promotes selective academic programmes and encourages individual students to come to school with their own belongings rather than share them among many. The advent of new technologies has not changed culture, notwithstanding rhetoric on group work and Web communities. Most schools have a bring-your-own-device policy or 1:1 system that actually encourages individual purchase and ownership.

Breaking down societal organisation premised on individualism is not a simple affair, for the cult of the individual and the demise of collective entities are intertwined with the growth of state control and market capitalism. The state and the market rely on the individual consumer as a source of spending power and in this vein exacerbate excesses of ownership (each individual has to have her own car, her own house, her own instruments, and so on), and the environment becomes saturated.[27]

A concerted effort to tackle the cycle of greed and individualism is happening in non-Western countries, such as Bolivia and India. Much of what these countries do serves as an example of where the future should take us if we are to preserve our planet.[28]

A number of organisations also offer educational materials to promote a sustainable mindset, such as the Ellen MacArthur Foundation and the Solar Impulse Foundation.[29] These examples pave the way for sustainable twenty-first century practice and education.

Some core features of an educational vision for regenerative systems include the following:

- Learners share books, resources and devices (for example in groups of four, with pedagogically sound rules for group interaction).
- Our youth are taught recycling as part of a design cycle process, with emphasis on sustainability and environmental impact.
- Schools and families teach, and model as case studies, historical, economic and geographic examples of sustainable practice at a number of levels.
- Young people are brought to look at economic expansionism, industrialisation, urbanisation and production-line development with a critical eye, always aware of externalities and environmental impact associated with such models.
- Schools, organisations and families ensure that they model recycling of paper, glass and other materials and avoiding of unnecessary consumption of plastic, water and electricity.
- Campuses set aside for students natural spaces to practice regenerative ecology (compost heaps, small-scale agriculture and so on).

Bafia and the White Rhino

What will become of the village of Bafia? One of two possible scenarios in the long term is that it will become more and more "modernised" as concrete goes up, more roads criss-cross the bush, forests are cut down and the few wild animals that try to live off the land are driven out to the last corners of rainforest in the country, if there are any left by then.

Or the population could decide to do a U-turn. They could seek to preserve the natural heritage of the land, its mighty trees and emerald grasslands. They would slow palm oil production, open natural reserves and develop alternative income streams around preservation and ecotourism. This scenario seems possible but unlikely. For this vision to become reality requires two forces: good governance and education. At least some part of those forces lies in the hands of some of you who are reading this page.

And the white rhino? What can we do to stop the poaching of one of Africa's big five? Goodwill is in plentiful supply, and a number of public figures, both South African and international, have raised awareness. However, the poaching continues, and no white rhinos will be left for our children to see.

Corruption and ignorance drive the forces behind the poaching of the rhino, who are harbor a crazed notion that its horn provides magical medicinal properties. They are enemies of a twenty-first century education. Education must address them, from the youngest generations to the eldest.

CONCLUSION

We arrive home after the shopping and take the bags out of the car, stock the fresh items in the refrigerator, pack away the vegetables and fruit. The various chemicals that we will use to clean the house are stocked away too. I read the synthetic ingredients on their plastic bottles, and they seem scary and harmful to life.

This consumerist pattern that our lives follow we share with the majority of the world's population. In every corner of the globe, people participate on the treadmill of buying, consuming and discarding, and in turn keep the economic machine running. Each household duplicates this consumerist behaviour alongside another household, creating a mass effect.

How to break away from this vicious cycle? How to live with less and consume less?

Clearly the effort must first be individual. Each person must be aware of what she is consuming, why such consumption is taking place and what the consequences will be. Then, an act of self-depriving discipline must take place. We need to walk rather than drive, settle for food that might not be the most immediately gratifying, invest in energies and products that are sustainable but often less ergonomically or practically satisfying than those that destroy the planet long term but meet our short-term needs. This part of sustainability is spiritual and speaks to each person's lifestyle. The tenets involved in this inner revolution that must take place for a more sustainable future are not unlike those found in many religious or ethical codes of conduct. They involve asceticism, austerity, patience, commitment and dedication to a cause.

In our schools and universities, at home and in the community, we can develop human beings who carry these qualities with them in their lives; we can design learning experiences that speak a message of balance and frugality that reaches the core of each person's values and sense of resilience.

The question is not just about how we consume, however. It is also about knowing what we consume and how human activity affects the planet, about scrutinising carefully, and fully understanding, the causes for which we vote, the political decisions that we take and the parties that we join. Debates on climate change, for example, are ideological and speak to the deep parts of the mind, the stores of critical thinking that will determine how astutely a young person is able to judge arguments and decide for herself which position to endorse. Schools, educational institutions and households must make available correct information on the environment so that young people do not consume or vote out of ignorance, but rather use knowledge and foresight. The curricula of economics, geography and the sciences must have a focus on sustainability in order to ensure this intellectual empowerment.

Once I've packed away the last produce from the shopping, I decide never to shop like this again, to spend more time investigating what it is exactly I am buying, even if this pursuit eats into my time. I decide to buy more at the local market on Saturdays and to curb the temptation to shop excessively and frequently at the supermarket.

Other steps must be consolidated, such as taking public transport and reducing energy consumption. If each individual were to embrace these tenets of environmentalism, surely we would move in the right direction. Larger groups and powers also need to agree to use renewable energy, to clamp down on overfishing and illegal poaching, to commit to reducing carbon monoxide emissions. In this light, the collective task seems so vast as to be almost impossible. But here is where hopelessness and cynicism must give way to a determination and an optimism that education can and must provide.

NOTES

[1] "According to Global Forest Watch, an online forest monitoring platform, Cameroon lost 657,000 hectares of forest between 2001 and 2014, with the annual rate of loss rising over the period to around 141,000 hectares in 2014" (Infocongo, 2017).

[2] A telling paragraph from Gaffney and Steffen's article "The Anthropocene Equation" explains the phenomenon scientifically:

> Over the last 7000 years the rate of change of temperature was approximately $-0.01°C$/century. Over the last hundred years, the rate of change is about $0.7°C$/ century (IPPC, 2013), 70 times the baseline – and in the opposite direction. Over the past 45 years (i.e., since 1970, when human influence on the climate has been most evident), the rate of the temperature rise is about $1.7°C$/century (NOAA, 2016), 170 times the Holocene baseline rate. (p. 3)

3 To give but one example, in 2015, the colossal Zachariae Isstrom Glacier in Greenland broke away from the main ice cap. At the time it was reported that the glacier holds "enough water to raise [the] global sea level by more than 18 inches … if it were to melt completely [and is] losing more than 5 billions tons of mass every year" (MIT, 2015).

4 A systematic literature review on the effects of climate change on animals conducted by Pacifici, Visconti, Butchart, Watson, and Rondinini (2017) estimated that "47% of terrestrial non-volant threatened mammals (out of 873 species) and 23.4% of threatened birds (out of 1,272 species) may have already been negatively impacted by climate change in at least part of their distribution".

5 United States Environmental Protection Agency records show that over 55,000 containers of radioactive waste were dumped in the Pacific between 1964 and 1970 (EPA, 2017). Furthermore, according to the United Nations, the dumping of radioactive waste was still done illegally off the coast of Somalia until recently (Milton, 2009).

6 The United States Strategic Command was able to track over 17,000 man-made objects orbiting the earth (NASA, 2016), and hundreds of millions of microscopic debris are believed to circulate the earth (ESA, 2013).

7 According to the World Ocean Review, marine biodiversity is "declining more rapidly than ever before in the history of the Earth [and] only a small fraction of the species in the deep sea and polar oceans have so far been identified" (World Ocean Review, 2017).

8 Despite everything we know about the potential horrors of nuclear warfare, in 2017 the American President Donald Trump made some alarmingly reckless comments about potential nuclear warfare, especially with regard to North Korea (Freedland, 2017), whilst American-Russian relationships continue to be strained and largely unpredictable.

9 Chomsky puts it strongly: "There is a huge public relations campaign in the United States, organized quite openly by Big Energy and the business world, to try to convince the public that global warming is either unreal or not a result of human activity" (Chomsky, 2016, p. 160).

10 Steffen, in an interview with the Australian National University, said, "The global economy can function equally well with zero emissions. Research shows we can feed nine billion people – the projected world population by 2050 – and reduce greenhouse gas emissions at the same time" (ANU, 2017).

11 Although there is a whole school of thought from Aristotle to Dewey on habituation and learning by doing, and although it is clearly true that every gesture to preserve the environment, no matter how small, is necessary and helpful.

12 This point is a fundamental one, not only related to sustainability. Much of what is needed in the turbulent climate of the early twenty-first century is related to the deep-seated well of character in which a person's values and sense of commitment lie. Educational experiences need to talk to this inner core for there to be a transformative response. This is not to say that real life simulations or experiences cannot access this inner core – very often they can. The point is that educators need to be mindful of the notion that it is by shifting values that there is real impact.

13 In an article by Asara et al. (2015), The authors promote the idea of degrowth as "a democratic and redistributive downscaling of the biophysical size of the global economy".

14 An author who has dedicated much time to investigating the dubious political and ethical underpinnings of consumerism is Naomi Klein. Her famous 1999 work, *No Logo*, spotlights unethical practices by multinationals, and her 2007 book, *The Shock Doctrine*, argues that a great many consumer populations are created through military intervention. These texts are worthy of study and discussion. Equally poignant is the film *The Corporation* (Achbar, Abbot, and Bakan, 2003), based on the book by Bakan.

15 Dosemagen puts it thus:

> The ease with which people can rapidly support environmental campaigns by clicking on links or buttons can be powerful for information sharing, but also has the potential to lead to a diffused environment movement in which most supporters only participate through acts of "clicktivism" that don't necessarily translate into environmental transformation.

CHAPTER 4

[16] An author who uncovers this curious, schizoid relationship well is J. M. Coetzee, particularly in the *Lives of Animals* (1999), a type of semi-fictional discussion of animal rights, *Life & Times of Michael K* (1983), a novel that plunges the reader into the harrowing details of what it means to kill an animal to eat it and *Disgrace* (1999), which unpacks the unsettling relationship between humans and dogs. The French philosopher Aymeric Caron has developed a philosophy based on respect for all living things and a re-evaluation of the role of human beings as alongside rather than above animals. He elaborates this philosophy in his 2016 book *Antispéciste* (Cayron, 2016).

[17] The results of a 2017 survey in which 2000 people were polled in the UK by the Prince's Countryside Fund found that one in eight young people had never seen a cow whilst only two in 10 claimed to have good or excellent knowledge of the country (The Telegraph, 2017).

[18] A powerful example is the Kruger National Park in South Africa, a natural reserve that spans over 50,000 square kilometres.

[19] A text that expresses the love a young person has for the wildness of nature is Gerald Durrell's *My Family and Other Animals* (1956), a book that opens the excitement, mystery and endless life pulse of the natural world to the reader.

[20] This European tradition of loving nature was strong with the Greeks and Romans, epitomised in famous texts celebrating the beauty of nature, such as Homer's *Illiad* and *Odyssey*, with their fantastic depictions of the sea and birds, or Lucretius' epic poem *De Rerum Natura*, a rich and obscure song in praise of the goddess of nature; and the tradition was revisited, with praise for all things natural by the grandfather of romantic philosophy, Jean-Jacques Rousseau, and with the gritty, sensual appreciation of nature that comes through in the writings of the British romantic poets (particularly Wordsworth and Keats).

[21] https://www.wartsila.com/twentyfour7/environment/africa-s-war-on-plastic

[22] Much postcolonial African literature treats this dichotomy well, for example, *The Joys of Motherhood* (1979) by Buchi Emecheta and *The Lion and the Jewel* (1962) by Wole Soyinka.

[23] It is common practice for primary schools to have vegetable patches or some other form of trivial exposure to the outdoors as part of a young person's education. Stronger models should be used, in which students spend extended amounts of time in uncultivated nature, exploring it deeply and coming to appreciate it.

[24] Berkes et al. (2000) see traditional ecological knowledge as the "relationships of living beings with one another and with their physical environment" (Mazzocchi, 2006). Semichison, an Aboriginal philosopher, puts it thus:

> When we touch the Earth and Sky we are reminded that all things, all creatures, indeed all life, shares the same source. We are part of that oneness. We are all relations. This is the Sacred Law. Being in harmony, learning, honouring, knowing, seeing, hearing, communicating, loving, teaching, living, working and sharing in gratitude, with Mother Earth, her diverse and wondrous life-forms, and each other is a Way of Life. (Semchison, 2001, p. 10)

Teila Watson, Murri woman singer and poet, says:

> Our people lived completely sustainably, and in balance with each other and country, for over 60,000 years. We kept our country clean through practices like fire-stick farming, we monitored our species of animals and plants through our totem systems. (Watson, 2017)

[25] This view is shared by a number of traditional farmers and herdsmen, such as Hungarian herders who suggest that "people should be encouraged to love nature, to see where they live" and that "young people should be taught to love nature" (Roué and Molnar, 2016, p. 43).

[26] A good example of this way of thinking, presented as an analogy between a woman's body and colonial territory, can be found in John Donne's famous poem *To His Mistress Going to Bed*, a piece of literature well worth studying not only for its prosody but for the way of thinking it portrays too:

> O my America! My new-found land,
> My kingdom, safeliest when with one man mann'd,
> My Mine of precious stones, My Empirie,
> How blest am I in this discovering thee!

[27] Yuval Harari points out:

> Over time, states and markets used their growing power to weaken the traditional bonds of family and community. The state sent its policemen to stop family vendettas and replace them with court decisions. The market sent its hawkers to wipe out longstanding local traditions and replace them with ever-changing commercial fashion. (Harari, 2014, p. 402)

[28] In his poignant essay *The Eve of Destruction*, Noam Chomsky asks, "What are people doing about it?" His response to this question is as follows:

> Those trying to mitigate or overcome these threats are the least developed societies – the indigenous populations, or the remnants of them; tribal societies; and the first nations in Canada… In fact, all over the world – Australia, India, South America – there are battles going on, sometimes wars. (Chomsky, 2016, p. 129)

He goes on to give examples of these battles or wars for the environment, always taking place in societies in which indigenous groups have stronger representative power than they do in most so-called developed countries. One is India, where "tribal societies" are "trying to resist resource-extraction operations that are extremely harmful locally" and the other two are Bolivia (which has encoded the rights of nature in its constitution) and Ecuador, where the government is actively preventing oil extraction.

[29] The work of the Ellen MacArthur Foundation (2017) on a circular economy can be used to stimulate educational programmes and school projects based on renewable energy. The group's approach to the economy of the future is that it should undergo "disruptive innovation" that stops waste-producing economic cycles of production and that offers new pathways that are renewable. The group works with certain educational organisations, such as the International Baccalaureate, on producing curricular material based on ecological principles.

Another organisation that proposes educational frameworks as an approach to clean and renewable industry is the Swiss-based Solar Impulse Foundation (2017), whose educational materials promote the understanding of, and innovation in, clean technologies.

REFERENCES

Achbar, M., Abbot, J., & Bakan, J. (2003). *The corporation.* http://thecorporation.com/

ANU [Australian National University] (2017). *Humans affect earth system more than natural forces.* http://www.anu.edu.au/news/all-news/humans-affect-earth-system-more-than-natural-forces

Asara, V., Otero, I., Demaria, F., & Corbera, E. (2015). Socially sustainable degrowth as a social-ecological transformation: Repoliticizing sustainability. *Sustainability Science, 10*(3), 375–384.

Baudrillard, J. (1970). *La société de consommation.* Paris: Folio.

California Institute of Technology (2015). *In Greenland, another major glacier comes undone jet propulsion lab.* http://www.jpl.nasa.gov/news/news.php?feature=4771

Cayron, A. (2016). *Antispéciste.* Paris: Don Quichotte.

Chomsky, N. (2016). *Who rules the world?* New York, NY: Metropolitan Books.

Coetzee, J. M. (1999). *The lives of animals.* Princeton, NJ: Princeton University Press.

Cohen, D. (2012). *Homo economicus: Prophète (égaré) des temps nouveaux.* Paris: Albin Michel.

Dosemagen, S. (2017). Social media and saving the environment: Clicktivism or real change? *Huffington Post.* https://www.huffingtonpost.com/shannon-dosemagen-/social-media-and-saving-t_b_9100362.html

Ellen MacArthur Foundation (2017). Website. https://www.ellenmacarthurfoundation.org/

EPA [Environmental Protection Agency] (2017). Website. http://www.epa.gov

ESA [European Space Agency] (2013). *How many space debris objects are currently in orbit?* http://www.esa.int/Our_Activities/Space_Engineering_Technology/Clean_Space/How_many_space_debris_objects_are_currently_in_orbit

Francis, P. (2015). *Laudato Si'.* Rome: Vatican. http://w2.vatican.va/content/francesco/en/encyclicals/documents/papa-francesco_20150524_enciclica-laudato-si.html

CHAPTER 4

Freedland, J. (2017). Trump has taken us to the brink of nuclear war: Can he be stopped? *The Guardian.* https://www.theguardian.com/commentisfree/2017/aug/09/trump-brink-nuclear-war-stop

Gaffney, O., & Steffen, W. (2017). The Anthropocene equation. *The Anthropocene Review, 4*(1), 53–61. doi:1710.1177/2053019616688022

Global Footprint Network (2017). *Biodiversity.* http://www.footprintnetwork.org/biodiversity/

Harari, Y. (2014). *Sapiens: A brief history of humankind.* London: Vintage.

Harvey, F. (2011). World headed for irreversible climate change in five years, IEA warns. *The Guardian.* https://www.theguardian.com/environment/2011/nov/09/fossil-fuel-infrastructure-climate-change

Herman, E. S., & Chomsky, N. (1988). *Manufacturing consent: The political economy of the mass media.* New York, NY: Pantheon Books.

Infocongo (2017). *Illegal logging drives deforestation in Cameroon.* http://infocongo.org/3013-2/

IPPC [International Plant Protection Convention] (2007). *The physical science basis* (IPCC Fourth Assessment Report, Working Group I Report No. 7.3.3.1.5, p. 527). http://www.ipcc.ch/report/ar5/wg1/

Mazzocchi, F. (2006). *Western science and traditional knowledge: Despite their variations, different forms of knowledge can learn from each other.* https://www.ncbi.nlm.nih.gov/pmc/articles/PMC1479546/

Milton, C. (2009). Somalia used as toxic dumping ground. *The Ecologist.* https://theecologist.org/2009/mar/01/somalia-used-toxic-dumping-ground

Minter, A. (2016). The burning truth behind an e-waste dump in Africa. *Smithsonian. com.* https://www.smithsonianmag.com/science-nature/burning-truth-behind-e-waste-dump-africa-180957597/

Klein, N. (1999). *No logo.* Toronto: Knopf Canada.

Klein, N. (2007). *The shock doctrine.* Toronto: Knopf Canada.

NASA (2016). *Orbital Debris Quaterly News, 20*(3).

Nature Conservancy (2015). *Rainforests: Facts about rainforests.* https://www.nature.org/ourinitiatives/urgentissues/land-conservation/forests/rainforests/rainforests-facts.xml

National Geographic (2017). Great pacific garbage patch. *National Geographic.* https://www.nationalgeographic.org/encyclopedia/great-pacific-garbage-patch/

Pacifici, M., Visconti, P., Butchart, S. H. M., Watson, J. E. M., Cassola F. M., & Rondinini, C. (2017). Species' traits influenced their response to recent climate change. *Nature Climate Change, 7*(3), 205. doi:10.1038/nclimate3223

Raven, P. H., & Berg, L. R. (2006). *Environment* (5th ed., p. 406). London: Wiley.

Roué, M., & Molnar, Z. (Eds.) (2016). *Knowing our lands and resources: Indigenous and local knowledge of biodiversity and ecosystem services in Europe and Central Asia* (Knowledges of Nature 9). Paris: UNESCO.

Save the Rhino International (2017). *Poaching statistics.* London: Save the Rhino International. https://www.savetherhino.org/rhino_info/poaching_statistics

Semchison, M. R. S. (2001). Ways of learning: Indigenous approaches to knowledge: Valid methodologies in education. *The Australian Journal of Indigenous Education, 29*(2), 8–10.

Solar Impulse Foundation (2017). Website. https://www.solarimpulse.com/

The Telegraph (2017). One in eight young people have never seen a cow in real life. *The Telegraph.* https://www.telegraph.co.uk/news/2017/07/31/one-eight-young-people-have-never-seen-cow-real-life/

United Nations (1992). *Convention on biological diversity* (No. 30619). Rio de Janeiro: United Nations.

Watson, T. (2017). Indigenous knowledge systems can help solve the problems of climate change. *The Guardian.* https://www.theguardian.com/commentisfree/2017/jun/02/indigenous-knowledge-systems-can-help-solve-the-problems-of-climate-change

World Ocean Review (2017). Website. https://www.worldwildlife.org

CHAPTER 5

POST-TRUTH POLITICS

I'm doing a spring clean in my apartment, the cyclical process of deciding what to keep and what to discard. I put books into the discard category only with difficulty. The reality is that a book already read will probably not be reread. It's heavy and bulky and tossing it could release much-needed shelf space. On the other hand, I feel guilty. I feel that by throwing a book away I diminish the cultural capital of my apartment, do away with the intellectual and emotional connection I've established with the past, culture and the world of ideas. Finally, I decide that I cannot throw the books out since my children are yet to read them. That principle seems sacred and incontrovertible.

As I have these thoughts, I realise that the book I was deliberating about was George Orwell's terrifying novel *1984*. I taught the novel for many years to high school students, insisting that along with Huxley's *Brave New World*, Golding's *The Lord of the Flies* and, Zamyatin's *We, 1984* was, and still is, essential reading on political ideology. The novel can be read at a number of allegorical and satirical levels. It is at once a criticism of propaganda, totalitarianism and Stalin's government. The most disturbing part of the novel is no doubt the torture sequence towards the end in which O'Brien, the party mastermind, manages to effectively brainwash Winston, the frail centre of consciousness, into believing that there is no such thing as truth.

In that sequence, O'Brien argues that truth is not objective, immutable and external to human viewpoints; it is a narrative that is controlled by a power group. I stop the spring clean and open Part 3:

> You believe that reality is something objective, external, existing in its own right. You also believe that the nature of reality is self-evident. When you delude yourself into thinking that you see something, you assume that everyone else sees the same thing as you. But I tell you, Winston, that reality is not external. Reality exists in the human mind, and nowhere else. Not in the individual mind, which can make mistakes, and in any case soon perishes: only in the mind of the Party, which is collective and immortal. Whatever the Party holds to be the truth, is truth. It is impossible to see reality except by looking through the eyes of the Party. (Orwell, 1949, p. 51)

Winston responds, arguing that simple objects that he has seen and can remember exist. O'Brien steadily increases the torture, and Winston starts to doubt the simplest of memories, exemplified in a photograph that he is quite sure he has seen but starts to doubt ever existed. Once O'Brein has tortured him into a state of submission and

CHAPTER 5

capitulation, he obediently repeats the dogma of the party, discards some thoughts as "false" and gives himself over to the party entirely:

> Anything could be true. The so-called laws of Nature were nonsense. The law of gravity was nonsense. "If I wished", O'Brien had said, "I could float off this floor like a soap bubble". Winston worked it out. "If he thinks he floats off the floor, and if I simultaneously think I see him do it, then the thing happens". Suddenly, like a lump of submerged wreckage breaking the surface of water, the thought burst into his mind: "It doesn't really happen. We imagine it. It is hallucination". He pushed the thought under instantly. The fallacy was obvious. It presupposed that somewhere or other, outside oneself, there was a "real" world where "real" things happened. But how could there be such a world? What knowledge have we of anything, save through our own minds? All happenings are in the mind. Whatever happens in all minds, truly happens.

Philosophy calls this line of thinking a type of radical idealism, whereby the empirical, material existence of objects is doubted and reality is seen as existing solely in the realm of ideas. Orwell's novel relates this philosophical notion to concrete examples that we have seen through time in the form of propaganda, manipulation by the media, state-controlled narratives, denialism and revisionism.

Alongside these political and historical examples is the phenomenon of relativism that characterises many contemporary positions, the idea being that there is no single truth but a number of truths, no master narrative but conflicting narratives, no objective reality but a set of opinions and perspectives that battle for prominence.[1] Relativism has marked, and arguably changed, our approach to history and philosophy in deep and potentially irreversible ways.

And when I put Orwell's dystopia aside and turn to the press to read about the presidential elections in France, the Brexit vote in Britain or Donald Trump's ascension to power in the United States, dubious words and phrases become apparent: "fake news", "counter-truths", "false claims", "alternate reality".

It appears that the idea of truth is fragile and needs to be explored fully; that we are living in an age in which different versions of the facts proliferate in a battle of one version against another, each relying on different sources, alternative sets of statistics and radically opposed readings of reality.

The world of education is challenged more than ever to equip young people with the knowledge, attitudes and competences to forge opinions in an age of relativism, when those opinions can be manipulated easily. Above all, I will argue in this chapter that young people must believe that there is such a thing as truth, that reality exists as an exterior, objective state and that those events sufficiently documented to be called historical fact must be considered real. This approach does not mean that we should become dogmatic; it does not mean that we should refuse to listen to alternative versions. It does mean, however, holding onto information that has been sufficiently elucidated and proven to be considered the truth.

LUCIAN

Years ago in a school at which I taught Theory of Knowledge, a student of mine, Lucian, did a presentation on the American rapper Tupac. More specifically, on how Tupac had been assassinated.

The point of the Theory of Knowledge presentation was for students to grapple with sophisticated questions about knowledge itself through a discussion of components of knowledge, such as justification, the nature of evidence, belief and truth.

Lucian was a portly boy who liked to wear American-style baseball and basketball tops. A shock of thick, curly black hair shot from his head like a wild, dark plant. He had a baby face, was pigeon-toed and would speak quickly in a high-pitched, nasal voice, never quite fully articulating all the syllables of each word. Nor did he pay particular attention to the rules of grammar. Words would follow one another in rapid succession, an unsettling continuum or stew of sound. Instead of saying, "I would now like to introduce you to …", he would say "Inowlikeintoduce".

He was lively and quick-witted, interested in computer programming. He invented a computer game that involved cutting through endless substrates of green matter that kept appearing. Despite his shortcomings with regard to articulateness, his creative mind and endless curiosity meant that he enjoyed Theory of Knowledge. On occasion he would catch me out, pointing out my errors or flaws in my arguments. His presentation on Tupac, however, went from the far-fetched to the fantastical to the ridiculous. He explained how the rapper had been silenced by either the CIA or the Illuminati or – and this was essentially his thesis – by both, seeing as the CIA was controlled by the Illuminati.

Lucian did not have a strong case but cited a string of websites, loosely correlated stories and a flurry of coincidences, which he presented as inextricably linked in a vast and sinister web of meaning. One of his strongest arguments was that the Illuminati symbol could be found on a number of different artefacts, suggesting linking: the dollar bill, the cufflinks of a politician, an advertising billboard, one of Tupac's rapper chains and another gangster's steering wheel. He also managed to find snippets of the rapper's lyrics that seemed to suggest that Tupac knew all along that he would be assassinated, and that he was aware that the government was made up of Illuminati. Of course, these same lyrics and symbols, presented in a different way, would have worked equally well to support an entirely different thesis. The premise of Lucian's position was the idea that the truth was hidden and protected, conspiritorially. To rely on conspiracy theory means that we can never really tell anyway and therefore might as well believe in conspiracies.

The students enjoyed the presentation, the dramatic air, the intrigue involving the world order. It was, after all, highly entertaining. But Lucian's presentation displayed deep problems, and as I listened to him dig himself deeper and deeper into the fantasy, I realised that we had to undo a number of his assumptions, one by one, and start all over again. I hope I managed to so by the end of the course. I would like to think that ultimately Lucian's approach to truth was less liberal, his thirst for substantiation more developed.

CHAPTER 5

Part of that educational process consisted in my asking critical questions directly after his presentation. He shifted nervously from one foot to another, coming back with, "Yeah, but", "Okay, I guess that's possible", and "Huh!". As this was a dummy run, I gave him a chance to rectify his approach; so the final performance was more credible and his grade better. In the second presentation, he almost reversed his position, pointing out how difficult it was for us to accept the death of anyone famous without imagining some sort of conspiracy. Above all, he was more careful about his facts and where they came from.

What would become of Lucian later in life? I wondered. We will come back to him later in this chapter.

WHAT IS TRUTH?

At the heart of the problem with Lucian's presentation and at the heart of the terrifying thrust of Orwell's *1984* is a glaring question: What is truth?

What do we mean by truth in the first place? This is the question (unanswered) that Pilate asks the Christ in the Bible, an ongoing debate in philosophy. Truth is by no means a simple word to define. In many ways, to define truth without some form of circular reasoning is impossible. Truth is something that is real and something that is real is the truth; truth is the opposite of falsehood while what is false is the opposite of what is true. At a purely intellectual level, this is one of the problems with truth: it is something of a given or axiom that cannot be defined beyond a conviction that there is something out there, that things happen and that what we experience is not an illusion.

One definition of truth that garners respect relies on the law of non-contradiction.[2] This means that a proposition cannot be a non-proposition at the same time (I cannot exist and not exist at the same time; you cannot be sitting in that chair whilst not sitting in it). The law of non-contradiction points to a rudimentary idea that if an object occupies a defined space in time, then it cannot simultaneously not occupy that same point in space and time.[3]

This seemingly incontrovertible stance has been challenged, though, through a number of paradoxes (*para* in ancient Greek, meaning "aside", and *doxa*, meaning "truth" – a paradox therefore being something that in a sense it true and untrue at the same time). Take, for example, the paradox of the stone (Mavrodes, 1963): if God were omnipotent, then he would be able to create anything. Therefore, God could create a stone so heavy that he himself could not lift it. However, if he could not lift the stone, then how could he still be omnipotent? Another famous paradox, ostensibly one of the original ones articulated by the philosopher Epimenides of Crete, is called the liar paradox. It starts, "All Cretans are liars". As Epimenides himself was from Crete, were his statement true, then it would have to simultaneously be a lie.

Philosophical tricks like these are purely theoretical and could be described as word games.[4] In more prosaic, day-to-day settings, however, things appear more straightforward, and truth can be defined in three different ways.

88

Correspondence Theory

The correspondence theory of truth states that the truth is the correspondence between a statement and a state of affairs. Were I to say, "The grass is green", and were that statement verified by someone checking the grass, we could say that it was true upon observing that, indeed, the grass is green. If I said, "The grass is long", and we saw that the grass was actually short, then we could say with conviction that my statement was false. Correspondence theory offers an empirical definition of truth and establishes those simple truths that can be established by observation or direct experience (through inductive reasoning).

The great advantage of this level of truth is that assertions can be tested and proven. Academic subjects that rely heavily on this definition of empirical truth include biology, in which observation is paramount, and human geography, in which trends and patterns are established after fieldwork and a number of observations.[5]

Correspondence truth is incontrovertible in that if a pencil drops and we see it dropping, it would be ridiculous and disingenuous to pretend that it did not drop. People's senses are not, however, always accurate.[6]

Coherence Theory

Coherence theory of truth is used when events cannot be corroborated by direct experience or observed evidence. Coherence theory of truth comes into play when a sentence coheres with a state of affairs that leads one to deduce what the truth must be, like guessing the missing piece of a puzzle through observing not the missing piece itself but all those pieces remaining.

To give some examples: We can only infer the temperature on Mars; we cannot test it directly. We can only deduce the distance from the earth to Venus, since we cannot make the voyage and count the kilometres. Coherence theory of truth is used in academic domains such as history (the past is not something that can be accessed directly; so we make educated guesses about the past by piecing together pieces of evidence to fill in the gaps), physics and mathematics (which are abstract exercises in logic, dealing with intangibles. In these epistemes (meaning "areas of knowledge"), we seek the values of missing variables, and the truth is based on epiphenomena and sets of evidence that must be brought together to give a coherent, truthful picture.[7] To arrive at conclusions using coherence theory of truth, we employ deductive thinking.

Pragmatism

One other definition of truth, slipperier and more troublesome than those mentioned, relies on the pragmatic theory of truth.[8] The idea is that correspondence and coherence theories tend to be related to statements and propositions. By establishing conduits between phrases that describe phenomena rather than the phenomena themselves, they are not actually saying anything useful about reality, if indeed there is such a

CHAPTER 5

thing as reality. Instead, these theories of truth are tied up in the structure and verity of statements. To move forward from this approach, rather than focussing on verbal propositions we should realise that truth and reality are social constructs, made up to suit a human group's beliefs and convictions.[9]

Pragmatism holds that which is true to be that which suits a community the best. Thus, that democracy is the best form of government, that freedom of speech or human rights or the pursuit of happiness are self-evident, are pragmatic truths. They cannot be verified or tested scientifically; they relate to what it is we want to achieve as a group of humans in space and time. This is the type of truth one will find in domains such as politics and law, the truth's being a social contract.

Whilst the pragmatic theory of truth can establish firm ground on non-scientific issues and allows us to make claims that are important socially, it is dangerous, since there is no ongoing, objective, external standpoint to clarify and verify its postulates. Instead, arguments can be made for or against a position; consensus can be achieved that might not actually be scientifically true but is more convenient because of is social "truth". If it find itself in the hands of dictators and wrongdoers, the pragmatic theory of truth becomes a power matrix, which makes people conform to contradictions, falsehoods and propaganda.

Famous social experiments have shown the extent to which individuals can bend the truth or behave immorally when faced with social pressure. Two key examples include the 1951 Asch conformity experiment, in which participants claimed that a line was of a different size to what it really was in order to comply with the false information other participants were deliberately giving. Another is the 1963 Milgram experiment in which participants were prepared to administer what they thought were lethal electric shocks to someone when told to do so by figures posing as medical specialists.[10]

So truth is by no means a simple concept to define, and it can be viewed in a number of different ways.

POSTMODERNISM AND TRUTH: RELATIVISTIC DISCOURSES

In philosophy, the approach to truth changes radically through time. Whereas earlier philosophers such as the ancient Greeks and Roman Stoics saw truth as pure form and associated truth with beauty and goodness, it was during and after the Enlightenment that notions of subjectivity came into prominence and began to affect the central idea of truth.

Nietzsche can be considered a turning point because of his radical perspectivism: a position that there is no such thing as truth and that reality is merely made up of beliefs, power and a genealogy of morals that can be traced through the development of language and religion.[11]

This approach informs various educational philosophies that influence the way we bring up young people today.[12]

We note the relativism of discourses in education when we compare the teaching of science in the world. For example, in Saudi Arabia, creationism is taught as truth, whereas evolution theory is described as dogma.[13] In the European Union, on the other hand, evolution theory is seen as the standard explanation for the origin and development of species.[14]

In the United States, the situation is more complex, since teaching creationism as scientific truth is described as unconstitutional in many states, but the situation is less clear in others, in which some schools clearly teach it.[15]

So where is the truth?

Whilst it is true that Darwin's theory is not 100% irrefutable scientific fact (since we cannot test the origin of species empirically, or use correspondence theory of truth), surveys have shown that 99% of 1,627 working PhD scientists and 99% of 1,246 active research scientists believe that human beings have evolved over time and effectively reject creationism (Rainie and Funk, 2015). Scientific evidence to the contrary remains scattered and tentative.

I would submit that, whilst debating alternative viewpoints in a classroom or around the dinner table is not bad, and to entertain some open mindedness is not bad, this activity should not present scientific and non-scientific phenomena as equivalent as to evidence and justification. We should not say that evolution theory and creationism are on equal footing. Similarly, whilst bringing young people to a deeper understanding that historical narratives are not necessarily givens because they have been more or less validated and supported by people in power for their own purposes, even in this more complex and nuanced case students should not be presented with different doctrines as though they are necessarily (and without criteria) on the same level of validity. Society has researched Darwin's theory of evolution for over 150 years, using objective scientific arguments and a generalisable system of references and method, and it has held firm against challenges; religious arguments for biological phenomena are based on unquestioned belief in certain texts and cannot be considered valid in the same manner.

When it comes to the arts, a relativistic discourse that argues that Shakespeare, Racine, Goethe and Dostoevsky have been studied and promoted merely because they form part of a dead-white-male, hegemonic canon and that they should therefore be replaced with more contemporary or indigenous texts is problematic. Such a position ignores the very reason great works of art should be studied in the first place: for the high quality of their content and form and the universality of their message. Although these authors might come from a historically favoured group, the group was large and the authors in question prevailed over others for a reason, inspiring minds across the globe for hundreds of years. Their prominence can be justified with rational arguments; the power of their vision and style is extraordinary and clear. A literature course includes enough space to study the Western canon alongside non-Western works without trying to relativise them and therefore impoverish some at the expense of others.

If scholars and educators do not hold onto consistent criteria for truth (justified empirical evidence or logical explanation), they encounter a slippery slope, leading easily to an "anything goes" scenario or, worse, a state of affairs in which authorities might manipulate versions of the truth to suit their purposes, since the controlling mechanism for establishing truth would no longer be external to them or objective.

For this reason students should understand the above-mentioned theories of truth – so that they do not take truth for granted or believe it to be fabricated out of thin air.[16]

HISTORICAL REVISIONISM

A big problem with the search for truth in education comes with the study of history. Here the agendas of ideology and nationalism will present information in more or less factual-seeming ways, and few mechanisms exist for verifying the truth of historical fact other than eyewitness accounts and forensic evidence, when available. Famous figures such as Voltaire and Napoleon summed up well these problems with studying history, in adages about history's being lies told by the victors.

Negationist approaches have marred the study of history, distorting the endeavour to ascertain the truth about the past. Two conspicuous examples relevant to education are as follows.

Holocaust and Genocide Denialism

That the World War II gas chambers either did not exist or were less important than commonly claimed and that history has exaggerated the extensiveness of Hitler's plan to exterminate all of Europe's Jews are theses that various authors have expounded. Robert Faurisson (1978, 1989) has claimed, essentially, that the gas chambers did not exist, and David Irving (1977) claimed that Hitler did not call for the extermination of European Jews. Whilst many countries regard these negationist positions as illegal (Irving, for example, has served prison sentences because of his claims), they still have currency and thus erode confidence in a clear statement about the past and encourage scholars and students to cast doubt on even the most incontrovertible facts.[17]

A number of politicians and statesmen have also engaged in Holocaust denial.[18]

Official Turkish accounts of the Armenian genocide have ranged from excluding important information to refusing to call it a genocide. This denialism trickles into history textbooks used at school.[19]

A relevant twenty-first century education must lead students to view representations of history as tenuous and ideological but at the same time necessarily dependent on factual evidence. Denialist discourses on genocide and the Holocaust should be identified and deconstructed.

Colonisation

Most schools teach the history of nineteenth century colonisation by European powers as less significant and violent that it was.[20] This practice prevents students from understanding the extent of its viciousness. When public authorities publically damn European colonial history, as they should, defenders of colonialism can generate a severe backlash, as examples have shown.[21]

Yoder (2011) points out that Japanese textbooks downplay the extent of Japanese imperialism in Asia (particularly with regard to the infamous Nanking massacre in China), whilst Israeli textbooks' depiction of Palestinians has been described as ideologically slanted (Peled-Elhanan, 2012). The well-known Pakistani textbook controversy of the 1970s involved a revision of Pakistani history so as to Islamise the past and essentially reclaim it from India (Jalal, 1995).

Such a state of affairs leaves educators with the responsibility to choose source material and textbooks that are as unbiased as possible. This is by no means straightforward, as it could be argued most convincingly that there is no such thing as a historically unbiased account. Yet, in choosing material, schools and teachers need to stand firm and avoid extreme relativism. Whilst it may be true that there is a grain of subjectivity and ideology behind everything, still one can and must distinguish between evidence that is largely objective and that which is downright mendacious. To say, for example, that the gas chambers did not exist is a lie and should not be called anything less.

Parents and mentors at home have a responsibility, too, to confine assertions about the past to those that are backed with evidence and to not promulgate false historical doctrines out of ignorance or hatred – not perhaps an easy undertaking, but then again, in an age of information most things can be looked up, and should be.[22]

In essence, facts concerning the past should be documented, recognised and reconciled, not swept under the carpet, minimised or reinvented. Young people need the tools of critical thinking that allow them to identify attacks on truth.

An interesting example of an approach to historical process that focussed on establishing the truth rather than versions of the truth was the 1994 Truth and Reconciliation Commission in South Africa, which asked perpetrators of atrocities committed during apartheid to confess. Indeed, one of the moral victories of South Africa is that apartheid was admitted and recognised. No one doubts that it happened.

PROPAGANDA

Education is, of course, more than a series of facts and scientific laws. It is a discourse and therefore prone to ideological positioning, explicitly or implicitly.[23] It should not surprise us that educational discourses tend to extol and legitimise the political and economic power structures in which they are embedded.

One might ask to what extent elements of propaganda colour education in general. The relationship between propaganda and education is the focus of a number of limited but relevant studies, which explain that education is about nurturing open-mindedness, whereas propaganda is about fossilising closed-mindedness.[24]

However, the putative nobility of education's aims does not prevent the mechanism of propaganda from being at work within education's channels of information distribution. Textbooks, curriculum, history and geography syllabi (particularly national history), religious education and the teaching of values can all be held up to scrutiny as pieces of propaganda. I say this because such educational decisions involve magnifying some facts and minimising others, selecting some pieces of information whilst omitting others, telling stories from a necessarily limited number of perspectives and promulgating what a society, group or organisation feels to be important. One might argue, perhaps rather cynically, that the more idealistic an education becomes, the more ideological it becomes and therefore the more prone to propaganda.[25]

Interestingly, the earliest theoretical works on propaganda such as Edward Bernays' (1928) seminal *Propaganda*, viewed it as a positive endeavour to forge positive opinions towards government and the nation. Woodrow Wilson's government essentially invented modern propaganda: his 1917 executive order was explicitly designed to shape the mindset of young men, to make them feel compelled to join the army and fight Germany in World War I (Daly, 2017). The art of propaganda (consisting of powerful images, simplifications, slogans, emotionally appealing scenarios, subliminal messages and exaggeration) thus started in the United States with an arguably noble intention, not in Orwellian single-party states or extremist European dictatorships as one might imagine. Ironically, Goebbels, the mastermind of Nazi propaganda, was openly influenced by the tactics Wilson's administration had used. This important background enables us to understand how widespread and normalised propaganda is, how the media use their extensive repertory of techniques of manipulation. It also reminds us that propaganda is not only used to promote hardline thinking but that it often shapes attitudes towards seemingly orthodox behaviours, such as consumerism and marketplace competition.

A lot of modern education speak emphasises collaboration, teamwork, creative and innovative thinking, new technologies, STEM and entrepreneurship. This emphasis is not ideologically neutral or intrinsically valid and truth-based. Major vested financial interests stand behind each of these premises, and a philosophy of capitalist economic production drives such practice and discourse. We could go so far as to talk of a type of propaganda at work. In any case, we should not view these trends uncritically, as reflecting simple truth.

Subtle propaganda is less about telling deliberate lies and more about selecting some pieces of information whilst omitting others, thereby promoting a skewed, partial and therefore inaccurate perception of reality. In particular, propaganda is about suggesting that a particular position is more than a subjective stance on reality, that it is, rather, true, all-encompassing and not to be doubted. Young people growing up in a media-saturated world need to understand the selective mechanism of news-making and infer some of the vested interests behind Reuters' selection of events to report. This ability to discriminate is especially important given that the control of Reuters has narrowed dramatically over the last 30 years.[26]

Herman and Chomsky's (1988) *Manufacturing Consent: The Political Economy of the Mass Media* remains essential reading for young people growing up in today's world, as in it we learn about the financial and ideological interests that lurk behind media selection of events on which to focus. The film version can also make interesting home viewing with children of 13 or older, as it will generate discussion and reflection.

If we believe fully in critical thinking, then the basic constituents of social organisation, those behaviours and patterns that we take for granted and therefore see uncritically as truth, should be held up to scrutiny and discussed in the classroom. Here is another reason to study philosophy in the twenty-first century; it is one of the few subjects, and possibly the only subject, that grapples with the epistemological, phenomenological and linguistic fundaments or normality, and that challenges and questions them.

CONTEMPORARY POLITICAL APPROACHES TO TRUTH

A disturbing development at the end of the first quarter of the twenty-first century has been the emergence of what is now called "post truth". The term was coined at the end of the twentieth century by the playwright, film producer and critic Steve Tesich[27] in response to the Reagan administration's covering up of the Iran/Contra scandal. The argument was that the general populace actually welcomed an inaccurate rendition of events, as it preferred not to have to face the truth.

The term has since been used widely, even featuring in dictionaries in response to the rise of Donald Trump in the United States and the Brexit vote in the United Kingdom. Both of these political phenomena involved unprecedentedly strong smear campaigns; mudsticks (meaning that untrue statements are made and then recanted, but with the full knowledge that the phenomenal and psychological effect of the initial, false information has affected perception); kickers (a technique Trump used in his presidential campaign whereby in a debate an opponent's statement is consistently concluded with a short insult or contradiction); and tabloid-press-style oversimplifications that sway public opinion, as was the case in the Brexit campaign in the United Kingdom.[28]

The Brexit Campaign

The June 2016 referendum in the UK, in which a narrow majority voted to leave the European Union, was fraught with misunderstandings, false promises and electoral campaigns full of untenable arguments.[29] Among the false claims characterising the referendum were promises about immigration levels' dropping should the UK leave the EU; millions of pounds of National Health Insurance gains weekly; huge savings on energy bills; and the revitalising of Britain as world leader in research.[30]

Of course, like all speculations, some of these might turn out to be true in the long run, and like all political analyses in which the viewpoint one endorses determines the choice of statistics and indices, statements like "Britain will be stronger" or "Britain will become a world leader" can be substantiated. These are not objective, scientific claims but opinions.

CHAPTER 5

The Brexit campaign promises are a good example of the use of statistics to tell stories that are inaccurate. The "vote leave" campaigners claimed that if the UK stayed in the EU, by 2030 the population would have grown by 5.23 million. This perspective hinged, however, on the assumption that Turkey, Albania, Montenegro, Serbia and Macedonia would all join the EU in 2020, by no means a foregone conclusion at the time the claims were made (Cooper, 2017).

But the most troublesome element of the entire Brexit referendum was the lack of clarity or understanding about what exactly the leave campaign was proposing – although this lack was in part due to the complex, hybrid nature of the EU in the first place.[31]

The Brexit vote has left us with educational lessons: the idea that on the one hand, modern electoral democracy often involves bending the truth or presenting scenarios that appear far more attractive and simplistic than they really are; and the idea, on the other, that any lack of clarity on what is being proposed for a vote needs to be investigated thoroughly by the voters and cleared up. At face value, the Brexit referendum process seems to reflect a society that is impatient to get through laborious processes and prefers sharp, short procedures to the cumbersome, intellectually draining endeavour of lengthy debate and analysis. It is perhaps in this regard that the Brexit experience is thoroughly twenty-first century in nature. Like social media feedback or oversimplification, it was rushed and based on impressions rather than deep truths.

Donald Trump

Unfortunately for the United States and the world, President Donald Trump is massively associated with falsehood, a symbol of a post-truth world.

According to journalist Daniel Dale (2017), US president Trump had made in his presidential campaign and first months in office 281 false statements. Politifact in 2017 awarded him their 2015 liar-of-the-year award for his campaign falsehoods. *New York Times* journalist Linda Qiu (2017) states, "In his first 100 days in office, President Trump has falsely boasted of attracting the largest inaugural crowd ever, cited a non-existent terrorist attack in Sweden and levelled an unproved accusation that his predecessor spied on him". The series of allegations made against Trump by former CIA director James Comey was met with an equally robust set of rebuttals and accusations by Trump's legal team. In essence, the scenario of one person's word against another's seems to epitomise the Trump paradigm: serious distortions of the truth and flat denial of contrary evidence or arguments.[32]

These are not the only examples. The 2017 presidential elections in France saw similar strategies, employed in particular by the far right. The day before the general elections, Emmanuel Macron was the victim of a cyberattack that "leaked" putatively false information about him and his party onto the Internet. Leaking was widespread during the 2017 US elections, too, as information about the Democrat candidate Hilary Clinton and Republican Donald Trump did the rounds of the Internet. In all of these cases, the identity of the authors of the leaks or the truth or falsity of the information in the leaks were not clear. The resulting impression, that someone is hiding or blurring the true story, creates a climate of mistrust that casts constant doubt on claims in general.

The Trump experience has given us a fundamental educational lesson: that one can go far in the world and have the backing of a majority of people when not actually telling the truth.[33] This lesson should not leave us cold or disabused but, on the contrary, should make us aware and sceptical, ready to deconstruct arguments, point out inaccuracies and debate openly before those who promulgate false ideas and who an ignorant majority votes into power.

Our response requires what Popper (1945) called an open society, that is to say, a society in which scientifically verifiable claims win the day and people subscribe to rational, objective standards rather than emotional sound bites and political strength. This vision is more easily described than accomplished and seems somewhat utopian. However, schools and other educational institutions can create microsocieties along these lines and thus influence the future actors of change to promote such a vision of society in the wider world.

Climate Change Controversies

Another important area in which post-truth dynamics play out is climate change. To what extent the planet is undergoing global warming and whether human activity can be targeted as the cause remain controversial, with positions that vary from the sceptical to the disingenuous.

The climate change debate is interesting to deconstruct and analyse because of the vested interests that drive positions. Those who deny global warming, or deny that particular instances of human industry cause it, have the backing of large corporations, frequently the very ones guilty of releasing damaging gases into the atmosphere. Climate change denial is a textbook example of "bad science", in which the process of scientific enquiry is premised on a subjective, financially driven effort to prove or disprove something rather than on a spirit of open-mindedness and observation.

Not only do lobbyists against climate change have the backing of corporations, but they also often officially represent the countries whose pollution is most damaging. The obvious example is the United States, a country with vested interests in oil trade and a number of dirty industries that drive lobbyists (often senators or official representatives at committees and conferences) to take dramatic stances against the whole idea of global warming.[34]

On the other side of the fence, those sounding the alarm bell tend to be academics and scientists, with little, if any, vested interest in their scientific results, which in itself would appear to make their claims more plausible. The scientific evidence is increasingly incontrovertible.[35]

The situation became so serious that in April 2017, thousands of scientists and activists congregated in Washington for a "March for Science". The feeling was that with governmental cuts in funding for organisations promoting environmentally sustainable practice, ideological pressure against climate change analysts and a general culture of denialism, the scientific community needed to band together to remind American society of the importance of the scientific method and manner of establishing truth.[36]

The climate change debate has a number of educational lessons within it, essentially how politics drives positions and interpretations of reality. Obama's Democratic administration took climate change seriously and was willing to act against Congress to clean up industries and human behaviour linked to the proliferation of greenhouse gases, whereas Trump's Republican administration has described the entire thesis of global warming as exaggerated and has gone about undoing much of the work done before. Young people now see politics' bending of the truth to suit agendas and are left wondering what to believe.

With objective criteria and a critical mindset, with the knowledge to identify and question sources, each individual will be armed to understand the world not in the way it is presented to us by politicians and corporations, but according to evidence.[37]

Bringing out Political Truth: Wikileaks and the Edward Snowden Phenomenon

Wikileaks, a non-governmental organisation founded by Julian Assange in 2006, regularly leaks government secrets onto the World Wide Web, its goal "to publish original source material … so readers and historians alike can see evidence of the truth" (Wikileaks, 2017). This leaking poses an ethical dilemma. On the one hand, the organisation claims to stand for freedom of expression and wishes to act as whistle-blower as to malpractice that is hidden from the public eye. On the other hand, however, the organisation is the subject of widespread criticism for its having disclosed private information, compromised security and breached information-protection protocols.

If we are living in a post-truth environment, then surely it will take organisations such as Wikileaks to uncover misrepresentations of the truth and bring out facts. However, because of the apparent ethical compromises involved, the situation is not so straightforward.

The Wikileaks phenomenon reminds us of the importance of social media in a post-deconstruction intellectual climate, in which the primary focus is apparently extreme relativism and manipulation, and in which politicians hide, bend and obscure the truth. The social media has somewhat changed the rules of the game, allowing for a broader forum of information distribution and access than ever before. Social media, like Wikileaks, takes on a life of its own, beyond the control of authors and spokespersons. The world of propaganda that Bernays and Goebbels dreamed of seems far more difficult today with the power of the Internet as a counterbalance.[38]

An education for critical thinking in the twenty-first century needs to go beyond the critical reception of primary source material. It requires investigating the dynamics of meaning-making through a problematizing of social media, which means that students need to grapple with several facts: that issues are debated in open fora; that different versions of facts will be bandied about on the Web; and that information is leaked comparatively easily. Finding the needle of truth in this cyber quagmire of a haystack means trying to distinguish reality as a representation of events and phenomena, taking into account that media and vested interests control the representation, and trying to figure out what lies behind that representation – like trying to identify the figures known only by the shadows they cast on the wall of Plato's cave in the famous allegory.[39]

This discussion is premised on the belief that there is some truth out there, that beyond the intertwined threads of narrative, a series of facts exists. Perhaps this belief is too simplistic, something Nietzsche would scorn. However, it is fundamental, for without it what would we teach? What would we believe in? What would be the ultimate purpose of an education? In the time of the Sophists, the cynical purpose of education was to equip individuals with the rhetorical techniques needed to persuade and convince others to believe in everything and anything, all things' being equal and the world's being without truth. That model offers no lasting motivation, or prospect, for education or for humankind.

LUCIAN AGAIN

I bumped into Lucian years later. As it happened, he was coming out of a cinema wearing a T-shirt with a giant kangaroo on it. We had a short conversation. He had gone to college and was a computer engineer earning a handsome salary. He told me that he travelled extensively and was married, that he missed his time at school.

I asked him what his favourite subject at school had been and to my surprise he answered, "Theory of Knowledge". "Why?" I asked. He paused to think through his response and then, to my surprise, said, "Because in Theory of Knowledge, we really got to think".

CONCLUSION

My spring clean has not been as successful as it should have been. I've spent the last hours in deep reflection, sitting on an all-too-comfortable sofa with Orwell's *1984* on my lap. I pick the book up again and read a passage from Part 2:

> Do you realize that the past, starting from yesterday, has been actually abolished? If it survives anywhere, it's in a few solid objects with no words attached to them, like that lump of glass there. Already we know almost literally nothing about the Revolution and the years before the Revolution. Every record has been destroyed or falsified, every book has been rewritten, every picture has been repainted, every statue and street and building has been renamed, and every date has been altered. And that process is continuing

CHAPTER 5

day-by-day and minute-by-minute. History has stopped. Nothing exists except an endless present in which the Party is always right. (Orwell, 1949, part 2, chapter 5, p. 14)

The passage sends shivers down my spine. Such a state of affairs cannot be, cannot be allowed to happen.

Outside it has become dark, and my eyes strain to read. I turn on the light and focus. Everything is where it was before my thoughts took me into darker places, away from the simple reality of the objects about me. Now they are here before me in stark clarity. How could anyone doubt their reality? I give the table in front of me a gentle kick, reminded of Dr. Johnson's famous response to Berkeley's radical idealism: he kicked a stone to refute the idea that things exist only in the mind. This table is here in my lounge, whether or not I am here to perceive it. I might not be able to prove this proposition, but it is a conviction I must uphold in order for anything to have any meaning at all.

How do we get this idea across to students in an age of post-truth politics, in an age in which competing discourses battle over the Internet, in which people can confirm their biases by searching for that which they want to believe? Above all, how do we keep younger generations hopeful that certain human constructs that are tied inexorably to the belief in truth – I'm thinking of social justice, equal opportunity, reducing the destruction of the planet and doing something useful with one's life – are goals to follow and not fleeting illusions?

I submit that we can accomplish this communication in four core ways:

- We need to teach that truth exists: through the study of history, scientific facts and logic.
- We need to teach critical appreciation of the media, including social media.
- We must avoid extreme relativism.
- We should resist obscurantism and strive for clarity.

I put *1984* back on the bookshelf and continue my spring clean.

NOTES

[1] The theses of pluralism, relativism and imminence form the thrust of postmodern philosophies, emanating from Nietzsche and continuing through such thinkers as Sartre, Foucault and Baudrillard.

[2] Established in its first iteration by Aristotle in his *Metaphysics*: "It is impossible that the same thing can at the same time both belong and not belong to the same object and in the same respect, and all other specifications that might be made, let them be added to meet local objections" (1993, pp. 19–23).

[3] Aristotle called this assertion indemonstrable in that it cannot be reasoned beyond its immediate premise, it is self-evident, constitutional and fundamental. Leibniz went on to call it the first principle.

[4] There are many; see for example Russell's barber paradox (1918) or Schrödinger's cat (1935).

[5] For most of the Enlightenment British Empiricists, especially David Hume, truth can only really be established through correspondence, in other words, through direct experience, testing and forensic verification.

[6] It is conceivable that we experienced an optical illusion (and Loftus has shown that human memory is extraordinarily fallible [1979]) or that acts of pressure or downright lying prevent the pure, observed

7   truth from being stated (people can be pressured into disbelieving what they saw or know). The notion can also be taken too far: Bishop Berkeley suggested that things might *only* exist when perceived, putting forward this notion in his adage *esse est percipi* (meaning "to be is to be perceived") (Berkeley, 1734), illustrated in the cunning, yet ultimately unanswerable, philosophical question, if a tree falls in a forest and no one is around to hear it, does it make a sound?
7   Coherence theory of truth, seen as the highest level of thought by continental European Enlightenment thinkers, most especially Kant and Leibniz, who saw reason as the supreme human gift, allows us to find the truth through mental calculations and pure logic rather than endless trial and error and physical experiences.
8   Explored primarily by the nineteenth century and early twentieth century American pragmatist philosophers William James, Charles Sanders Pierce and John Dewey.
9   "The real, then, is that which, sooner or later, information and reasoning would finally result in, and which is therefore independent of the vagaries of me and you. Thus, the very origin of the conception of reality shows that this conception essentially involves the notion of a community, without definite limits, and capable of a definite increase of knowledge" (Peirce, 1868, CP 5.311).
10 Kuhn's seminal *The Structure of Scientific Revolutions* (1962) shows not only how scientific revolutions essentially progress as paradigms – in other words, large interconnected units of thought, much in the fashion of coherence theory of truth – but also, disturbingly, through the consensus and often tacit political and social cohesiveness of a scientific community, in other words, through pragmatism. Kuhn's study remains essential reading for a relevant, critically minded education in the twenty-first century.
11 For Nietzsche, partly in response to the discourse of positivism (that sees scientific proof as absolute) "facts is precisely what there is not, only interpretations" (1967, § 481).

This relativistic position influenced the French school of twentieth century postmodern philosophers, such as Foucault and Baudrillard, who all continued with this idea, situating truth as a "regime" (Foucault, 1975, p. 30) or positing that the "value of thought lies not so much in its inevitable convergences with truth as in the immeasurable divergences which separate it from truth" (Baudrillard, 1995, p. 94).

These cryptic statements have had their influence on educational theory too, for example, the New Sociology of Education movement throughout the 1970s (Young, 1971, 1976) viewed curriculum choices as hegemonic and reflective of European cultural dominance. The response has been to valorise multiple perspectives and not to privilege any single narrative as absolute: "As each voice is brought into the choir, the category of the privileged 'knower' becomes smaller, each strongly bounded from one another, for each 'voice' has its own privileged and specialised knowledge" (Maton, 1998, p. 17).

12 Such as social constructivism (a community of learners build up knowledge according to their perspectives and experiences) and inquiry-based learning (students "discover" knowledge on their own premises and through selected experiences and experiments). It has also been at the core of many educational reforms that seek to displace Western canonical knowledge with alternative types of knowledge, particularly in the humanities (see Break [2017] for an example from Ontario of Shakespeare's being ousted from a curriculum to make space for indigenous Canadian literature).
13 Nevertheless, in the West appeared what is called 'the theory of evolution' which was derived by the Englishman Charles Darwin, who denied Allah's creation of humanity, saying that all living things and humans are from a single origin. We do not need to pursue such a theory because we have in the Book of Allah the final say regarding the origin of life, that all living things are Allah's creation" (Burton, 2010, p. 26).
14 In a 2007 report, member states agreed "to promote scientific knowledge and the teaching of evolution and to oppose firmly any attempts at teaching creationism as a scientific discipline" (Harmon, 2011).
15 In a speech to Congress in 2017, US vice-president Mike Pence said the following:

> Charles Darwin never thought of evolution as anything other than a theory. He hoped that someday it would be proven by the fossil record but did not live to see that, nor have we, ... And now that we have recognized evolution as a theory, I would simply and humbly ask, can we teach it as such and can we also consider teaching other theories of the origin of species? (Pence, 2002)

[16] Truth rests on a system of thoughts and mechanisms, and there are different types of truth: this needs to be taught at an age-appropriate level (about 15 years old) through courses in philosophy, epistemology or history.

[17] What is particularly disturbing in these negationist positions is not only that what is being refuted, relativised or belittled is the death of millions of people, but that basic historical phenomena are painted as the fabrication of ideologically driven agendas, as if to say that history is nothing but a politicised façade.

This is complex, because in many instances this is precisely what history is (for example, subjective accounts of war, nationalist accounts of political relations and constantly evolving discourses on ancient history, changed by carbon-testing results and increasingly sophisticated forensics). However, to use such a nuanced and sophisticated argument to deny commonly known and accepted, widely corroborated issues is to cast meaning-making and the most basic of claims into doubt. When such substantive matters are tampered with, the entire fabric of truth is damaged.

[18] These include Franjo Tudjman (former president of Croatia), who questioned the number of Jews killed in the Holocaust (1989), Mahmoud Ahmadinejad, former president of Iran, who went so far as to describe the Holocaust as a "myth" (Vick, 2005).

[19] For more details, see Akçam (2006). These positions translate themselves into textbooks and classroom discourse: in a 2014 article, Akçam points out:

> Textbooks characterize Armenians as people 'who are incited by foreigners, who aim to break apart the state and the country, and who murdered Turks and Muslims'. Meanwhile, the Armenian Genocide – referred to as the 'Armenian matter' in textbooks – is described as a lie perpetrated in order to meet these goals, and is defined as the biggest threat to Turkish national security.

He goes on to say that these textbooks are filled with "blatant errors".

[20] In a series of interviews, many British academics concurred that British colonialism needs to be taught more truthfully. They included Daniel Branch, head of history, University of Warwick; Anthony Seldon, vice-chancellor of the University of Buckingham; Ashley Jackson, professor of Imperial and Military History, King's College London; Esme Cleall, lecturer in the history of the British Empire, University of Sheffield; Pippa Virdee, senior lecturer in modern South Asian history, De Montfort University (Owen, 2016).

Andrea Major from Leeds University states that there is:

> ... a collective amnesia about the levels of violence, exploitation and racism involved in many aspects of imperialism, not to mention the various atrocities and catastrophes that were perpetrated, caused or exacerbated by British colonial policies and actions.... We need better education and more open public debate on all aspects of British colonial history 'warts and all' – not as an exercise in self-flagellation, but as a means of better understanding the world around us and how we are perceived by others. (quoted in Owen, 2016)

This trend can be viewed as part of a larger design, which is the dismantling of Eurocentric meaning-making of history and education that still dominates worldwide curricula, telling the story of the world from a Western perspective. Hickling-Hudson views this perspectivism as particularly distortive:

> Eurocentric education is stratifying and racist. It suppresses knowledge, distorts learning and persuades Europe and its diaspora of their putative superiority. The experience of education in the era of decolonisation indicates that socialization in neo-colonial ideas of race is still hegemonic. (Hickling-Hudson, 2006, p. 215)

[21] For example, French president Emmanuel Macron, before being voted into office, described France's colonisation of Algeria as a crime against humanity and was faced with a barrage of virulent criticism from the extreme right, who described it as "backstabbing", but also from the centre right: former prime minister François Fillon described Macron's statement as "hatred of our history" and "perpetual repentance" (Mcpartland, 2017). So the forces at work are not necessarily in favour of statesmen or

textbooks telling the truth about colonialism. The conquest of Algeria by France did, after all, involve the death of over 800,000 Algerians (Kiernan, 2007), although admitting this fact is frowned upon.

[22] Chomsky warns us that "historical amnesia is a dangerous phenomenon not only because it undermines moral and intellectual integrity but also because it lays the groundwork for crimes that still lie ahead" (2016, p. 43).

[23] Michaels Apple's *Ideology and Curriculum* explores how curriculum design has always carried some social project with it, in the Western context usually acculturation, the privileging of technical skills and the specialising of labour (Apple, 2004, pp. 65–66).

[24] Wooddy's (1935) article "Education and Propaganda" differentiates propaganda from education by pointing out that the former is essentially untrue – or is at least wanton exaggeration – and has a narrower ideological purpose than does education, whose purpose is the broader project of enculturation, which nonetheless aims for a more truthful rendition of the facts. Wooddy's view might be somewhat naïve: propaganda and education coalesce since they share the aim of shaping minds and attitudes through emphasis and selection.

[25] The International Baccalaureate's Learner Profile (IB, 2013) is an example: the value of "risk-taking" is described as a quality that all learners should strive to embody. One might argue that this is a culturally and ideologically slanted position, that taking risks is not necessarily a desirable trait in all cultures. Yet, it is presented as a universal truth.

[26] According to Frugaldad (2011), 90% of American media was in the hands of over 50 companies in 1953, whereas by 2011 those media companies were owned by only six companies. Clearly, this narrowing of avenues of information damages the possibilities of learning the full truth and of having open, critical exchange as to the relative advantages and disadvantages of competing political agendas.

[27] We are rapidly becoming prototypes of a people that totalitarian monsters could only drool over in their dreams. All the dictators up to now have had to work hard at suppressing the truth. We, by our actions, are saying that this suppression is no longer necessary, that we have acquired a spiritual mechanism that can denude truth of any significance. In a fundamental way we, as a free people, have freely decided that we want to live in some post-truth world (Tesich, 1992).

[28] Two studies of so-called post-truth politics that focus on Trump and Brexit are Matthew d'Ancona's *Post-Truth: The New War on Truth and How to Fight Back* (2017) and Evan Davis' *Post-Truth: Why We Have Reached Peak Bullshit and What We Can do About It* (2017). The shared analysis of these works is that structural political systems such as plebiscites that narrow issues to binary systems, the effects of the media and social media and relatively recent ideologies of relativism such as postmodernism have brought about a post-truth culture.

[29] A central figure in this obfuscation was the populist Nigel Farage, whom many journalists and analysts accused of mendacity. More discerning voices, less interested in scapegoats and more intent on establishing structural analyses, like Roger Scruton (2017), have reminded their readers that historical political figures such as Sir Edward Heath and Harold Wilson were guilty of exaggerations and misleading statements in the past. *Nil novum sub solem* ("there is nothing new under the sun").

[30] A. C. Grayling's (2007) *Democracy and Its Crisis* points out just how undemocratic the Brexit vote actually was, in its campaigning style and in the constitutional mechanics of how it was adopted.

[31] Claims were made that the UK would stay in the single market whilst leaving the EU, that the UK would position itself with a leave vote but would then spend years negotiating the terms of its leave. Furthermore, positions were adapted or even modified substantially as soon as the vote results came through: one had the idea that many of the campaign slogans and promises were bluffs that rested on the assumption that the UK population would not actually vote to leave. When the referendum results showed an intention to leave, it was not without panic and a series of contradictions that political leaders reacted.

[32] So much has been written about Trump's administration and the truth that a special series of articles called "Trump and the Truth" was published on the website of *The New Yorker* (2018).

[33] This phenomenon is nothing new. It can be found in Machiavelli's *The Prince* (1532), a cynical political manual dedicated to the Medici leader Lorenzo the Magnificent, in which lying is actively promoted as a highly effective political instrument. In a famous passage, the author advises the great

CHAPTER 5

leader to behave not only like a lion – in other words, with courage and statesmanship – but also like a fox, who is cunning and deceitful.

[34] An example is Jim Inhofe, who described climate change as "the greatest hoax ever perpetrated against the American people" (Goldenberg, 2015). More specifically, climate change denialism appears to emanate from Republican or right-wing forces in the United States. According to Xifra (2016), over 90% of academic or policy papers that put climate change into doubt originate from right-wing constituencies. These groups tend to receive handsome funding (several hundreds of millions), usually indirectly, from major corporations (Brulle, 2014).

[35] For example, the US Environmental Protection Agency (EPA, 2017) released a paper, "Endangerment Finding", in which it showed that carbon pollution was affecting climate change. The government response was to release a counterclaim in a white paper that fundamentally contradicted the EPA's findings. The white paper, backed by Trump's administration, has been described as "terrible" and "false" (Nuccitelli, 2017), most especially for the manner in which it attempts to disregard the effects of greenhouse gases.

[36] Naomi Oreskes, a Harvard professor of History of Science said: "I can't think of a time where scientists felt the enterprise of science was being threatened in the way scientists feel now" (St. Fleur, 2017).

[37] When it comes to scientific facts or situations that can be verified through experimentation, the best type of scientific trial known to us is the double-blind, randomised, controlled trial (Torgeson, Torgeson, and Brown, 2010). Such high-quality methodology should drive statements on truth, rather than idle speculation, politically inspired haggling or vested interests.

[38] A 2008 report on Facebook by Universal McCann stated, "The idea that we live in a simplistic world where there is a small group of 'influencers' who dictate the agenda to everyone else is no longer true thanks to social media" (Marantz, 2016).

[39] Baudrillard, in habitually and unhelpfully cryptic style, puts it thus:

> For reality is an illusion, and all thought must seek first of all to unmask it. To do that, it must itself advance behind a mask and constitute itself as a decoy, without regard for its own truth ... Reality must be caught in the trap, we must move quicker than reality. (Baudrillard, 1995, p. 99)

REFERENCES

Akçam, T. (2006). *A shameful act: The Armenian genocide and the question of Turkish responsibility.* New York, NY: Metropolitan Books.

Akçam, T. (2014). Textbooks and the Armenian genocide in Turkey: Heading towards 2015. *The Armenian Weekly.* http://armenianweekly.com/2014/12/04/textbooks/

Apple, M. (20014). *Ideology and curriculum.* New York, NY: Routledge.

Aristotle (1993). *Metaphysics, books Γ, Δ, and E.* (C. Kirwan, Trans. and notes). Oxford: Clarendon.

Asch, S. E. (1951). Effects of group pressure on the modification and distortion of judgments. In H. Guetzkow (Ed.), *Groups, leadership and men* (pp. 177–190). Pittsburgh, PA: Carnegie Press.

Baudrillard, J. (1995). *The perfect crime.* London: Verso Books.

Berkeley, G. (1734). *A treatise concerning the principles of human knowledge.* London: Jacon Tonson.

Bernays, E. (1928). *Propaganda.* New York, NY: H. Liveright.

Break, J. (2017). Ontario school board tosses Shakespeare for indigenous writers. *National Post.* http://news.nationalpost.com/news/canada/ontario-school-board-tosses-shakespeare-for-indigenous-writers

Brulle, R. (2014). Institutionalizing delay: Foundation funding and the creation of U.S. climate change counter-movement organizations. *Climatic Change, 122,* 681–694. https://doi.org/10.1007/s10584-013-1018-7

Burton, E. K. (2010). *Evolution education in Muslim states: Iran and Saudi Arabia compared.* http://www.academia.edu/870964/Evolution_Education_in_Muslim_States_Iran_and_Saudi_Arabia_Compared

Chomsky, N. (2016). *Who rules the world?* New York, NY: Metropolitan Books.
Cooper, C. (2017). EU referendum: Immigration and Brexit—what lies have been spread? *The Independent.* https://www.independent.co.uk/news/uk/politics/eu-referendum-immigration-and-brexit-what-lies-have-been-spread-a7092521.html
Dale, D. (2017). Trump said 19 false things in his speech on the Paris climate accord. *The Star.* https://www.thestar.com/news/world/2017/06/05/donald-trump-has-said-100s-of-false-things-heres-all-of-them.html
Daly, C. B. (2017). How Woodrow Wilson's propaganda machine changed American journalism. *Smithsonian.* http://www.smithsonianmag.com/history/how-woodrow-wilsons-propaganda-machine-changed-american-journalism-180963082/
d'Ancona, M. (2017). *Post-truth: The new war on truth and how to fight back.* London: Ebury Press.
Davis, E. (2017). *Post-truth: Why we have reached peak bullshit and what we can do about it.* London: Little, Brown.
Foucault, M. (1975). *Discipline and punish.* London: Pantheon.
Fourisson, R. (1978, November 1). Les chambres à gaz, ça n'existe pas. *Le Matin de Paris.*
Fourisson, R. (1989). My life as a revisionist. *The Journal of Historical Review, 9*(1), 97.
Frugaldad (2011). Media consolidation: The illusion of choice (infographic). http://www.frugaldad.com/media-consolidation-infographic/
Goldenberg, S. (2015). Republicans' leading climate denier tells the Pope to butt out of climate debate. *The Guardian.* https://www.theguardian.com/environment/2015/jun/11/james-inhofe-republican-climate-denier-pope-francis
Grayling, A. C. (2017). *Democracy and its crisis.* London: Oneworld.
Harmon, K. (2011). Evolution abroad: Creationism evolves in science classrooms around the globe. *Scientific American.* https://www.scientificamerican.com/article/evolution-education-abroad/
Herman, E. S., & Chomsky, N. (1988). *Manufacturing consent: The political economy of the mass media.* New York, NY: Pantheon Books.
Hickling-Hudson, A. (2006). Cultural complexity, post-colonialism and educational change: Challenges for comparative educators. *International Review of Education, 52*(1–2), 201–218.
IB [International Baccalaureate] (2013). *Learner profile.* http://www.ibo.org/contentassets/fd82f70643ef4086b7d3f292cc214962/learner-profile-en.pdf
Irving, D. (1977). *Hitler's war.* London: Hodder & Stoughton.
Jalal, A. (1995). Conjuring Pakistan: History as official imagining. *International Journal of Middle East Studies, 27*(1), 73–89.
Kiernan, B. (2007). *Blood and soil: A world history of genocide and extermination from Sparta to Darfur.* New Haven, CT: Yale University Press.
Kuhn, T. (1962). *The structure of scientific revolutions.* Chicago, IL: University of Chicago Press.
Loftus, E. (1979). *Eyewitness testimony.* Cambridge, MA: Harvard University Press.
Marantz, A. (2016). Trump and the truth: The viral candidate. *The New Yorker.* http://www.newyorker.com/news/news-desk/trump-and-the-truth-the-viral-candidate
Maton, K. (1998, March). *Recovering pedagogic discourse: Basil Bernstein and the rise of taught academic subjects in higher education.* Paper presented at the Knowledge, Identity and Pedagogy Conference, University of Southampton, Southampton, UK.
Mavrodes, G. (1963). Some puzzles concerning omnipotence. *Philosophical Review, 72,* 221–223.
Mcpartland, B. (2017). Macron causes uproar by saying France's colonisation of Algeria was 'crime against humanity'. *The Local.* https://www.thelocal.fr/20170216/frances-colonisation-of-algeria-was-crime-against-humanity
Milgram, S. (1963). Behavioral study of obedience. *Journal of Abnormal and Social Psychology, 67*(4), 371–378. doi:10.1037/h0040525
Nietzsche, F. (1967). *The will to power* (W. Kaufmann, Trans. and commentaries). New York, NY: Random House.
Nuccitelli, D. (2017). Climate contrarians want to endanger the EPA climate endangerment finding. *The Guardian.* https://www.theguardian.com/environment/climate-consensus-97-per-cent/2017/may/02/climate-contrarians-want-to-endanger-the-epa-climate-endangerment-finding

CHAPTER 5

Orwell, G. (1949). *Nineteen eighty-four*. London: Secker & Warburg.
Owen, J. (2016). British Empire: Students should be taught colonialism 'not all good', say historians. *The Independent.* http://www.independent.co.uk/news/education/education-news/british-empire-students-should-be-taught-colonialism-not-all-good-say-historians-a6828266.html
Peirce, C. S. (1868). Some consequences of four incapacities. *Journal of Speculative Philosophy, 2*, 140–157.
Peled-Elhanan, N. (2012). *Palestine in Israeli school books: Ideology and propaganda in education.* London: Tauris.
Pence, M. (2002). Theory of the origin of man. (107th Congress, 2nd Session Issue: Vol. 148, No. 93—Daily edition). https://www.congress.gov/congressional-record/2002/7/11/house-section/article/h4527-1?q=%7B%22search%22%3A%5B%22%5C%22mike+pence%5C%22%22%5D%7D&resultIndex=190
Politifact (2017). Donald Trump's file. *Politifact.* http://www.politifact.com/personalities/donald-trump/
Popper, K. (1945). *The open society and its enemies.* London: Routledge.
Qiu, L. (2017). Fact-checking President Trump through his first 100 days. *New York Times.* https://www.nytimes.com/2017/04/29/us/politics/fact-checking-president-trump-through-his-first-100-days.html?_r=0
Rainie, L., & Funk, C. (2015). *An elaboration of AAAS scientists' views.* Washington, DC: Pew Research Center. http://www.pewinternet.org/2015/07/23/an-elaboration-of-aaas-scientists-views/
Russell, B. (1918). The philosophy of logical atomism. In J. G. Slater (Ed.), *The collected papers of Bertrand Russell, 1914–19* (Vol. 8). London: Routledge.
Schroedinger, E. (1935). *The present situation in quantum mechanics: Quantum theory and measurement.* Princeton, NJ: Princeton University Press.
Scruton, R. (2017). Post-truth? It's pure nonsense. *The Spectator.* https://www.spectator.co.uk/2017/06/post-truth-its-pure-nonsense/
St. Fleur, N. (2017). Scientists, feeling under siege, march against Trump policies. *New York Times.* https://www.nytimes.com/2017/04/22/science/march-for-science.html
Tesich, S. (1992). A government of lies. *The Nation.* https://www.highbeam.com/doc/1G1-11665982.html
The New Yorker (2018). Trump and the truth. *The New Yorker.* June 4 & 11, 2018 issue. http://www.newyorker.com/topics/trump-truth-fact-checking-investigation
Torgerson, D. J., Torgerson, C. J., & Brown, C. (2010). Randomized Controlled Trials (RCTs) and non-randomized designs. In J. S. Wholey & H. P. Hatry (Eds.), *The handbook of practical program evaluation* (3rd ed.). Chichester, CA: Jossey-Bass.
Tudjman, F. (1989). *The horrors of war: Historical reality and philosophy.* New York, NY: M. Evans.
Xifra, J. (2016). Climate change deniers and advocacy: A situational theory of publics approach. *American Behavioral Scientist, 60*(3), 276–287. doi:10.1177/0002764215613403
Yoder, R. S. (2011). *Deviance and inequality in Japan: Japanese youth and foreign migrants.* Bristol: Policy Press.
Young, M. F. D. (Ed.) (1971). *Knowledge and control: New directions for the sociology of education.* London: Collier-Macmillan.
Young, M. F. D. (1976). Commonsense categories and curriculum thought. In R. Dale, G. Esland, & M. Macdonald (Eds.), *Schooling and capitalism: A sociological reader.* London: Routledge.
Vick, K. (2005). Iran's president calls Holocaust 'myth' in latest assault on Jews. *Washington Post.* http://www.washingtonpost.com/wp-dyn/content/article/2005/12/14/AR2005121402403.html
Wikileaks (2017). Website. http://www.wikileaks.org
Wooddy, C. (1935). Education and propaganda. *Annals of the American Academy of Political and Social Science, 179*, 227–239. http://journals.sagepub.com/doi/abs/10.1177/000271623517900129

CHAPTER 6

KNOWLEDGE

I'm writing with a ballpoint pen on rich, thick paper. With only one book on my table, no computer, no cell phone and no Internet connection, if I am to write, then I have no choice but to commit myself to what I know: how to spell, how to use grammatical rules and – perhaps most pertinent – what I can remember and draw from the recesses of my mind.

Whereas under normal circumstances I would settle for an inkling, a half-formed notion that I could then verify and complete with a Google search, here I must wrestle with my working memory to get it to retrieve from my long-term memory the necessary word, date, name, quotation, formula, law, anecdote or concept that lies there, entire, hidden but not entirely forgotten.

I'm in rural Cameroon. Tall, lean, sinewy workers hack at the savannah with pangas, children draw well water and transport it in buckets on their heads, palm fronds dot the misty horizon. Not only must one rely on one's mind to navigate ideas here, one must also live without the sugar, food rich in grease, hot running water and recreational distractions of the so-called developed world. In this place, fortitude, character, adaptability and patience carry you. Life here is simple, but it's not for the faint at heart. And here is part of the twenty-first century, too.

And so it is that humans without the comforts, enhancements and crutches of industrialisation, fending for themselves without supermarkets, fridges, television, band connection, delivery service and endless technical specialists, are left with what they are physically, mentally, culturally, socially and spiritually – with what, at the end of the day, they really know.

Thus we come to the question of the core knowledge that young people should develop in a twenty-first century education. What should they know? And what, therefore, should feature in curricula across the globe? What should change, what should be left out and what should remain? How confident can we be in tampering with aspects of schoolroom teaching and learning that are no longer relevant? Or that require changing?

In this chapter, by knowledge I mean strictly intellectual or academic knowledge. I'm not referring to the affective and psychomotor domains (these are discussed in other chapters). I am referring to the cognitive domain, and more specifically to the information that students should encounter, appreciate and learn. I am thus talking about the factual and conceptual content of subjects such as languages, literature, the humanities, mathematics, sciences and the arts. Discussing the "what" forces us to look at the "how" too, since the two are inextricably linked.

© JOINTLY BY IBE-UNESCO AND KONINKLIJKE BRILL NV, LEIDEN, 2018
DOI:10.1163/9789004381032_006

CHAPTER 6

Sarah

I had a student from Poland, Sarah, in a philosophy class. Tall, with piercing eyes and cropped blonde hair, she spoke with a low, almost growling voice as she argued points, wrestled with ideas or disagreed with something someone had said.

She seemed to know just about everything. Whenever we needed a historical date, such as that of the Second French Revolution, or a synopsis of the legacy of a historical figure, such as Julius Caesar, Sarah stood head and shoulders above her age-peers.

In fact, it was unsettling just how much Sarah knew and could recite from the repertoire of school knowledge: science, the arts, social sciences, literature and mathematics. She was an all-rounder. One day I asked where she had acquired all this information, how it was that she knew so much. She shrugged and said that knowledge was important in her family.

I'm not a teacher who believes that knowing dates and facts is enough in education, but I do think that knowing dates and facts is important, because it allows you to harness knowledge fluently and with automaticity. Sarah, gifted in retaining information after one or two repetitions, and large amounts of it, proved my point whenever we had class debates. Whether we were discussing artificial intelligence, Marxism, capital punishment or vegetarianism, Sarah would wipe the floor with her opponents: she would substantiate all her points and could poke holes in others' arguments by pointing out their factual errors.

Because no one else had the facts at their fingertips, although some would do a quick Google check, few could counter Sarah's arguments or contradict her. She commanded debates more through facts than through pure argumentative skills. In fact, what are argumentative skills if you cannot back them up with facts?

When Sarah backed up her arguments with facts, her delivery was rapid-fire, an impressive peppering with information that came at you fast and furious. She would gesticulate passionately as she explained what had happened in history, why something had worked or not worked, exactly which twist and turn had shaped a certain process.

I'll come back to Sarah and what became of her later in the chapter.

SKILLS VERSUS KNOWLEDGE

In today's popularised educational discourse, a serious and pervasive misconception is that less time should be spent on acquiring knowledge so that more time is freed up for developing skills. This idea is particularly widespread in the argument specific to twenty-first century skills (QCA, 2007, p. 114; Robinson, 2012; Department for Education and Skills, 2003, p. 11; Trilling and Fadel, 2012; Mitra, 2013; IB, 2015).

Education should emphasise, so the argument goes, not mere knowledge retention but rather critical thinking, creativity, collaboration, communication, "soft skills" and entrepreneurship. Opportunity costs are such that teachers need to cut out content in order to free up enough time for the development of skills.

The idea is rooted in the thoughts of many distinguished educators and philosophers who have concluded, understandably, that what is important is less the basis of factual knowledge and (much) more what one actually does with it.[1]

What we should retain from this discourse is that skills stemming from knowledge are more fundamentally important than isolated knowledge. In other words, knowing a lot is not enough in itself; one needs to be able to deal with new knowledge and make decisions in life using old knowledge. This claim is understandable and valid, understandable particularly since many of the figures making these points were subjected to a facts-heavy, Victorian-style curriculum in which little time was set aside for the application of critical and creative thinking or applied doing. Dickens' famous Gradgrind in the novel *Hard Times* epitomised this sterile, superficial approach. Gradgrind wants "nothing but the facts" from his students. The reaction to this view has been to point out that education is much more than filling students' heads with facts.

The position that considers what one does with knowledge as more important than mere absorption and retention does not usually, of course, favour dispensing with knowledge altogether. It does not say that knowledge is not crucial. To draw an analogy, if one says that what is important in a house is less the bricks than the way that they are cemented together, one still admits that without bricks there will be no house (that is, does not say that there should be no bricks).

The position is not always interpreted in favour of retaining knowledge, however; many modern educational authorities (from the early twentieth century to the present) see knowledge not just as less important than its application. They go so far as to see mere factual knowledge as an impediment to skills, seeing the two as separate and as in a state of mutual tension. These proponents of skills over knowledge have almost come to see pure factual knowledge, in its bare, declarative form, as a dirty word.

This radical skills-instead-of-knowledge perspective paints a dichotomy (a false one) between dreary rote learning, testing, teacher talk and drill on the one side and on the other, a more forward-looking approach based on constructivist learning theory, full of exciting projects, student discussions, group work and creativity.[2]

The romantics had an idea that human beings have an innate propensity for learning and should be freed from the shackles, socially imposed, of having to regurgitate facts. An education would then allow them to think for themselves. This romantic idea has become second nature in many schools, particularly in primary education, where time is given over to play, creativity and not too much drilling of facts.[3]

Thus, in 2017, permeating many educational viewpoints is a strong anti-knowledge ideology, which not only no longer regards knowledge as the core basis of thinking, but also often regards it as an impediment to higher-order thinking. This view is particularly strong among technophiles, who argue that new technologies and Internet connection can, and will, replace old-fashioned, learnt-by-heart knowledge.[4]

CHAPTER 6

Irrelevant Knowledge

A related faction in this anti-knowledge discourse is keen to point out that one of the main problems of a knowledge-based curriculum is that some knowledge is irrelevant and should not be learned in the first place, as it will never be used.[5]

After all, why learn trigonometry, the names of rivers or even basic arithmetic and handwriting in an information age when technology can do it for you?[6] Sugata Mitra takes the argument to considerable lengths:

> You know, an average boy from an average school in a poorer area would go out for a job interview, and the employer says, 'What can you do well?' And he'll say, 'I have good handwriting, my grammar's excellent, I can spell properly and I can do arithmetic in my mind'. Well, if I was the boss I would think: I don't care about your handwriting, everything's done on computers. Grammar is not particularly important, we deal with the Chinese and the Americans who don't bother about grammar at all, as long as it makes sense. Spelling is corrected by the computer and you don't need to know anything about arithmetic. In fact the less arithmetic you do in your head the better. (Cadwalladr, 2015)

What the Research Tells Us

Both of these positions – that knowledge should be reduced to make way for skills and that we should cut out knowledge deemed extraneous or irrelevant – are misguided.

Firstly, skills cannot be dissociated from knowledge. What we call skills are the application and synthesis of knowledge; skills do not simply exist independently of knowledge. Cognitive psychology has demonstrated this point experimentally a number of times, from the 1960s to the present.[7]

When someone has built up sufficient knowledge to solve problems well, they can be described as experts (as opposed to novices).[8]

Cognitive psychology has shown us that we store and retrieve information in mental schemata that are related to contexts and domains, which are learnt and known ways of organising information, invariably attached to a subject domain or concrete practices and experiences.[9]

Much research has been conducted to prove this point (Egan and Schwartz, 1979; Jeffries, Turner, Polson, and Atwood, 1981). "Results suggest that expert problem solvers derive their skill by drawing on the extensive experience stored in their long-term memory and then quickly selecting and applying the best procedures for solving problems" (Kirschner, Sweller, and Clark, 2006, p. 76).

Research has also shown us how critical it is for young readers to consolidate general knowledge if they are to become skilled readers. In effect, unskilled readers with extensive background knowledge on a topic will outperform skilled readers with less background knowledge.[10]

So to say that one should free up the curriculum from factual knowledge to concentrate more on skills, or that the purpose of an education is not to impart facts but to develop skills, is to propose the unworkable. In reality, given what we know about learning, performance and the way the mind works, skills and knowledge are two sides of the same coin.

The other argument, that some kinds of knowledge are more useful than others, is interesting and, of course, to a certain extent is borne out in practice. Clearly, choices need to be made in putting together a syllabus, and it will include some topics, themes or phenomena to teach instead of others. The latter parts of this chapter outline what I think a good knowledge base for the twenty-first century would look like in the humanities and literature.

The reason we should not aim to remove facts from the curriculum is that we simply do not know which are going to be useful and for which purpose. Furthermore, the more factual information we give students, the more we arm the brain, strengthen the necessary fibre to give it skilful muscle.[11]

Another problem with cutting down supposedly irrelevant knowledge is the question of what exactly to replace it with. If the new, relevant knowledge is contemporary and cutting-edge, then it is less likely to be a worthwhile investment, as it may be a fad that will come and go.[12]

The idea that instead of absorbing facts and dates students should be simulating real-world problem-solving and behaving like entrepreneurs, that they should act like real researchers engaged with "hands-on" knowledge and working through research projects, makes sense intuitively but in reality might turn out to involve a significant waste of time. The reason is that experts in the field do not work through problems the way children or teachers do in a classroom.[13]

Of course, to demonise all real-life simulations in the classroom per se would be excessive. Many are well designed,[14] and I have argued that real-life simulations can be used to create greater empathy and reduce prejudice (Hughes, 2017). However, we should embrace these types of projects for their real value (mainly motivational and imagination-inspiring), and they should not take over the curriculum. They are not the most effective way of developing knowledge in children, and we certainly should not assess them as anything more than competence simulations. In the real world, experts working on problems tend to employ different neural and cognitive circuitry than do children.

Whereas children approach problem-solving in a protracted, hit-or-miss fashion,[15] experts, on the other hand, are working with large amounts of knowledge that they have acquired through years of learning and practice. They have well-oiled ways of organising that information.[16]

So arguing over which bits of knowledge should be taken out of the curriculum in order to permit concentrating on "skills" is a red herring. What schools should be doing, most especially in the twenty-first century when humanity stands on the shoulders of so many historical giants and there is so much to know, is increasing students' knowledge but doing so in conceptual ways so as to allow for schematic, succinct, powerful treatment of information, thus getting more across and ensuring that even more is learnt.

The question should not be how to reduce the teaching of facts so as to allow more time for creativity and critical thinking, but rather how to concentrate meaningful creativity and critical thinking into the teaching of facts, which would require teaching in such a way that moments of applied knowledge are powerful and feel worthwhile, not dragged out and trivial. To put it bluntly, more time is needed on fundamental knowledge development and less time – well focussed – on skills.

The argument for reducing the amount of declarative knowledge learnt in the twenty-first century classroom is that it can be looked up on the Internet. This argument is, however, misleading, because isolated searches without context or associated knowledge will lead to nothing meaningful.[17]

And in the final analysis, who is to say that knowing the periodic table of elements off by heart, what a spinning jenny was, why riverbeds are formed the way they are or the capitals of the world's countries is a waste of time? We can't know what will become useful in life, which connections will be made and which fact will turn out to be valuable. Concretely, the more you know, the broader your base for thinking and doing. Therefore, an education for the twenty-first century must have knowledge at its core.

BLOOM'S TAXONOMY REVISED ... AGAIN!

Bloom's taxonomy (1956, revised in 2001 by Anderson et al.), a massively influential, quoted and used model of cognitive architecture that describes levels of thinking, from factual to abstract, makes clear – though it's the subject of some criticism – that the basis of much curriculum is knowledge and memory.[18]

However, the taxonomy, while describing knowledge as "important" as an educational objective, also describes it as "basic" and therefore a low level of cognition upon which the rest of higher cognitive architecture rests. Bloom explains that from the perspective of assessment, knowledge is essentially about factual recall, which is a rudimentary facet of cognitive activity.[19]

Knowledge and understanding receive the label "lower-order thinking", as opposed to "higher-order thinking" (analysis, synthesis, evaluation, creativity). I would argue that this categorising of knowledge has had a most unfortunate effect and is misguided. It gives one the impression that knowledge and understanding are less important than higher-order thinking.[20]

It has also contributed to the idea that knowledge and memory are not necessarily required as a foundation on which higher-order thinking can be built. In fact, lower-order thinking is seen as something of an obstacle. Some constructivist analyses of educational practice describe a reliance on recall and knowledge disparagingly, actually arguing that they are not prerequisites for higher levels of thought.[21]

On the other side of the debate, many of the research findings in cognitive psychology do not confirm this hypothesis but suggest, to the contrary, that foundational knowledge must be consolidated for it to be applied in modes of higher-order thinking (Tuytens and Devos, 2011; Timperley, 2008; Hill et al., 2005; Sadler et al., 2013, for example, all see strong content knowledge as a necessary condition of good learning). So the idea that less time should be spent on "lower-order thinking" in the form of factual-knowledge transmission needs to be considered carefully for its full implications.

Concretely, if students know less, what will they apply? What will they synthesise? With which criteria will they be able to evaluate? How exactly can one be a critical thinker without knowing anything? And what sort of creativity will occur without knowledge of technique, composition, past examples and domain-related limitations and possibilities? Anyone who observes a debate – surely a good example of higher-order analytical thinking – knows that those who excel are those who are able to substantiate their arguments with strong factual knowledge.

In order to rectify this situation, I would suggest that the descriptors used in Bloom's taxonomy be modified: rather than "lower-order thinking", the base of the cognitive pyramid should be called "foundations of thinking". Rather than "higher-level thinking", the top echelons of the pyramid should be described as "modes of thinking" so as to see them for what they really are – varieties of applied knowledge.

I would argue that a strong educational experience is one in which an emphasis on knowledge and understanding comes first and then come chances to apply that knowledge, once the student has learnt and mastered it, in analytical, synthesising, evaluative and creative ways. This is a pattern that should be repeated not only in courses that might last one or two years (such as an undergraduate degree or school leaving certificate), but also, developmentally, through a child's entire time in school, from the primary years (strong knowledge base) to the end of secondary school (continued knowledge but with more application of that knowledge). E. D. Hirsch's core knowledge curriculum embraces this premise, as do all those who advocate a strong approach to numeracy, literacy, and firm intellectual bases in the early years of schooling and in the ground level of any course. In a phrase, the idea is knowledge first, skills later.

This is not to say that there should be no debating, creative work, problem-solving or enquiry learning in the primary years, but rather that these should be the exception rather than the rule; they should be special moments when knowledge that has been mastered can be used in meaningful ways. This approach will make those creative moments more powerful and relevant, since they will be rigorously knowledge based, not empty of substance and therefore trivial. Since these moments would be exceptional and memorable in the child's mind, the child would more likely appreciate them than if they were overused and represented the norm. Indeed, nothing is more dreary than too much of any strategy in education. It would be a pity to kill the excitement of project-based learning, creativity or enquiry by overdoing it.

None of my argument means that primary schooling must be boring or sterile, with the teacher frontloading students with dry factual information. Children can master knowledge through a broad repertoire of strategies and techniques (hot-seating,

CHAPTER 6

games, quizzes, interviews, knowledge maps, online adaptive tests and battles and so on).[22] What must guide these experiences is a knowledge consolidation objective rather than a skills development objective.

THE ROLE OF THE TEACHER

At the centre of this debate is the role of the teacher. The skills-over-knowledge position sees the teacher a little like this: if we are to focus on skills that are deemed to be relevant for the future and twenty-first century skills such as critical thinking, creativity, communication and collaboration, the role of the teacher is as a facilitator and guide (McWilliam and Taylor, 2016), not an instructor, since knowledge can be found elsewhere and students should be spending their time developing the way that they search for knowledge and using the knowledge they find in innovative ways. The teacher's role will be to comment on learning strategies, suggest communication strategies, model approaches to learning and facilitate reflection on learning. This leads to the constructivist paradigm in which the teacher speaks less than the student, asks questions and generally exercises "minimally invasive pedagogy", as Sugata Mitra (2015) calls it.

If, on the other hand, the view of a twenty-first century education is that students should not only know things but know a huge amount, the teacher's role becomes more central: the teacher needs to test knowledge and make sure that it is being learnt well. The implication is that the teacher becomes more of a coach, one who knows a lot and is interested in imparting that knowledge to students. The emphasis is less on how good the students are at communicating and applying problem-solving strategies and more on their integrating, understanding and being able to recall declarative and procedural knowledge. The teacher in this model will inspire the students not by technical learning facilitation but by being someone who masters the body of knowledge in question, sparking students to want to master that area of knowledge – or another – themselves. The implication is that this type of teacher should be well qualified in the domain content taught and, above all, highly knowledgeable about subject content.

What the Research Tells Us

That teacher content knowledge is fundamental is no secret. It has been corroborated by much research,[23] and it stands to reason. After all, "teachers cannot help children learn things they themselves do not understand" (Ball, 1991, p. 5).

This is not to say, however, that mere knowledge of academic content is enough by itself. Clearly, academic knowledge must be fused with pedagogical technique, since teachers need strong academic background knowledge not only of their domain, but also of cognitive science.[24]

Much quality research has shown through different types of study that an effective position on teacher development is to reinforce teachers' academic knowledge and understanding in areas in which students' misconceptions are the greatest (Timperley et al., 2007; Blank and de las Alas, 2009; Sadler, 2013). In other words, the best situation is one in which teachers are strongest where students are weakest, allowing for scaffolding and instruction that really adds value.

Even though a teacher may be highly knowledgeable, and even though knowledge remains foundational in education, classroom practice should not consist of nothing but lectures and the broadcasting of information. Indeed, the fact that teachers know a lot does not warrant their depriving students of any opportunity to use their own thinking skills to get to the right piece of knowledge.[25]

So just as the student of the twenty-first century needs to know a huge amount, the teacher needs to be pushed further, to know not only a huge amount about her subject, but about pedagogical techniques, too. The classical, intuitive and research-corroborated techniques of clear sign-posting, knowing how to give feedback to each learner for her to move forward, differentiating instruction, modelling correct responses and designing relevant and appropriate ways of allowing students to learn (multiple assessment points) are requirements for a teacher to be not just good, but great.

Parents and mentors outside of the classroom, too, can help by making sure that children reflect on what they have learnt at school and discuss the implications of their learning at home. Just getting young people to talk about and recast their knowledge as a way of refreshing it is a useful exercise.

ROTE LEARNING

One common misconception in the popular discourse about good teaching is that it is not about learning things off by heart, test after test, or about boring drills, the idea being that students should absorb knowledge in more subtle, hands-on ways.

However, as attractive as this idea might be intuitively, it does not stand up to what we know about memory consolidation thanks to advances in neuroscientific research. Memories depend on neural connections (synapses) that become reinforced through repetition. To be more specific, information should be repeated in a certain way for it to be effectively stored in memory. We know that the most effective way of memorising information is through Ebbinghause's famous 1885 "spacing effect" (Bahrick, Bahrick, Bahrick, and Bahrick, 1993).

Research (Appleton-Knapp, Bjork, and Wickens, 2005) has shown how, through study-phase retrieval, "if learners are allowed to forget the information in between study and restudy, that restudy episode triggers retrieval of the first episode and thus constitutes a much more potent learning event" (Bjork and Yan, 2014, p. 20). It seems disingenuous to acknowledge that great athletes and concert musicians arrive at their level of expertise through thousands of hours of practice (in fact deliberate practice, meaning that the focus in the practice is on weak areas; see Ericsson et al., 1993) but not to see that this repetition is necessary in the classroom for general or domain specific knowledge.

CHAPTER 6

By going back over information again and again and making sure that it is interleaved – meaning that it is alternated with other pieces of knowledge – we learn to memorise it and recall it more easily. Most learners need between five and eight repetitions to master something (gifted individuals can do it in fewer, but they are an exception). In much the way that a drama student will spend weeks pacing up and down and learning her lines off by heart, or the way someone trying to learn a new language will find herself coming across the same rules, words and phrases until she has mastered them, students must consolidate neural connections through repetition and will need a good teacher, mentor or coach to create appropriate learning conditions for such repetition.[26]

Most creative teachers would rather not spend their time repeating information or having students repeat it; they would rather have students design space rockets, paint landscapes or invent stories. However, the skilled practitioner will devise subtle ways of ensuring that students repeatedly bring back information stored in long-term memory, while shielding them from having to do sheer verbal regurgitation, endless testing or textbook learning by heart.

I have a sneaking suspicion that in a post-constructivist world, full of inquiry learning and creativity, many young people rather enjoy being made to learn things off by heart and being tested on them. In a school where I worked, it was not without irony that the teachers designed clubs for students on entrepreneurship, computer coding and human rights debating but the students started up their own club on quizzing each other on general knowledge, which led to quiz nights and was a runaway success, more so than some of the putatively twenty-first century clubs set up by teachers.

I believe the explanation is that to have learnt (not just learned but learnt as in "having it taped") is empowering; it makes you stronger and more confident, more knowledgeable. For the same reason, I believe that factual tests are important for all types of learning, be they in school, university, the professional domain or after workshops. If learners are not tested, what is to keep them from tuning out and retaining little, if anything? Frequent tests build powerful dendritic spines in the brain.

A TWENTY-FIRST CENTURY EDUCATION

So what is it that students should be learning in the twenty-first century? Some argue that the age-old subjects should continue to feature strongly in curricula: "Mastery of fundamental subjects and twenty-first century themes is essential for students in the twenty-first century. Disciplines include: English, reading or language arts; World languages; Arts; Mathematics; Economics; Science; Geography; History; Government and Civics" (Partnership for 21st Century Skills, 2017). Others suggest that we need to "rethink the significance and applicability of what is taught, and simultaneously to strike a better balance between the theoretical and the practical" (Fadel, 2016). We might need to include "modern disciplines such as Technology & Engineering, Media, Entrepreneurship & Business, Personal Finance, Wellness,

Social Systems, etc.", making sure that these are "accommodated as a normal part of the curriculum, not as ancillary or optional activities" (Fadel, 2016).

I would argue that science and mathematics, whilst integrated with technology and the principles of engineering, will include much of the core knowledge that

Table 1. A twenty-first century international canon for history and the arts

	History	Literature	Philosophy
Concepts	Language, Writing, Agriculture, belief systems		
Africa	Ancient Egypt & Phoenicia	*Cultural Atlas of Ancient Egypt* (Baines & Malek)	*The Book of the Dead*
Asia	Ancient & imperial China & India	*Ancient India: In Historical Outline* (Jha)	*The Upanishads*
Oceania	Aboriginal culture	*Papunya School Book of Country and History* (8–14 year olds)	*Ancient and Modern: Time, Culture and Indigenous Philosophy* (Muecke)
Middle East	Sumeria & Persia	*Gilgamesh, The Histories* (Herodotus), *The Shahnameh* (Ferdowsi)	*Teachings of Zoroaster and the Philosophy of the Parsi Religion* (Kapadia)
Europe	Greece & Rome	*The Illiad* & *Odyssey* (Homer), *Parallel Lives* (Plutarch)	*The Republic* (Plato), *The Meditations* (Marcus Aurelius)
Americas	Native Americans	*An Indigenous Peoples' History of the United States* (Dunbar-Ortiz)	*The Wisdom of the Native Americans* (Nerburn)
Concepts	Empires		
Africa	Kingdoms of Africa (Nok, Awkar, Fulani, Hausa, Zulu)	*Chaka* (Mofolo)	*The Desert Shore: Literatures of the Sahel*, Vol. 3 (Wise)
Asia	Han dynasty & Mughals	*The Baburnama* (Babur)	*The Analects* (Confucius)
Oceania	Peoples of Polynesia & Micronesia	*A History of the Pacific Islands* (Campbell)	*Hawaiian Mythology* (Beckwith)
Middle East	Early Islam and the Ottoman Empire	*Osman's Dream* (Finkel)	*Seyahâtnâme* (Celebi), *On the Perfect State* (Al-Farabi)
Europe	Middle Ages & Renaissance	The Bible, *The Inferno* (Dante), The great tragedies (Shakespeare), poetry of John Donne	*The Confessions* (St. Augustine), *Discourse on Method* (Descartes), *The Prince* (Machiavelli)

(Continued)

CHAPTER 6

Table 1. (Continued)

	History	*Literature*	*Philosophy*
Concepts	Empires		
Americas	Inca, Mayan & Aztec kingdoms; conquistadors	*Conquistador* (Levy)	*The Popol Vuh* (Tedlock trans.)
Concepts	Power and territory		
Africa	The scramble for Africa & colonisation	*The Lion and The Jewel* (Soyinka), *Things Fall Apart* (Achebe), *Heart of Darkness* (Conrad), *King Leopold's Ghost* (Hochschild)	*Imperialism: The Highest Stage of Capitalism* (Lenin), *Writings on Empire and Slavery* (Tocqueville)
Asia	The East India Company and colonisation of India	*The Honourable Company* (Keay)	*Autobiography* (Gandhi), *The Jail Notebook and Other Writings* (Bhagat Singh), *Dream of the Red Chamber* (Cao Xueqin)
Oceania	Cooke, Tasmania & colonisation of Australia	*Blue Latitudes: Boldly Going Where Captain Cook Has Gone Before* (Horwitz), *The Fatal Shore* (Hughes)	*Two Treatises of Government* (Locke)
Middle East	The Sykes-Picot Agreement & Balfour Declaration	*Seven Pillars of Wisdom* (Lawrence), *The Arab Awakening* (Antonius)	*The State of the Jews* (Herzl), *The Prophet* (Gibran)
Europe	Enlightenment & Industrial Revolution	*Hard Times* (Dickens), *Pride and Prejudice* (Austen), *The Brothers Karamazov* (Dostoevsky), *Madame Bovary* (Flaubert), *Industry and Empire: The Birth of the Industrial Revolution* (Hobsbowm)	*The Communist Manifesto* (Marx and Engels), *The Twilight of the Idols* (Nietzsche), *The Origin of Species* (Darwin)
Americas	American colonisation, independence & Civil War	*Moby Dick* (Melville), *The Metaphysical Club* (Menand)	*Walden* (Thoreau)
Concepts	War and independence		
Africa	Post-colonisation	*Long Walk to Freedom* (Mandela), *Season of Migration to the North* (Salih), *The Cairo Trilogies* (Mahfouz)	*African Philosophy: An Anthology* (Eze)

KNOWLEDGE

Table 1. (Continued)

	History	Literature	Philosophy
Asia	Independence and Communism	*Midnight's Children* (Rushdie), *The God of Small Things* (Roy),	*The Little Red Book* (Mao), *Orientalism* (Said), *The Master of Go* (Kawabata)
Oceania	The plight of modern Aborigines and Maoris	*A Secret Country* (Pilger), *The Bone People* (Hulme), *The Whale Rider* (Ihimaera)	*Tikanga Whakaaro: Key Concepts in Maori Culture* (Barlow)
Concepts	War and independence		
Middle East	Afghanistan, Arab Spring, Palestine & Israel, Iraq war	*Woman at Point Zero* (Nawal El Saadawi), *The Shaping of the Modern Middle East* (Lewis)	*Murderous Identities* (Maalouf)
Europe	WW1, WW2, Cold War	War poets (Owen, Sassoon), *1984* (Orwell), *Death in Venice* (Mann)	*Nausea* (Sartre)
Americas	WW1, WW2, Cold War	*The Great Gatsby* (Fitzgerald), *Who Rules the World* (Chomsky), *Beloved* (Morrison), *One Hundred Years of Solitude* (Marquez)	*Labyrinths* (Borges)

has been taught for the last century. Whilst a number of new education pundits call for new topics in the sciences, students must still master the essentials so as to be operating from a solid basis when they grapple with more sophisticated applications in their later academic or professional lives.

What has changed, and will change in the future, is the depth and technological application involved in many of these STEM areas.[27] None can be cut back or thrown out, because they are essential building blocks to understanding the physical world.

Literature, arts and the humanities, on the other hand, require more ideological choices. What sort of canon might we consider in the twenty-first century, an age of globalisation? In the table above I suggest what it might entail in order to ensure a coverage that is at once intercultural, balanced, relevant to current world political fault lines, canonical and rich in its transferrable patterns and concepts.

The age group towards which a school targets these units would depend on the school's aims and objectives. The literature indicated tends to suit mature minds but could be broken down for younger readers.

SARAH

What became of Sarah, my ace student who seemed to know everything?

CHAPTER 6

We had expected she would study law at university, as it was her passion. Since she could access and manage large amounts of information with ease and dexterity, I and my colleagues in University Guidance thought that she would become a great advocate or judge. She received offers from the London School of Economics and Columbia.

Years later, Sarah surprised me one day by visiting my school. She was still much the same physically and superficially, but after a few minutes talking to her, I realized she had a new mellowness, of the type that comes with maturity, as well as a serenity that she had not seemed to possess in high school. She seemed at peace with her surroundings. She had developed a subtle, wise expression and manner.

She said she had turned her back on law and was studying to become a teacher. Given her interest in knowledge and learning, I was not surprised. As we spoke, I realised that her passion for knowledge had liberated her from the base, materialist ambitions that drive so many. She was interested in knowledge and how to transmit it, not in glamour or riches.

Perhaps the most powerful aspect of knowledge is that it puts you under its spell and gives you a purpose that is noble and free of the chthonian currents that for the most part drive the world. When you fall in love with knowledge, you are bound to be happy, even if you live in misery. You can look at trees, waves breaking on the shore, statues, buildings and people with depth and understanding. Knowledge is a higher force.

CONCLUSION

A small black iguana rushes across a wall until it finds the yellowish-green slice of sunlight that bathes it in a peaceful, pleasant warmth. The creature's triangular red and orange head bobs rhythmically. A lizard's behaviour here and now, governed by instinct, sun and the will to survive, is exactly as it was dozens, hundreds, thousands and even millions of years ago. The winds of change blow across the face of the earth, and yet so many of the elements and forces, the principles and fundamentals that the ancient Egyptians, Sumerians, Phoenicians and Greeks observed, about agriculture, number, alphabet, political organisation, religion, language, and so on, have not changed and probably never will.

The iguana spots a winged insect 10 centimetres to its left. Its cold, reptilian eye is riveted on the nervous fluttering of the insect's diaphanous wings and the gentle probing of its emerald antennae. Once the insect has folded its wings into a neat braid on its back and has taken to licking its serrated forearms, fully concentrated on this act of grooming, the iguana darts and seizes it in its mouth. The action, involving four steps and a carefully focussed bite, takes but a fraction of a second. It is an act of mastery, no doubt born of hours of practice and millennia of adaptation.

I put my pen on the table and browse through a UNESCO document. It reads, "Quality education fosters creativity and knowledge, and ensures the acquisition of the foundational skills of literacy and numeracy as well as analytical, problem-solving and other high-level cognitive, interpersonal and social skills" (UNESCO, 2015).

KNOWLEDGE

One word stand out: "foundational", from the Latin *fundare,* meaning "to lay a base". What sort of base will our grandchildren's education rest upon? I wonder. A line of poetry by Alexander Pope appears to me, something I had once learned off by heart. At the time, memorising it had seemed pointless, without relevance, but now as I recall it, the words ring true:

A little learning is a dangerous thing;
Drink deep, or taste not the Pierian spring:
There shallow draughts intoxicate the brain,
And drinking largely sobers us again.

NOTES

[1] Here are examples of this notion in the mouths of educational authorities:

> The teacher is not in the school to impose certain ideas or to form certain habits in the child, but is there as a member of the community to select the influences which shall affect the child and to assist him in properly responding to these influences. (Dewey, 1941, p. 8)

> What is of paramount important in the pre-university stage is not what is learned but learning how to learn … What matters is not the absorption and regurgitation either of facts or pre-digested interpretation of facts, but the development of powers of the mind or ways of thinking which can be applied to new situations and new presentations of facts as they arise. (Alec Peterson [IB, 2010]) And in the form of a criticism of a facts-filled education:

> Education, thus becomes an act of depositing, in which the students are the depositories and the teacher is the depositor.… But in the last analysis, it is the people themselves who are filed away through the lack of creativity, transformation and knowledge in this (at best) misguided system. (Freire, 1996, p. 52)

[2] Here are some citations from various bodies and figures that display this problematic interpretation, downplaying knowledge itself (my added italics mark the anti-knowledge stance): "*My object is not to give him science* but to teach him to acquire science when needed" (Rousseau, 2010, p. 358). An oft-quoted aphorism from the English poet W. B. Yeats, the sort of thing some educators will tag to their e-mails, tells us that *"education is not the filling of a pail,* but the lighting of a fire". "The [IB Middle Years Programme] assessments themselves will also be innovative, *replacing the traditional imperative to memorise* with a desire to understand, to apply concepts, to relate to global contexts …" (Hegarty, 2016, p. 101).

One can analyse the process at work – as do Daisy Christodoulou (2014), E. D. Hirsch (2006) and Theodore Dalrymple (2010) – as an ideological position that started with the early romantic ideas of Jean-Jacques Rousseau, took hold at the turn of the twentieth century with Friedrich Froebel, Edward Claparède, John Dewey and Maria Montessori (as an experimental method, namely, inquiry-based learning) and became a strong educational paradigm with widespread application from the 1950s to the present through the constructivist movement (citing chiefly the 1930s Soviet pedagogue Lev Vygotsky, who was resuscitated by Harvard scholars in the 1970s).

[3] Dalrymple (2010) bemoans the massively influential Spens report for the effect it has had on British pedagogical philosophy (the italics are mine): "The Primary school curriculum should be thought of in terms of activity and experience *rather than knowledge* to be acquired and facts to be stored" (Spens Report of 1937 in Dalrymple, 2010, p. 23).

[4] Examples of this radical anti-knowledge perspective include:

> Knowledge does not make you skilled. (Boulet, 2015 – part of the elearning industry web page)

121

CHAPTER 6

> The world no longer rewards people just for what they know – search engines know everything. (Schleischer in Fadel, Bialik, and Trilling, 2015, p. 1)

> I have yet to talk to a recent graduate, college teacher, community leader, or business leader who said that not knowing enough academic content was a problem. In my interviews, everyone stressed the importance of critical thinking, communication skills, and collaboration. (Wagner, 2008)

> The industrial and subsequently the digital revolution have had dramatic and widespread impact, changing the way we think, live, and work. Education, however, has not always changed commensurately. The burgeoning knowledge economy and resultant change in employment structures have highlighted the fact that our 'unknown unknowns' (the things we don't know that we don't know) vastly outnumber the things we do know and know we know. Education must prepare learners for these changing working environments, increasingly based on the manufacture, distribution, and consumption of information. (Griffin, 2016)

5   Examples of this world view:

> A twenty-first century curriculum cannot have the transfer of knowledge at its core for the simple reason that the selection of what has become required has become problematic in an information-rich age. (Association of Teachers and Lecturers, 2007)

> Knowledge is the dimension most emphasized in the traditional view of curriculum and content. Yet as collective knowledge increases, curriculum has not successfully kept up. The current curriculum is often relevant neither to students' disengagement and lack of motivation nor to societal and economic needs. (Fadel, 2016)

> Knowledge is changing so fast that we cannot give young people what they will need to know, because we do not know what it will be. Instead we should be helping them to develop supple and nimble minds, so that they will be able to learn whatever they need to. (Claxton, 2013, p. 1)

6   The 2017 YouTube video "Don't Stay in School" by Boyinaband went viral (over 13 million views in under a year). The rap argues that instead of teaching useless knowledge such as quadratic equations, prime numbers, details on mitochondria, knowledge of Shakespeare and Henry VIII, schools should focus on useful issues such as law, how money is made, negotiating a mortgage or personal health. Charles Fadel argues that "tough choices must be made about what to pare back in order to allow for more appropriate areas of focus (for instance in Maths, more statistics and probabilities, and less trigonometry)" (Fadel, 2016).

7   Chase and Simon (1973) showed conclusively how chess experts rely on hundreds of learnt configurations (and not on stand-alone analytical or logical thinking). This has been confirmed in more academic disciplines, such as physics (Chi, Feltovich, and Glaser, 1981; Larkin, McDermott, Simon, and Simon, 1980), in which participants with knowledge of the subject interpret problems correctly using learnt theory and not in intuitive, erroneous ways: problems solved without knowledge will be solved poorly.

8   Hatano (1990) and Newell (1990) have pointed out how much clearer, more procedural and effective experts' problem-solving skills are than novices'. This edge essentially comes from the extensive knowledge bank experts are able to activate.

9   See, for example, Baxter and Glaser (1998), or for the specific example of the importance of mathematical knowledge in solving algebraic problems, Sweller and Cooper (1985).

10 Schneider and Korkel (1989), Recht and Leslie (1988) and Singer, Revlin and Halldorson (1990) have shown how background knowledge predicts reading skill. This case is also made in E. D. Hirsch's masterful *The Knowledge Deficit* (2006, p. 90).

11 Wollet, Spiers, and Maguire (2009) have found that the amount of memorisation to which London taxi drivers commit their brains actually increases the size of their hippocampus. This study's hypothesis was reinforced in a later study (Jabr, 2011). So knowing a lot, even if the substance is

arguably trivial (and this is an ideological argument), does have an impact, literally changing brain morphology.

Daisy Christodolou puts it well in *Seven Myths about Education* (2014):

> To make a scientific breakthrough, first of all you have to reach the frontiers of knowledge in your discipline. As scientific knowledge has advanced over the decades, that frontier has got further and further away, which means that it takes researchers more and more time to reach it. What this should show us is that making a new scientific discovery requires an intimate understanding of what has gone before. (p. 54)

[12] Larry Sanger, co-founder of Wikipedia, points out that he did much better at 17 to learn US history than WordPerfect and BASIC because what he "learned about history will remain more or less the same, subject to a few corrections; skills in WordPerfect and BASIC are no longer needed" (Sanger, 2011).

[13] Kirschner, Sweller, and Clark, paraphrasing Kyle (1980) put it thus:

> Scientific inquiry is a systematic and investigative performance ability incorporating unrestrained thinking capabilities after a person has acquired a broad, critical knowledge of the particular subject matter through formal teaching processes. It may not be equated with investigative methods of science teaching, self-instructional teaching techniques, or open-ended teaching techniques. Educators who confuse the two are guilty of the improper use of inquiry as a paradigm on which to base an instructional strategy. (2006, p. 79)

[14] Such as the IMMEX (Interactive Multimedia Exercises) programme in which students pretend they are forensic scientists and receive feedback on their problem-solving strategies as they go along (see Vendlinski and Stevens, 2000).

[15] For example, the research of Kaiser, Proffitt and McCloskey (1985); Seigler (1998) or Fay and Klahr, (1996). Significantly, "one of the most important findings from detailed observations of children's learning behavior is that children do not move simply and directly from an erroneous to an optimal solution strategy.... Instead, they may exhibit several different but locally or partially correct strategies.... They also may use less-advanced strategies even after demonstrating that they know more-advanced ones, and the process of acquiring and consolidating robust and efficient strategies may be quite protracted, extending across many weeks and hundreds of problems" (Pellegrino, Chudowski, and Glaser, 2001, p. 81).

[16] According to Pelligrino, Chudowski, and Glaser (2001):

> Experts have acquired extensive stores of knowledge and skill in a particular domain. But perhaps most significant, their minds have organized this knowledge in ways that make it more retrievable and useful. In fields ranging from medicine to music, studies of expertise have shown repeatedly that experts commit to long-term memory large banks of well-organized facts and procedures, particularly deep, specialized knowledge of their subject matter... Most important, they have efficiently coded and organized this information into well-connected schemas. These methods of encoding and organizing help experts interpret new information and notice features and meaningful patterns of information that might be overlooked by less competent learners. These schemas also enable experts, when confronted with a problem, to retrieve the relevant aspects of their knowledge. (pp. 72–73)

[17] "You Can Always Look it Up" is the sardonic title of one of E. D. Hirsch's articles on the topic. The point is that in order to look something up, you need to know what you are looking for:

> Imagine an expert and a novice looking up the entry 'planet' on the Internet and finding the following: Planet – any of the non-luminous bodies that revolve around the sun. The term 'planet' is sometimes used to include the asteroids, but excludes the other members of the solar system, comets, and meteoroids. A well-informed person would learn a good deal from this entry, if, for example, he was uncertain about whether asteroids, comets, and meteoroids should be called planets. A novice, even one who 'thinks scientifically', would learn less.

123

CHAPTER 6

> Since he wouldn't know what planets are, he probably wouldn't know what asteroids, comets, and meteoroids are… Yes, the Internet has placed a wealth of information at our fingertips. But to be able to use that information – to absorb it, to add to our knowledge – we must already possess a storehouse of knowledge. (Hirsch, 2000, p. 2)

[18] It says on page 28:

> Probably the most common educational objective in American education is the acquisition of knowledge or information. That is, it is desired that as the result of completing an educational unit, the student will be changed with respect to the amount and kind of knowledge he possesses. Frequently knowledge is the primary, sometimes almost the sole kind of, educational objective in a curriculum. In almost every course it is an important or basic one.

Bloom explains in his handbook that knowledge can be subdivided into many different types – it is by no means only declarative but can be considered as a method of approaching and storing information. "Knowledge, as defined here, involves the recall of specifics and universals, the recall of methods and processes, or the recall of a pattern, structure or setting" (p. 201). Humans use knowledge that has been understood and apply it in various ways, eventually at the higher order thinking levels of analysis, synthesis, evaluation and (for Anderson et al., who revised the taxonomy in 2001), creativity.

[19] "For measurement purposes, the recall situation involves little more than bringing to mind the appropriate material. Although some alteration of the material may be required, this is a relatively minor part of the task" (p. 201).

[20] Bloom himself makes the argument in the handbook: "The emphasis on knowledge as little more than remembering or recall distinguishes it from those conceptions of knowledge which involve 'understanding', 'insight,' or which are phrased as 'really know' or 'true knowledge' (p. 29).

[21] Here are some examples:

> The term 'higher order' skills is probably itself fundamentally misleading, for it suggests that another set of skills, presumably called 'lower order,' needs to come first. This assumption – that there is a sequence from lower level activities that do not require much independent thinking or judgment to higher level ones that do – colors much educational theory and practice. Implicitly, at least, it justifies long years of drill on the 'basics' before thinking and problem solving are demanded. Cognitive research on the nature of basic skills such as reading and mathematics provides a fundamental challenge to this assumption". (National Research Council, 1987, p. 8)

> The notion that students have to be immersed in 'lower-level' factual and procedural knowledge BEFORE they can do 'higher-level' thinking work doesn't comport with what we know from cognitive research. (Mcleod, 2017)

Exactly what cognitive research Mcleod is referring to – apart from the 1987 National Research Council position – is not entirely clear. It is true that much educational discourse on problem-solving focusses on the strategies of processing information strategically through working memory rather than emphasising the need to access long-term memory. The idea is that higher order thinking processes can, and should be, taught in and of themselves as metacognitive and application processes, independent of knowledge. This movement leads to discrete courses in study skills, critical thinking or problem-solving that stand outside of disciplines.

[23] In Cotton (1988), we read:

> Higher cognitive questions are not categorically better than lower cognitive questions in eliciting higher level responses or in promoting learning gains; Lower cognitive questions are more effective than higher level questions with young (primary level) children, particularly the disadvantaged; Increasing the use of higher cognitive questions (to considerably above the 20 percent incidence noted in most classes) produces superior learning gains for students above the primary grades and particularly for secondary students; Simply asking higher cognitive questions does not necessarily lead students to produce higher cognitive responses. (p. 4)

[24] Blank (2013) and his team of researchers, using meta-analysis research methodology, reviewed more than 400 published studies of professional development, coded 74 and analysed 16 (p. 52) to come to the conclusion that the primary element of effective programmes was content focus. Coe et al. (2014) in the Sutton Report state that "the most effective teachers have deep knowledge of the subjects they teach, and when teachers' knowledge falls below a certain level it is a significant impediment to students' learning" (p. 2). Hill et al. (2005) found fairly high correlations between mathematics teachers with low levels of knowledge content and low-scoring students. To be fair, the research does not always indicate this. Rockoff et al. (2011) have shown that there is no real corollary between student performance and the academic qualifications of their instructors.

[25] "As well as a strong understanding of the material being taught, teachers must also understand the ways students think about the content, be able to evaluate the thinking behind students' own methods, and identify students' common misconceptions" (Coe et al., 2014, p. 2).

[26] "Basically, any time that you, as a learner, look up an answer or have somebody tell or show you something that you could, drawing on current cues and your past knowledge, generate instead, you rob yourself of a powerful learning opportunity" (Bjork and Bjork, 2011, p. 61).

[27] There are other important conditions for good memory consolidation, such as contextually emotional cues, enough sleep and a healthy lifestyle.

[28] UNESCO's International Bureau of Education has developed seven macro competences for the twenty-first century: lifelong learning, self-agency, interacting with diverse tools and resources, interacting with others, interacting in and with the world, trans-disciplinarity and multi-literateness (Marope, Griffin, and Gallagher, 2017).

REFERENCES

Anderson, L. W., & Krathwohl, D. R. (Eds.) (2001). *A taxonomy for learning, teaching and assessing: A revision of Bloom's taxonomy of educational objectives.* New York, NY: Longman.

Appleton-Knapp, S. L., Bjork, R. A., & Wickens, T. D. (2005). Examining the spacing effect in advertising: Encoding variability, retrieval processes, and their interaction. *Journal of Consumer Research, 32*, 266–276.

Association of Teachers and Lecturers (2007). *Subject to change: New thinking on the curriculum.* https://www.atl.org.uk/advice-and-resources/publications/subject-change-new-thinking-curriculum

Bahrick, H. P., Bahrick, L. E., Bahrick, A. S., & Bahrick, P. E. (1993). Maintenance of foreign language vocabulary and the spacing effect. *Psychological Science, 4*, 316–321.

Ball, D. L., & Hill, H. C. (2009). Measuring teacher quality in practice. In D. H. Gitomer (Ed.), *Measurement issues and assessment for teaching quality.* Washington, DC: Sage Publications.

Barahal, S. (2008). Thinking about thinking: Pre-service teachers strengthen their thinking artfully. *Phi Delta Kappan, 90*(4), 298–302.

Baxter, G. P., & Glaser, R. (1998). Investigating the cognitive complexity of science assessments. *Educational Measurement: Research and Practice, 17*(3), 37–45.

Bjork, R. A., & Yan, V. X. (2014). The increasing importance of learning how to learn. In M. A. McDaniel, R. F. Frey, S. M. Fitzpatrick, & H. L. Roediger (Eds.), *Integrating cognitive science with innovative teaching in STEM disciplines.* St. Louis, MO: Washington University. https://bjorklab.psych.ucla.edu/wp-content/uploads/sites/13/2016/04/BjorkYan_IncreasingImportanceOfHowToLearn.pdf

Blank, R. K. (2013). What research tells us: Common characteristics of professional learning that leads to student achievement. *JSD, 34*(1), 50–53. https://learningforward.org/docs/default-source/jsd-february-2013/blank341.pdf?sfvrsn=2

Blank, R. K., & de las Alas, N. (2009). *Effects of teacher professional development on gains in student achievement: How meta analysis provides scientific evidence useful to education leaders.* Washington, DC: Council of Chief State School Officers.

Bloom, B. S. (Ed.) (1956). *Taxonomy of educational objectives: The classification of educational goals* (Handbook 1: Cognitive domain). New York, NY: McKay.

Boulet, G. (2015). *The difference between knowledge and skills: Knowing does not make you skilled.* https://elearningindustry.com/difference-between-knowledge-and-skills-knowing-not-make-skilled

CHAPTER 6

Bransford, J., & Stein, B. (1984). *The ideal problem solver*. New York, NY: W. H. Freeman.
Brookhart, S. (2010). *How to assess higher order thinking skills in your classroom*. Alexandria, VA: ASCD. http://www.ascd.org/Publications/Books/Overview/How-to-Assess-Higher-Order-Thinking-Skills-in-Your-Classroom.aspx
Cadwalladr, C. (2015). The 'granny cloud': The network of volunteers helping poorer children learn. *The Guardian*. https://www.theguardian.com/education/2015/aug/02/sugata-mitra-school-in-the-cloud
Chase, W. G., & Simon, H. A. (1973). Perception in chess. *Cognitive Psychology, 1*, 33–81.
Cheng, P. W., & Holyoak, K. J. (1985). Pragmatic reasoning schemas. *Cognitive Psychology, 17*(4), 391–416.
Chi, M. T. H., Feltovich, P. J., & Glaser, R. (1981). Categorization and representation of physics problems by experts and novices. *Cognitive Science, 5*, 121–152.
Christodolou, D. (2014). *Seven myths about education*. London: Routledge.
Claxton, G. (2013). *Learning to learn: A key goal in 21st century curriculum*. http://www.cumbria.ac.uk/Public/Education/Documents/Research/ESCalateDocuments/QCAArticlebyGuyClaxton.pdf
Coe, R., Aloisi, C., Higgins, S., & Elliot Major, L. (2014). *What makes great teaching? Review of the underpinning research*. London: Sutton Trust. http://www.suttontrust.com/researcharchive/great-teaching/
Common Core Standards (2017). Website. http://www.corestandards.org/
Cotton, K. (1988). *Classroom questioning*. http://educationnorthwest.org/sites/default/files/ClassroomQuestioning.pdf
Dalrymple, T. (2010). *Spoilt rotten: The toxic cult of sentimentality*. London: Gibson Square.
Department for Education and Skills (2003). *21st century skills: Realising our potential: Individuals, employers, nation*. Norwich, UK: HSMO.
Dewey, J. (1941). *Education today*. London: George Allen & Unwin.
Egan, D. E., & Schwartz, B. J. (1979). Chunking in recall of symbolic drawings. *Memory and Cognition, 7*, 149–158.
Ericsson, K. A., Krampe, R., & Tesch-Römer, C. (1993). The role of deliberate practice in the acquisition of expert performance. *Psychological Review, 100*(3), 363–406. http://dx.doi.org/10.1037/0033-295X.100.3.363
Fadel, C. (2016). *Redesigning the curriculum for a 21st century education*. Boston, MA: Center for Curriculum Redesign. http://curriculumredesign.org/wp-content/uploads/CCR-FoundationalPaper-Updated-Jan2016.pdf
Fadel, C., Bialik, M., & Trilling, B. (2015). *Four-dimensional education: The competencies learners need to succeed*. Boston, MA: Center for Curriculum Redesign.
Fay, A., & Klahr, D. (1996). Knowing about guessing and guessing about knowing: Preschoolers' understanding of indeterminacy. *Child Development, 67*, 689–716.
Freire, P. (1996). *Pedagogy of the oppressed*. London: Penguin.
Griffin, P. (2016). *Curriculum in a knowledge economy* (IBE Learning Series lecture, 18 October). Geneva: UNESCO International Bureau of Education.
Hatano, G. (1990). The nature of everyday science: A brief introduction. *British Journal of Developmental Psychology, 8*, 245–250.
Hegarty, G. (2015). Assessing the MYP: EAssessing year 5 students. In M. Hayden, J. Thompson, & J. Fabian (Eds.), *MYP new directions*. Woodbridge, UK: John Catt Educational.
Hill, H. C., Rowan, B., & Ball, D. L. (2005). Effects of teachers' mathematical knowledge for teaching on student achievement. *American Educational Research Journal, 42*(2), 371–406.
Hirsch, E. D. (2000). You can always look it up … Or can you? *American Educator*. http://www.aft.org/pdfs/americaneducator/spring2000/LookItUpSpring2000.pdf
Hirsch, E. D. (2006). *The knowledge deficit: Closing the shocking education gap for American children*. New York, NY: Houghton Mifflin.
IB [International Baccalaureate] (2010). *The history of the IB*. Cardiff: IB. http://www.ibo.org/globalassets/digital-tookit/presentations/1711-presentation-history-of-the-ib-en.pdf
IB (2015). *Guide to MYP eassessment*. Cardiff: IB. https://jdosher.weebly.com/uploads/3/7/3/8/37387871/guide_to_myp_eassessment.pdf

Jabr, F. (2011). Cache cab: Taxi drivers' brains grow to navigate London's streets. *Scientific American.* https://www.scientificamerican.com/article/london-taxi-memory/

Jeffries, R., Turner, A., Polson, P., & Atwood, M. (1981). Processes involved in designing software. In J. R. Anderson (Ed.), *Cognitive skills and their acquisition* (pp. 255–283). Hillsdale, NJ: Lawrence Erlbaum.

Kaiser, M. K., Proffitt, D. R., & McCloskey, M. (1985). The development of beliefs about falling objects. *Perception & Psychophysics, 38*(6), 533–539.

Kirschner, P. A, Sweller, J., & Clark, R. E. (2006). Why minimal guidance during instruction does not work: An analysis of the failure of constructivist, discovery, problem-based, experiential, and inquiry-based teaching. *Educational Psychologist, 41*(2), 75–86.

Kyle, W. C. (1980). The distinction between inquiry and scientific inquiry and why high school students should be cognizant of the distinction. *Journal of Research on Science Teaching, 17*, 123–130.

Larkin, J. H., McDermott, J., Simon, D. P., & Simon, H. A. (1980). Expert and novice performance in solving physics problems. *Science, 208*, 1335–1342.

Marope, M., Griffin, P., & Gallagher, C. (2017). *Future competences and the future of curriculum: A global paradigm shift.* Geneva: UNESCO International Bureau of Education.

Marzano, R. J., Pickering, D. J., & Pollock, J. E. (2001). *Classroom instruction that works: Research-based strategies for increasing student achievement.* Alexandria, VA: Association for Supervision and Curriculum Development.

Mcleod, S. (2017). *Do students need to learn lower-level factual and procedural knowledge before they can do higher-order thinking?* http://bigthink.com/education-recoded/do-students-need-to-learn-lower-level-factual-and-procedural-knowledge-before-they-can-do-higher-order-thinking

McWilliam, E., & Taylor, P. (2016). *Personally significant learning.* http://www.ericamcwilliam.com.au/personally-significant-learning/

Mitra, S. (2013). *SOLE: How to bring self-organized learning environments to your community.* http://www.ted.com/pages/835

Mitra, S. (2015). Minimally invasive education: Pedagogy for development in a connected world. In P. Rothermel (Ed.), *International perspectives on home education: Do we still need schools?* (pp. 254–277). London: Palgrave Macmillan.

National Research Council (1987). *Education and learning to think.* Washington, DC: National Academy Press.

Newell, A. (1990). *Unified theories of cognition.* Cambridge, MA: Harvard University Press.

Partnership for 21st Century Skills (2017). *Framework for 21st century learning.* http://www.p21.org/our-work/p21-framework

Pellegrino, J., Chudowsky, N., & Glaser, R. (2001). *Knowing what students know: The science and design of educational assessment.* Washington, DC: National Academy Press.

QCA [Qualifications and Curriculum Authority] (2007). *The national curriculum.* London: QCA.

Recht, D. B., & Leslie, L. (1988). Effect of prior knowledge on dood and poor readers' memory of text. *Journal of Educational Psychology, 80*(1), 16–20.

Robinson, K. (2012). *Changing education paradigms.* https://www.ted.com/talks/ken_robinson_changing_education_paradigms

Rockoff, J. E., Jacob, B. A., Kane, T. J., & Staiger, D. O. (2011). Can you recognize an effective teacher when you recruit one? *Education, 6*(1), 43–74.

Rousseau, J. J. (2010). Emile, or on education. In C. Kelly (Ed.), *The collected writings of Rousseau* (Vol. 13, C. Kelly and A. Bloom, Trans.). Hanover, NH: Dartmouth College Press.

Sadler, P. M., Sonnert, G., Coyle, H. P., Cook-Smith, N., & Miller, J. L. (2013). The influence of teachers' knowledge on student learning in middle school physical science classrooms. *American Educational Research Journal, 50*(5), 1020–1049.

Sanger, L. (2011). *An example of educational anti-intellectualism.* http://larrysanger.org

Schneider, W., & Korkel, J. (1989). The knowledge base and text recall: Evidence for a short-term longitudinal study. *Contemporary Educational Psychology, 14*, 382–393.

Siegler, R. S. (1998). *Children's thinking* (3rd ed.). Upper Saddle River, NJ: Prentice Hall.

Singer, M., Revlin, R., & Halldorson, M. (1990). Bridging inferences and enthymemes. In A. C. Graesser & G. H. Bower (Eds.), *Inferences and text comprehension* (pp. 35–52). San Diego, CA: Academic.

Sweller, J., & Cooper, G. A. (1985). The use of worked examples as a substitute for problem solving in learning algebra. *Cognition and Instruction, 2*, 59–89.

Timperley, H. (2008). *Teacher professional learning and development*. Educational Practices Series 18. Geneva: UNESCO International Bureau of Education & International Academy of Education. http://www.ibe.unesco.org/fileadmin/user_upload/Publications/Educational_Practices/EdPractices_18.pdf

Timperley, H., Wilson, A., Barrar, H., & Fung, I. (2007). *Teacher professional learning and development: Best evidence synthesis iteration.* Wellington: Ministry of Education. http://www.educationcounts.govt.nz/publications/series/2515/15341

Trilling, B., & Fadel, C. (2012). *21st century skills: Learning for life in our times.* New York, NY: Wiley.

Tuytens, M., & Devos, G. (2011). Stimulating professional learning through teacher evaluation: An impossible task for the school leader? *Teaching and Teacher Education, 27*(5), 891–899.

UNESCO (2015). *Incheon declaration.* Incheon, Korea: World Education Forum 2015. https://en.unesco.org/world-education-forum-2015/incheon-declaration

Vendlinski, T., & Stevens, R. (2000). The use of Artificial Neural Nets (ANN) to help evaluate student problem solving strategies. In B. Fishman & S. O'Connor-Divelbiss (Eds.), *Proceedings of the fourth international conference of the learning sciences* (pp. 108–114). Mahwah, NJ: Erlbaum.

Wagner, T. (2008). *Even our "best" schools are failing to prepare students for 21st-century careers and citizenship.* http://www.tonywagner.com/244

Woollett, K., Spiers, H. J., & Maguire, E. A. (2009). *Talent in the taxi: A model system for exploring expertise.* London: The Royal Society. doi:10.1098/rstb.2008.0288

CHAPTER 7

CHARACTER

The lights are down, and the audience is hushed. Tension, energy and anticipation are palpable in the dark hall. We are no longer in the tame, matter-of-fact world of school, but rather in the timeless other universe of a dramatic production. Parents, grandparents, siblings and peers grow impatient in the penumbra of the lit stage, fidgeting in their seats as they wait for the opening bars of music, for the spotlight to fall on the lead actor.

And when that strong beam of light brings to life the actor before us, the person standing there no longer appears to be a child but rather a grown adult, radiating energy and purpose, lifted not only by confidence, but also by the extraordinary power of potential actualised for the first time.

Few things are as exhilarating as the sight of a young person rising to the challenge of a theatrical performance, taking on someone else's persona and mastering artistic expression. The experience is transformative; the parents see themselves through their children in a new way, and the children playing someone else have shed their habitual, childish ways and grown into something more mature, more dramatic. The power of art makes them larger than life. This overcoming of the self represents much of what the educational process is striving for; that is, to lead someone out of her present state and into a more knowledgeable and competent self, a greater and better self. In any case, this process forms the root of the word *education*: to lead out.

I look around at the audience, faces lit by the stage lights, eyes gleaming with pleasure and pride. What is it that creates this magic? My mind drifts to some big questions haunting our world. How and when will we change our consumerist behaviour so as to slow down the destruction of the planet? How do we prepare young people to enter a paradoxical and fast-changing world that is at once more threatening and more full of opportunities than ever before? How can we as educators and parents prepare our children to be part of the world's rich tapestry and to work together towards a brighter future for humanity? The answer to many of these questions seems to lie in the gaze of the audience, its sheer enthrallment, its utter captivation. If something can catch the attention of so many people the way this play can, then surely something within the play – or in the way that it is being put on – can give us clues as to how to educate for the mid-twenty-first century. For what we need is a force or vision that can cause human beings to federate across frontiers and can cause them to focus together on a certain number of issues so as to address and solve them. And for this, we need character.

CHAPTER 7

It also occurs to me that the artistic production itself embodies and illustrates many of the competences and approaches of a desirable twenty-first century education. On stage you see collaboration, teamwork, communication, creativity and confidence. These are some of the outward signs we look for in a well-educated person and a well-functioning society, as much research and theory show.

DISCIPLINE

So what is it in the play that brings out these competences? Will putting on dramatic productions be enough to bring students to the type of learning experience that will equip them for our times? We would like to think that through positive experiences, expressive and creative pedagogy, student choice and confidence-boosting feedback and teamwork we will arrive at the finished person or society that is so well symbolised by a masterful theatrical production. From the time of European romanticism at the end of the Enlightenment to this day, the dominant, all-powerful paradigm of education – naturalistic, inquiry-based, constructivist, with the learner at the centre – has given us a series of beliefs about good learning that confirms this desire.

Surely, however, the pathway is uncomfortable and rugged that leads to mastery and to the depth of character we are aiming for.

For into the opening night of the high school musical, as the actors and their parents know, went a lot of pain, exhaustion, repetition, discipline, anti-democratic directorial instruction. The students were not asked to come to rehearsals, at a time convenient to them, they were not presented with their lines in such a way that they would seem more meaningful or connected to their interests. If they were late for rehearsals the teacher director would fly into a rage and might even drop them from the cast.[1]

The students collaborate well on stage during the performance, but to get there they were not asked to collaborate freely during rehearsals; on the contrary, they were told what to do, explicitly, by a master who dictated every step. Even if the production were to have reflected a more democratic ethos, it would still have been held together and controlled by one person whose authority and word were final. And as in any enterprise that pushes the learner to truly stretch herself beyond perceived limits, as though she were in a gruelling long-distance race, the process held moments of disappointment at the level of the casting; moments of disillusionment in which the task seemed too much and the actor would break into a sob; long stretches of time lost waiting in the aisles to appear on stage, patiently waiting for one's cue. The whole process was a sacrifice, for other things had to be dropped to make the performance what it was.

And on the night, of course, if a song comes out flat or lines are forgotten, if an actor trips up or forgets her cue, the humiliation will be great, the audience ruthless in its laughter, its silence or its scattered, insincere applause. Perhaps this is the most powerful of all the elements of the performing arts: acquiring knowledge of what is good and what is not. No one can sweep failure under the carpet: the show undergoes the acid test of public judgement.

The Paradox

Here, as just described, lies an enigma and a paradox: that the most mysterious and significant part of character education is produced not in pleasure but in some form of pain. This idea has been propounded by a great many philosophers and thinkers through time.[2]

Any parent knows some sort of structure, authority and hardship are necessary for a child's moral, if not intellectual, education to succeed. To develop strength of character in our children, we would not simply spoil them and ask them what they felt like doing. We must parent our children not by overindulging them but by making them strong, with a firm inner compass that will not lead them astray when they enter the world alone and storm clouds brew on the horizon. No parent wants to see her child discouraged, deflated, demoralised or unhappy, but without these formative educational moments (which should nonetheless be supportive and humane), character will not be wrought and empowered.

This "no pain, no gain" truism appears more complex when we turn our attention to formal education and the role of the teacher.

It is a paradox because on the one hand we want students to be happy, to be fulfilled and to feel safe in schools. Conditions that make learners feel comfortable increase the likelihood of creative thinking and fluid expression. We condemn the idea of a Victorian classroom based on humiliation, corporal punishment and fear, and rightly so. It was the model of education for much of the last 300 years and led many to hate school.[3]

At the same time, however, if we wish to strengthen our students to be not only resilient in the world but ultimately happy and productive, we cannot turn education into a seat of instant gratification or an amusement park, cannot allow children to grow without restrictions or careful guidance, cannot dance around children with all sorts of limp praise while they spend hours playing games on their iPhones. Such ultra-permissiveness will create weakness, lack of direction, low tolerance of hardship and acceptance of low standards.

There is evidence that spoilt children grow to be less resilient and less fulfilled in their adult lives.[4]

Participants in studies identified many of the attributes of their own upbringings as spoilt children, and these attributes can be associated with a loose, unchallenging school structure: lack of rules, soft structure, overnurturing, no chores and being entertained.

Concomitantly, there is research that shows how educational experiences that create resilience reap greater all-round educational rewards, including academic gain.[5]

Clearly the education that we provide young people needs to empower them to survive and excel in a highly challenging environment. So we need to do what we

CHAPTER 7

can to develop the inner strength and staying power that will be necessary for them to be happy and successful as adults. At the same time, schools, parents, mentors and social institutions need to strike a balance between an educational experience that honours children by pushing them further and one that is too hard and breaks them. This balancing needs to take into account varying cultural contexts in which parent expectations, societal pressures and different types of goals or perceptions of success further complicate matters.

How to Create Self-Discipline in Students

I recommend four easy ways to create self-discipline in students.

Be disciplined yourself. Teachers should model discipline by always being on time, being scrupulous about handing back work in a timely manner, caring about themselves and others in a systematically disciplined manner. Parents need to be disciplined in spending time with their children, putting them to bed on time, not responding to tantrums and responding to crises in calm, measured ways.

Establish a clear routine with fair rewards and consequences. Teachers should have classroom rules that are well communicated and systematically upheld. If teachers apply these rules consistently and deal with student work and attitudes according to these rules, students will learn to appreciate and abide by the rules. Children do not respect hypocrisy and double standards any more than adults do, and they must be offered a consistent system that is agreed-upon and maintained. This idea applies to parents as well as to teachers.

Stretch young people. The teacher, like the parents, should push children to improve, to not settle for second best. However, we cannot ask students more than to do their best and should not drive young people into the ground, not reach the point at which pushing could become counterproductive. Teachers should openly appreciate and valorise hard work. Instruction should differentiated one student from another so that each individual student is being pushed a little further at every step.

Value patience. Discipline is strictly correlated to time: the disciplined person knows how to wait, stave off passions and control impulsiveness. Working towards a goal or trying to perfect oneself requires enormous reserves of patience, which means that teacher and parents should not be afraid to make young people wait, sit in silence and ultimately accept that they cannot have what they want immediately.

ETHICS

Let us come back to the high school musical. At the end of the applause at the last performance, the students gather around a microphone sheepishly, as if all of a sudden their dramatic personae have faded and they have returned to their fragile, unsure, 15-year-old selves. One lead actor clears her throat and says, "Now we would like to thank a few special people without whom this production would never have been possible". Thanks and praises abound, and some who worked behind the scenes stand one by one to be bathed in a cascade of applause, while others come to the stage to receive flowers that the students have bought for them. When the director comes on stage, she shares anecdotes about the production and congratulates the students on their performance. Thick emotion runs palpably though the hall. The audience gets to its feet for one last ovation.

This seems like the obvious way to end a major production. It can be considered a convention. What it is premised on, however, is thankfulness and generosity – values that should not be taken for granted. These values represent principles that we hope young people will incorporate into their way of being as they grow at school and when they go out into the world to partake in its activities as citizens. Other ethical values were also at work for the production to be its eventual resounding success: for example, caring for other people (being patient with actors and giving them moral support) and being honest (letting the director know when there is a problem).

Ethics comes from the Greek word *ethika*, meaning "customs" (morals comes from the Latin word *morales*, also meaning "customs" and is, essentially, the same thing, although some philosophers consider morals a more cultural and temporal than ethics, which they see as broader and more universal in scope). Interestingly, ethics is related to *ethos*, meaning "stables" in ancient Greek; so the place to which the horses return – a type of stability. (The Roman word for stables, *stabilum*, further anchors this notion of stability.) Indeed, there can be no ethics without there existing a bedrock of stable values.

Ethical behaviour is behaviour that considers other people and operates within a social network. An ethical person is preoccupied with the effects of her or his actions on other beings and wants to ensure that she or he is acting for positive, good reasons with good consequences.

Education should be nurturing the right values in young people too, so that the actions they take and the way they apply their knowledge and talents will be ethical and not harmful. If all we are doing is giving our students technique and understanding of systems, what will prevent them from employing these in the service of greed, disregard for others and exploitation?

This idea is well summarised in the quotation by the French writer Rabelais, who wrote, "Science sans conscience n'est que ruine de l'âme", meaning that science (used here to mean reason and learning generally) in the absence of an ethical conscience is the ruin of the soul. Rabelais (1532, 1534) put this warning in his masterpiece, *Gargantua et Pantagruel*, to remind enthusiasts of the Renaissance that the accumulation of knowledge and science that was accelerating during the period needed to be conjugated with righteousness and wisdom. A similar warning issued during the Renaissance is artfully represented in the extraordinary painting *The Ambassadors* by Hans Holbein the Younger (1533). The painter mocks the vanity

CHAPTER 7

of Renaissance men, with their loss of spirituality (a crucifix is barely perceptible in the background behind a curtain) and the inevitability of their death (a *memento mori* appears oddly strewn across the canvas through a brilliant technique whereby it can be seen only from an angle, again to suggest its hidden presence that haunts earthly success with its pomp and circumstance).

We also know from the Holocaust that individuals who have benefitted from the highest educational standards and cultural traditions of art, philosophy and science can behave like the worst barbarians. Philosopher and literary critic George Steiner put it well in his chilling statement, "We know that a man can read Goethe or Rilke in the evening, that he can play Bach and Schubert, and go to his day's work at Auschwitz in the morning" (Steiner, 1967, p. 15).

In a world in which war, exploitation, destruction of the ecosystem and endless examples of human cruelty abound, education is an area that can make a difference if we ensure that it offers practices that allow students to grow in their ethical dimension, to take the right decisions and to consider the plight of other people in their adult lives. Unfortunately, the socio-economic structure that is in place models, for the most part, individualistic accumulation of assets accomplished with (or because of) little deep consideration for other people or beings.[6]

And since the existentialist revolution in philosophy (its precursor, Nietzsche, set the tone in the late 1800s, but it is really after the World War II that it dominates the Western intellectual scene), freedom of choice has pushed higher-level ethical questions to one side and left a supremely subjective individual in the centre of any ethical decision. This development has led to a moral vacuum within a landscape of moral relativism.[7]

Although awareness of many of the man-made problems that the world is in seems to be growing, through platforms such as social media, which allow for a network of social activism and awareness-raising, and whilst movements in social entrepreneurship claim to be helping other people while ensuring that investors profit,[8] the politico-economic model that predominates is still strong, and we see only fringe humanitarian activity to counter it.

Education does not necessarily need to create a generation of people who will deliberately and dramatically go against the status quo or engage in radical social activities that are completely off-centre. In fact, the student revolutions of May 1968 and the resultant anti-establishment positions popularised in the late 1960s and the 1970s did little to prevent the neoliberal policies of the 1980s that drive the economic model that is with us today. These anti-establishment movements were less about caring for other people than they were rhetorical and ideological discourses of violence and disruption directed against figures of authority, such as the state.

The type of ethical behaviour that schools should seek to encourage in students in the twenty-first century needs to be subtler, less ideological. It needs to empower young people to treat others in a humane fashion no matter their position, culture, status or social identity. Immanuel Kant's categorical imperative (whereby any action should be worked out to be universally replicable and should always involve consideration of other people as ends rather than means to an end) would be a starting point for designing this type of ethical philosophy.

The way we provide education should give young people the experiences and tools necessary to ensure that they grow up to become competent professionals operating in mainstream society with a strong moral compass, that their decisions will be guided by an idea of what it means to be human and will not be cold and calculating.

VALUES IN SCHOOLS

So what does this approach translate into in schools?

Religious Education

The most obvious response is religious education. Whether in a Jewish school, Catholic school, madrassa or Gaudiya Vaishnavism establishment, it seems clear that a religious educational institution will embrace, or at least should embrace, strong ethical principles. Religious education binds students together under a common set of values (the word religion comes from *religio* in Greek, meaning "to bind together"). It has the powerful faculty, through providing a belief system in cosmic and spiritual matters, of giving students confidence, strength and an inner compass to guide them through the storm.

Of course, the problem with this religious model of education is that it is culturally specific and therefore exclusivist: a Christian school, for example, excludes Jewish students, a Jewish school excludes Christian students and so on. To be clear, I am not suggesting that schools will not admit students of another faith. Many religious schools claim to be multi-faith, especially in the UK, with its Lockean liberalist tradition of religious pluralism and tolerance anchored in the 1689 English Bill of Rights. I am suggesting, however, that the traditions and rituals of a religious school will speak to, and privilege, those in whom its religious practices have been inculcated and thus will not address the needs of all students, will not offer a universal, generalisable doctrine. To give a personal example, I attended a Catholic school, even though I am not a Catholic. We said the Hail Mary every morning, which was for all students, but when it came to chapel, only the Catholic students were required to partake in the Holy Communion. The Hindu, Protestant, Muslim, agnostic or atheist students would kick our heels at the bench, while the others went to the priest to receive their bread and wine. At the back of our minds was a feeling that not everyone was the same, that some students had greater access to school culture and identity than did others.

This type of situation seems inevitable sooner or later in a religious school that opens its doors to students of other faiths, since the central tenets of any religion will be based on stringent dogma that require sworn adepts to strictly adhere to a single system, not many systems at the same time. For this reason, religious education, which can provide students a strong moral backbone, is a necessarily sectarian model and thus troublesome in a discussion about education for all students.

We have also seen countless models of religious educational experiences that have not necessarily led to more ethically responsible graduates but that, on the contrary, led to a hatred of all things religious. Many of the most outspoken atheist philosophers attended religious schools or had some sort of religious formation: Nietzsche's father was a Lutheran pastor; Simone de Beauvoir attended the Institut Catholique de Paris; Benedetto Croce grew up in a strict Catholic environment. It might be that religious zealousness can have the countereffect of turning young people away from religion.[9]

Kohlberg's Stages of Moral Development

Kohlberg (1976, 1981) has written extensively on moral education, using a Piagetian model of moral development. It says that in order to reason in a genuinely moral fashion, individuals must break out of egocentrism. Educational practice, then, needs to take students to states of group awareness in which atomisation and individualism give way to something greater and more collective. Kohlberg cites as the basis of a moral education an appreciation of the importance of justice.[10]

Kohlberg argues that the most developed stages of moral reasoning (the "post-conventional" stage) cannot be realistically expected of students before they reach the age of 20. Therefore, according to his model, schools need to take time to build up students' conceptions of morality and need to create environments that provide students opportunities to appreciate and value justice progressively.[11] This model implies an increasingly abstract and maturely reasoned code of conduct that could be used by schools and students in successive years of their schooling, starting with the basic and specific, extending gradually, as students mature, to the universal and abstract. It also implies that teachers and administrators need to be careful to model fair and just responses to behaviour.

Non-Western Models of Character Education

One might also reflect on non-Western alternative forms of ethical reasoning, such as the Southern African philosophy of Ubuntu, meaning that a person is a person because of other people, thereby anchoring ethical practice in communal behaviour and an adherence to collective needs (see Eze, 2010). The African notion of the extended family as a caring community suggests a model that would allow students to feel respected and cared for. The African conception of justice is more restorative than is the Western model, which is more disciplinary. Restorative justice in a school context would mean that the emphasis in school rules should be on restoring dignity or comfort to someone who has suffered humiliation or discomfort in a situation, rather than using the offender as a scapegoat or example for others.

Confucianism, with its focus on the Chun-Tzu, roughly translated as "gentleman", puts character development at the centre of education, arguing that for the good of the individual and for the good of society as a whole, developing a selfless, honourable and trustworthy character should be main purpose of an individual's grooming.

Islamic culture, according to the French philosopher Abdennour Bidar (2015, 2016), offers a vision of "fraternity" that can bring about social renewal and greater individual character growth. Bidar emphasises a secular model of fraternity centred on respectful living together and solidarity.

Values-Based Schools

Some school systems openly promote an education for values, for example, the International Baccalaureate programmes, which all subscribe to a learner profile that advocates 10 values.[12] The United World Colleges Movement claims in its mission statement to "inspire our students to create a more peaceful and sustainable future through education" (UWC, 2017). Both of these school systems insist on service learning as a means to increase empathy and some sort of social commitment.

Some schools organise themselves in extremely democratic ways, with an emphasis on group discussion about moral dilemmas and how to find positive outcomes, thereby exposing students to mediation and dialogue as well as to ethically sound principles. These include such American examples as the Just Community Schools, based on Kohlberg's theory (see Power, Higgins, and Kohlberg, 1989) and a number of small schools based on the premise and functioning of direct democracy.[13]

Other examples include the Steiner or Waldorf schools (the names are interchangeable), which function according to the philosophy of the late nineteenth century, early twentieth century Austrian anthroposophist philosopher Rudolf Steiner. In these schools, students' choice and freedom are cherished, as students are guided through an education that claims to bring them to actualise their potential.[14]

A European example of a school with a pedagogical philosophy based on ethics is the Early Childhood Education Reggio Emilia movement, which is centred on exploring the different modes of expression very young children possess, so that these can be made visible and appreciated. The approach is based on Emmanuel Levinas' concept of the ethics of an encounter.[15]

How to Develop Ethics in Schools

Among the examples given, based on existing research and on practice in schools that I have led, I would suggest these five core steps towards an education for ethical behaviour and being:

Openly communicated values. Schools should not be afraid to make their philosophy clear. The school's mission statement should be distributed widely, repeated and known by students. Although some might criticise this approach as cosmetic, it is not by remaining silent about that which a school stands for that any real educational process will take place. Institutions need to have a clear, ethical vision. Research on prejudice has shown that it can be reduced when institutions make it clear that they regard each person as equal in value (Hughes, 2017). This is a stance that should be celebrated and modelled.

Dialogue. Schools should be places in which – through assemblies, debates, communities of inquiry, staff meetings, mediation, classroom and small group discussions – moral dilemmas, community issues and disciplinary problems are shared and discussed. Meeting this goal involves strategies conducive to sharing of ideas (such as good chairing, methods to ensure equal participation) and a philosophy of generous, active listening. Although critical thinking can be associated with robust exchange, it is important not to turn public discussion into displays of mental power, that is, occasions in which aggressive debating techniques are applauded as they run individuals into the ground, shame and humiliate them.

Service learning. A service learning programme allows students to learn about themselves and other people, as they interact with them and investigate how they can contribute to other people's well-being. Every student should be expected to be involved in some service learning activity with a clearly established philosophy behind it. Students should not be left to think that they are merely helping people less fortunate than themselves but should embrace service learning opportunities as learning adventures that stretch their understanding of others and themselves.[16]

Role models. Many, if not most, of the figures we learn about in history are kings, emperors, dictators or generals, who often represent some form of imperialist violence. Schools need to counterbalance this ideology and can inspire students to be more ethical in their outlook and actions by exposing them to role models who are known for ethical acts and positions. Schools can invite activists, humanitarians, philosophers and advocates for a better world to address students through a speakers series. Schools send a message to students by the types of guests and public figures they celebrate. Similarly, schools should reward not just academic excellence in assemblies, prize giving, honour rolls and graduations; they should publicly celebrate students' ethical actions, such as community and service work and acts of kindness towards others.

Social commentary. Although it is not necessarily easy, and it can be contentious or even polemical, schools should offer critical social commentary on current events, so that students understand what the institution's values are and how those relate to events taking place in the world. The school leadership should condemn wars, environmental disasters and acts of violence and hatred, and the school community should commemorate the victims of atrocities in a suitably dignified manner. Implementing this recommendation can become complicated because of ideological choices: many schools fear irking parents and fear appearing to have a political agenda. One stumbling block is the questions raised: Which atrocities? Which wars? Why commemorate some and not others? And if we are going to take time out of learning to discuss every item in the news, we will not get through a single day of classical instruction. However, if the school promotes ethical behaviour but has nothing to say or do about daily ethical transgressions in the real world, it will not be living by its word. Therefore, choices have to be made and discussions have to be had about events that are in geographic proximity to the school or of particular historic or symbolic value to the community.

EMOTIONAL INTELLIGENCE

One other element of character that should be discussed is emotional intelligence, in other words, the ability to recognise, understand and manage one's own emotions and the emotions of other people (Goleman, 1995, 1998). This skill is important for a number of fairly self-evident reasons. For one, human beings operate in a social network and need to know how to restrain their emotions lest they offend others or come to emotionally-charged, rash decisions. This path involves self-regulation and self-restraint. For another, knowing how to read other people's emotions is important because it allows for higher levels of sensitivity and empathy.

Emotional intelligence is a powerful dimension of human competence that is central in defining human and organisational culture.[17]

Daniel Goleman's (2017) popularised Emotional Intelligence Quotient allows individuals to test themselves in five domains (knowing your emotions; managing your own emotions; motivating yourself; recognising and understanding other people's emotions and managing relationships), and so-called "social and emotional learning" programmes are run in a number of schools, focussing on the managing and awareness of emotions.

Research underpins the idea that emotional intelligence underpins academic success.[18]

Being emotionally aware and sensitive makes you a better communicator, a better listener and a subtler negotiator. Human relationships are primarily emotional affairs (although we would like to think that decisions are driven by reason), and so it stands to reason that schools should do as much as they can to develop emotional awareness in students. One simple and effective way of doing this is to model behaviours that are measured and emotionally controlled: teachers and school leaders should not allow strong emotions to cloud judgement. This restraint is particularly important in the domain of assessment, since emotional predispositions towards particular students (such as anger, strong affection or pity) can lead to rater bias and distorted overall evaluation. At every step of the assessment process, evaluators need to be reminded of the unreliability of their perceptions because of the presence of emotions.

At another level, not only teachers and schools leaders, but also parents, mentors and coaches should be aware of the changing emotional states of the young people they are committed to, as this will help them understand student behaviour and motivation more accurately. In this regard, teachers need to see themselves as more than mere agents of the transmission of knowledge and skills: they need to build up a relationship with their students that is strong enough that they can detect when students are upset, angry, bored, highly motivated or afraid. Decades of research have shown that there are universal emotional traits, recognisable across ethnic and cultural lines, but we also know that little training in emotional intelligence goes into teacher preparation. Schools can counter this lack by organising professional development that allows teachers opportunities to become more expert in their recognition of emotions. Many profile tests and psychometric assessments in the field of industrial psychology include items that test participants on their emotional intelligence and give them relevant formative feedback.[19]

When it comes to developing students' social and emotional intelligence, courses within the school programme should allow for discussion of emotions, different strategies for recognising and negotiating emotions and ways of appreciating and valorising the role of emotions in cognitive processes, such as critical thinking and creativity. This work can be done through a mentor programme in which teachers work regularly with small groups of students on questions of relationships, self-management, approaches to learning, self-awareness and empathy. Or the work can happen in academic subjects, in which some time and consideration is given to the emotional dimension of decision-making in history. To find examples, schools might consider how some emotional or socially-driven agenda was at work in the actions and words of great historical figures (briefly considering Ivan the Terrible, Winston Churchill, Nelson Mandela and Indira Ghandi from an emotional perspective can be elucidating); the role of the emotions as a way of knowing in the arts; or the psychological dimension of emotions in social science courses such as human geography, economics and philosophy. That is to say, time can be put aside within subject areas to look at the domain from the perspective of emotions.[20]

The Cultural Dimension of Emotions

We should not lose sight of the cultural relativity of emotions in society. At the risk of overgeneralising, it does not seem totally unreasonable to say that in northern cultures in the West (Nordic, English, Dutch and German, for example), open displays of emotions are less culturally common than in the Mediterranean. In traditional Japanese culture, open displays of emotion are not encouraged, whereas on much of the African continent, expressive displays of emotions around core social events such as marriages and funerals are celebrated and make up a key part of those cultural identities. Schools should not assume that the Anglo-Saxon model (dampened emotions in public, open displays in certain social gatherings such as parties, an emphasis on critical thinking and highly controlled emotions in the workplace) is the norm: it is merely one cultural expression. I say this because part of being emotionally and socially intelligent is being receptive to different cultural paradigms, so that behaviours are not judged out of ignorance but with some wider understanding of the different ways that emotions operate in different societies. Schools that emphasise extroversion, outward-facing confidence or staged celebrations of achievement and the self might misinterpret certain quieter behaviours, patterns of self-abnegation and modesty as lack of effort or low community involvement when in reality they are related to cultural norms and expectations.

How Can Schools Develop Social and Emotional Learning?

Most authors on social and emotional learning concur as to the areas that should be underlined within school programmes to ensure that social and emotional learning happen.[21]

Here are four steps that schools can take to bolster social and emotional leaning within their communities:

Have a social and emotional learning programme. It could include a programme coordinator with overall accountability for social and emotional learning; a weekly course (such as a mentor programme) in which discussions and learning on emotions in particular take place; and some form of feedback on social and emotional learning to students and parents in the form of reports or regular oral feedback.

Model emotional intelligence. School leaders and teachers should model behaviour that is measured, empathetic, emotionally sensitive; assemblies and public celebrations should be culturally sensitive and tuned in to the emotions of students and all members of the community (including thanking people for their work, showing solidarity and sharing good news).

Focus on the role of emotions in different areas of learning. Courses should weave into the fabric of their design some reflection on, and discussion of, the role of emotion as a way of knowing. This inquiry can be particularly rewarding when it leads to a more accurate and profound analysis in the study of literature, art, history and the social sciences. Key questions that can stimulate this type of reflection: What is the role of emotion in this case? Explain how emotions might have acted on X's decision-making in this case. What do you think the emotional response to this piece of legislation might be from such-and-such a constituency? Explain how you would feel if this were to happen to you?

Ensure ongoing professional development for teachers and school leaders. It can include standard teacher training (conferences, workshops, visiting speakers, degree courses or online evaluations); regular discussions about emotions in the workplace or in the student body with specialists such as counsellors and the school psychologist; discussion groups in which members of the community are given a chance to discuss their emotions, how they respond emotionally to decisions taken by the administration and how the school could be a more emotionally sensitive institution.

CHAPTER 7

BRINGING THE PIECES TOGETHER IN CHARACTER EDUCATION

Why Is Character Important?

John Dewey claimed that the aim of education is growth or development, both intellectual and moral. Ethical and psychological principles can aid the school in the greatest of all constructions – the building of a free and powerful character" (1964, p. 207). Other sources point to the centrality of character development as an educational goal.[22]

What Do the Theory and Research Say about Character?

Standard historical definitions of character involve the three elements I have developed in this chapter (discipline, ethics and emotional intelligence) in different strains.

For Plato, one core purpose of life was to live the good life or *eudaimonia*, achieved through a virtuous existence with an appreciation of truth, beauty and goodness: all considered inherently knowable elements (Books II and III of his *Republic)*. Aristotle similarly believed that character (*êthos*) is essentially virtue (Book II, *Nichomanean Ethics*). Virtue for the ancient Greeks was not only a moral definition; it also implied excellence and mastery. The Roman Stoics, like Marcus Aurelius and Seneca, continued with the idea of character's being a state of virtue but extended the idea to acceptance of the world and, consequently, a type of inner fortitude brought about by humility and temperance. Thus, for the ancient Greeks and Romans, character was fundamentally about discipline and ethics.

The philosophers of the Middle Ages, Renaissance and Enlightenment took, in various ways, the idea of character to the level of kindness towards other people. Kant's categorical imperative, whereby a person should always be treated as an end and never as a mere means to an end, emblematises this position, which can be found in Christian theology through to Enlightenment reasoning. The emphasis on character through the models from the eleventh to the eighteenth centuries was on ethics. From the nineteenth century, with the philosophy of Nietzsche onwards, at least in the West, character came to be synonymous more with willpower and determination and less with Judaeo-Christian ethics.

Non-Western definitions of character vary, but many emphasise interactions with others and the way one is defined through the actions one takes towards others. I spoke of Confucianism's *Chun Tzu*, or gentleman, who acts with regard for those around him and the Southern African philosophy of Ubuntu, which holds that a person is a person because of other people, relying on a communal definition of humanity. Buddhist conceptions of character involve a fluid identity, challenged and shaped by transient phenomena (*dhammas*) that mean one seeks to meditate on aspects complementary to one's state to achieve balance (for example, the person driven by hatred should meditate on goodwill and so on). In Muslim thought, a noble character will be utterly devoted to God and manifest kindness to other people. We see how these definitions focus more on emotional intelligence as a hallmark of character.

Contemporary definitions of character incorporate many of these historical and cultural definitions.[23]

Established research and theory thus correspond with what I have argued: that the three essential facets of being that should be evoked and stimulated in character education are discipline, ethics and emotional intelligence. These three components come together to define a person's drive, values and interactions with people.

The Process of Character Development

From the outset, we can consider a series of relationships that follow one another in the development of character, beginning with a set of ideas and finishing in action.

First, a cultural or institutional system causes someone to think or believe in a system of values, which is latent and ideated. Second is the actual content of those values, which we can consider when defining character: for example, what exactly do we mean by good?[24] Third is motivation, or in other words, strength of character. It involves conviction, courage and determination. Finally is the praxis or action you take – in other words, being committed to a cause. Schools need to support young people in each of these steps, which take the student from inner thoughts to outer actions.

BELIEFS	VALUES	DISPOSITIONS	ACTIONS
Religious dogma	Kindness	Motivation	Service to others
Philosophical ideas	Honesty	Resilience	Political activism
Political doctrines	Faithfulness	Temperance	Social activism
Cultural conventions	Generosity	Self-discipline	Charity
Beliefs wrought from personal experience	Compassion	Stoicism	Consciousness raising
	Empathy	Courage	Mediation
Institutional values	Respect	Risk-taking	Professional conduct
Family values	Humility	Curiosity	

Figure 1. Processes of character actualisation

Plato thought that the young person would know goodness directly and empirically but only start to understand it intellectually at a mature age. Aristotle, on the other hand, believed that character (*êthos*) would developed through experience, or more precisely habituation, a process in which the repetition of actions would make those actions second nature (Book II, *Nichomanean Ethics*).

Developing students' character is a subtle undertaking, which requires a multifaceted approach. Kohlberg counsels a developmental approach, so that students gradually become more and more invested and aware of their values and potential as agents of change.[25] Carol Dweck's work on mindsets (1999, 2006, 2012) emphasises student self-belief: she argues that a growth mindset – as opposed to a fixed mindset –

is one that exemplifies a "can do" attitude and encourages students to take risks and thrive on challenge. It can be achieved with the right school culture and discourses.

In the following list, I summarise the steps that I have suggested in this chapter for the development of the subcomponents of character. Activities to stimulate the mentioned areas would be age-appropriate and adapted to school contexts and curricula frameworks.

- Be disciplined yourself as a teacher/mentor/parent.
- Establish a clear routine with fair rewards and consequences.
- Stretch young people.
- Value patience.
- Openly communicate your or your institution's values.
- Value dialogue.
- Promote service learning.
- Choose the right role models.
- Give some social commentary on current and historical events.
- Have a Social and Emotional Learning Programme.
- Model emotional intelligence.
- Focus on the role of emotions in different areas of learning.
- Ensure ongoing professional development for teachers and school leaders.

Figure 2. Thirteen recommended steps for character growth in schools

A Case for the Performing Arts and Physical Education

One area of learning that deserves attention because of the natural way that it reinforces what we might call character – at least the elements of self-discipline and rigour – is the performing arts. The ancients knew this and placed particular value on the role of music in education: "Music has a power of forming the character, and should therefore be introduced into the education of the young" (Aristotle, *Politics*, Book VIII, section 5). If schools have strong performing arts programmes, they will offer students opportunities to improve themselves and develop confidence as they learn to take the right steps towards performance excellence.

Similarly, some form of athletic activity, so dear to the ancients, remains to this day an essential pathway towards strength of character, self-discipline and mastery. Plato, in his *Laws* and *Republic*, made clear that a Spartan diet of athletics was a cornerstone of a good education, not only for the fitness that it ensures but also for the noble virtues of courage and perseverance that it stimulates in the individual. Competitive sports allow students to develop some psychological fortitude, whereas more recreational sports allow for relaxation and offer a counterbalance to the pressurised world of academia.

Both physical education and the arts need to feature strongly in a good education. Some research tells us that physical education does not necessarily correlate with high academic achievement (Podulka Coe et al., 2006) and there is disagreement about whether the arts do.[26] I feel, however, that the point lies elsewhere. It is not so much whether sports and the arts in isolation are predictors of academic success that is important; it is more the intrinsic qualities they bring with them.

The performing arts and physical education appear to be all the more essential in the twenty-first century landscape, with its excesses of indirect human contact via social media – perhaps sheltering individuals from the skills needed and developed through face-to-face interaction – and with the majority of jobs' being in the services sector and involving little physical challenge and low levels of energetic physical activity.

CONCLUSION

The musical is over, and it is time to go home. As the audience disperses, I move to the stage to congratulate the director. Just before I reach her, one of the main actors, a young girl still in costume with glitter in her hair, appears before me as she picks her way through the crowd to reach her friends and family. I congratulate her on her outstanding performance. With a trembling whisper, nothing like the powerful, soaring voice with which she dominated her performance, she thanks me for my praise.

What touches me is not only the sincerity of her thanks – she has been affected by the praise in a humble, deeply human manner – but also the simple politeness and grace with which she responds. "Oh, thank you so very much. I greatly appreciate that", she says sheepishly. Here again I am struck by the dichotomy between the bold, larger-than-life performance of the actor, so full of self-discipline, and the modest, generous personality of the student, so full of emotional intelligence and the right ethical values.

Connecting these elements, like a bridge between the vertiginous mountains of discipline and the soft, flowing valleys of ethical conduct and emotional intelligence, is character. Character is a bridge that reinforces confidence and hope; it is the central pathway that will motivate and allow students to actualise their learning in meaningful ways. It is particularly important in a turbulent and complex twenty-first century that needs people with energy, hope and vision.

NOTES

[1] A good example is the great film director Stanley Kubrick, who was notoriously dictatorial and uncompromising in his treatment of actors. The result of this trait of character was some of the finest cinema ever produced.

[2] The ancient Greek philosopher Aristotle in his *Politics* (Book VIII, Section V) said that "learning is no amusement, but is accompanied with pain". Blind and deaf American novelist Hellen Keller stated in her journal, "Character cannot be developed in ease and quiet. Only through experience of trial and suffering can the soul be strengthened, ambition inspired, and success achieved" (1938, p. 60). British prime minister Benjamin Disraeli described the three pillars of learning as "seeing much, suffering much, and studying much" (Disraeli, 1841).

CHAPTER 7

3   One need only read the autobiography of Roald Dahl, *Boy* (1984), or to consider Charles Dickens' novel *Nicholas Nickleby* (1839) or Ingmar Bergman's film *Fanny and Alexander* (1982) to be reminded of the horror that it is for a young person to live in the shadow of a sadistic, frustrated, cane-swinging adult. The English novelist W. Somerset Maugham said, "It is not true that suffering ennobles the character; happiness does that sometimes, but suffering for the most part, makes men petty and vindictive" (Maugham, 1919, p. 64).

4   In 1988, Bredehoft et al. designed a questionnaire for adults who considered themselves to have been overindulged as children, if whom 124 identified themselves as previously overindulged and associated themselves with the following problems: "not knowing what is enough, overeating and gaining weight, money management problems, parenting and childrearing conflicts, conflicts with interpersonal boundaries, difficulty in decision-making, poor self-esteem, poor health, and being involved in excessive activities" (Bredehoft, Illsley Clark, and Dawson, 2002, p. 4).

5   In 2007, Duckworth et al. conducted a controlled study using over 1000 participants to show how graduates at the West Point Military Academy who stayed the course and were successful, did so because of resilience ("grit") rather than academics or other measures. In another study, 20 college graduates with certified learning difficulties listed the need to persevere under challenging circumstances as a vital component for postsecondary success (Skinner, 2004). Colangelo, Assouline, and Gross (2004) argue that many American students are not challenged enough because of an ideology that holds them back out of fear of acceleration. By not challenging students enough, American society is losing countless opportunities to stretch gifted learners further than they will eventually go.

6   Thomas Piketty's *Capital in the Twenty-First Century* (2014) has shown how income and capital inequality are growing and have never been higher. Studies on corruption have shown that it is a worldwide problem that does not show any signs of diminishing (Transparency International, 2016). The critical work of Noam Chomsky (2016) has argued for the last 40 years that Western foreign policy and a globalised world economy continue to exacerbate patterns of exploitation, while media lulls most citizens into a state of complacency and apathy.

7   As Poole says:

> Liberalism has given up trying to discover what constitutes the good life: it leaves it in the domain of individual choice. It has limited itself to providing a theory of justice. This self-abnegation has left it without anything worthwhile to say on the vast range of moral issues… The arbitrariness which liberalism concedes to the good cannot but return to infect the domain of justice… The failure of liberalism to deliver a theory of justice shows the need for 'some' limits to the pluralism it espouses. (Poole, 1991, pp. 85–86)

8   See, for example the model of Ashoka (2017) or the Goodwall project (2017).

9   Richard Dawkins, who was educated in a Church of England school, puts it thus:

> I think there is a great deal to be said for religious education in the sense of teaching about religion and biblical literacy. Both those things, by the way, I suspect will prepare a child to give up religion. If you are taught comparative religion, you are more likely to realise that there are other religions than the one you have been brought up in. And if you are taught to read the bible, I can think of almost nothing more calculated to turn you off religion. (Richard Dawkins, cited in AZ Quotes, 2017)

10 He says:

> The aim of moral education should be to stimulate people's thinking ability over time in ways which will enable them to use more adequate and complex reasoning patterns to solve moral problems. The principle central to the development of stages of moral judgment, and hence to proposals for moral education, is that of justice. Justice, the primary regard for the value and equality of all human beings and for reciprocity in human relations, is a basic and universal standard. (Kohlberg and Hersch, 1977, p. 56)

[11] Kohlberg's model has been criticised by Gilligan (1982) as being too masculine. She sees it as missing the essentially female attribute of caring and argues that his vision is too centred on an objective reasoning rather than on deep empathy.

[12] Students and teachers should aim to be "inquirers, knowledgeable, thinkers, communicators, principled, open-minded, caring, risk-takers, balanced and reflective" (IB, 2013a).

[13] See Althof (2003). Althof and Berkowitz describe these types of schools as being "theory driven, heavily influenced by psychology, designed to promote the development of moral reasoning stages and well-researched" (Althof and Berkowitz, 2006, p. 497).

[14] The movement is premised on

> the belief that humanity has the wisdom to transform itself and the world, through one's own spiritual development. To that end, Waldorf Education holds as its primary intention the ideal of bringing forth – in every child – his or her unique potential in a way that serves the further development of humanity. (Waldorf, 2017)

Conflicts are dealt with through a communal approach:

> A Waldorf class is something like a family. Problems between teachers and children, and between teachers and parents, can and do arise. Schools typically work to resolve such problems through a conflict resolution or grievance procedure. With the goodwill and active support of the parents and the teacher concerned, schools do make the necessary changes needed to ensure the best situation for all concerned. (Waldorf, 2017)

Waldorf schools have been criticised on a number of counts, the mystic and possibly delusional philosophy of their founder Rudolf Steiner with his belief in reincarnation and racist theories give the schools the reputation, among harsh critics it should be said, of being esoteric and new-fangled (see Cook, 2014).

[15] Dahlberg and Moss (2005). Gunilla Dahlberg describes an educational philosophy that places centrality on the act of listening as an ethical approach to learning. Active listening is "a form of listening that builds on a serious engagement and inquisitiveness in the here-and-now event… This takes us beyond a tendency to think in either-or terms. It is a trusting and affirmative listening that welcomes an infinity of possible responses" (Dahlberg, 2012, p. 226). Dahlberg contrasts this approach with the ethics of neoliberal interaction: "Such an openness requires attitudes that do not rely on a scheming or transactional mentality – the kind of thinking that characterizes the marketplace and purely contractual relationships" (p. 226).

[16] For steps involved in quality service learning, see Hughes and Acedo (2017).

[17] Salovey and Mayer (1990) define emotional intelligence as "intellectual processes involved in the recognition, use, understanding, and management of one's own and others' emotional states and the ability to use those feelings to motivate, plan, and achieve" (Brooks and Nafukho, 2006, p. 12); whereas Brooks and Nafukho point out that emotions play a far more prominent role in our understanding of organisational culture in the contemporary workplace:

> Over the past 15 years, new technology has allowed breakthroughs in brain research that has increased our understanding about the mutual interaction between feelings (affect) and cognition (thought). Defining the nature and significance of this interplay between thought and emotion is at the heart of the emerging research on emotional intelligence. HRD [Human Resource Development] professionals continually grapple with the issues associated with organizing, motivating, enhancing, and evaluating human activity; emotional intelligence research can inform HRD practices within organizations. (Brooks and Nafukho, 2006, p. 122)

[18] A meta-analysis by Durlak et al. (2011) of 213 school-based, social and emotional learning programmes involving 270,034 students showed an "11-percentile-point gain in achievement" as well as a great many behavioural and emotional gains among students. Zins et al. (2007) have researched and shown the scientific relationship between social and emotional depth and school success.

CHAPTER 7

For the OECD, "social and emotional skills" are predictors of student success, according to research in Canada, Korea, New Zealand, Norway, Sweden, Switzerland, the United Kingdom and the United States. They come to the conclusion that "social and emotional skills are particularly important drivers of social outcomes, such as health, civic engagement, and subjective well-being" (OECD, 2015, p. 1).

[19] For a rich discussion of the way that educational institutions can integrate emotional intelligence into learning, see Newton (2014).

[20] A course that focusses on emotions specifically as a way of knowing is the International Baccalaureate's Theory of Knowledge course (see IB, 2013b).

[21] These areas of agreement can be summarised as follows, as articulated by CASEL (Collaborative for Academic, Social, and Emotional Learning):

Self-awareness: recognizing and labeling one's feelings and accurately assessing one's strengths and limitations.

Self-management: regulating emotions, delaying gratification, managing stress, motivating oneself, and setting and working toward achieving goals.

Social awareness: showing empathy, taking others' perspectives, and recognizing and mobilizing diverse and available supports.

Relationship skills: clear communication, accurate listening, cooperation, nonviolent and constructive conflict resolution, and knowing when and how to be a good team player and a leader.

Responsible decision making: making ethical choices based on consideration of feelings, goals, alternatives and outcomes, and planning and enacting solutions with potential obstacles anticipated. (Elias et al., 2016)

These skills and values need to be brought together in a structural fashion so that the development of social and emotional learning is explicit, with levels of accountability and evaluation.

[22] According to Fadel, Bialik, and Trilling (2015), character education is a necessity because it can: "build a foundation for lifelong learning; support successful relationships at home, in the community, and in the workplace; develop the personal values and virtues for sustainable participation in a globalized world" (p. 81). A fairly detailed study by Berkowitz and Bier (2007), involving 64 empirical studies and five meta-analyses concluded that "character education can effectively positively impact a range of risk behaviors, a set of prosocial competencies, various school outcomes including academic achievement, and social-emotional competencies" (2007, p. 42).

[23] Berkowitz sees character as "an individual's set of psychological characteristics that affect that person's ability and inclination to function morally" (Berkowitz, 2002, p. 48). The Centre for Curriculum Redesign (2015) associates the following words with character: agency; attitudes; behaviors; dispositions; mindsets; personality; temperament; and values. Wilson's definition emphasizes a communal value systems and interpersonal attributes:

It is the internalization of the moral principles of a society, augmented by those tenets personally chosen by the individual, strong enough to endure through trials of solitude and diversity. The principles are fitted together into what we call … the integrated self, wherein personal decisions feel good and true. (Wilson, 1998, p. 245)

Kiel, on the other hand, focusses more on certain types of moral values, namely "integrity, responsibility, forgiveness, and compassion" (Kiel, 2015, p. 32).

[24] From a universal perspective, "good" will necessarily entail respecting and helping other people and leading a life that is healthy and not destructive.

[25] A similar developmental approach has been designed by Perry (1970), gradually scaffolding steps that take students from simple ideas to more complex ideas and eventually to action.

[26] Eisner (2010) questions the idea, whereas Catterall (2015) reinforces it; both scholars base their approach on an analysis of data.

REFERENCES

Althof, W. (2003). Implementing 'just and caring communities' in elementary schools: A Deweyan perspective. In W. Veugelers & F. K. Oser (Eds.), *Teaching in moral and democratic education* (pp. 153–172). Bern: Peter Lang.

Althof, W., & Berkowitz, M. W. (2006). Moral education and character education: Their relationship and roles in citizenship education. *Journal of Moral Education, 35*(4), 495–518.

Aristotle (1999). *Politics.* B. Jowett, trans. Kitchener, Canada: Batoche Books.

Ashoka (2017). Website. https://www.ashoka.org/en

AZ Quotes (2017). Richard Dawkins quotes. http://www.azquotes.com/quote/529803

Berkowitz, M. W. (2002). *The science of character education.* Conshohocken, PA: John Templeton Foundation. http://media.hoover.org/sites/default/files/documents/0817929622_43.pdf

Berkowitz, M. W., & Bier, M. (2007). What works in character education. *Journal of Research in Character Education, 5*(1), 29–48.

Bidar, A. (2015). *Plaidoyer pour la franternité*. Paris: Albin Michel.

Bidar, A. (2016). *Quelles valeurs partager et transmettre aujourd'hui?* Paris: Albin Michel.

Bredehoft, D. J., Illsley Clarke, J., & Dawson, C. (2002, November). *Relationships between childhood overindulgence and parenting attributes: Implications for family life educators.* Paper presented at the National Council on Family Relations Annual Meeting. http://citeseerx.ist.psu.edu/viewdoc/download?doi=10.1.1.567.1809&rep=rep1&type=pdf

Bredehoft, D. J., Mennicke, S. A., Potter, A. M., & Clarke, J. I. (1998). Perceptions attributed by adults to parental overindulgence during childhood. *Journal of Marriage and Family Consumer Sciences Education, 16*, 3–17.

Brooks, K., & Nafukho, F. M. (2006). Human resource development, social capital, emotional intelligence: Any link to productivity? *Journal of European Industrial Training, 30*(2), 117–128.

CASEL [Collaborative for Academic, Social, and Emotional Learning] (2015). Website. http://www.casel.org/

Catterall, J. S. (2015). Does experience in the arts boost academic achievement? A response to Eisner. *Art Education.* http://www.tandfonline.com/action/showCitFormats?doi=10.1080%2F00043125.1998.11654333

Center for Curriculum Redesign (2015). *Character education for the 21st century: What should students learn?* http://curriculumredesign.org/wp-content/uploads/CCR-CharacterEducation_FINAL_27Feb2015.pdf

Chomsky, N. (2016). *Who rules the world?* New York, NY: Metropolitan Books/Henry Holt.

Colangelo, N., Assouline, S. G., & Gross, M. U. M. (2004). *A nation deceived: How schools hold back America's brightest students.* Iowa City, IA: University of Iowa Press.

Cook, C. (2014). Why are Steiner schools so controversial? *BBC.* http://www.bbc.com/news/education-28646118

Dahlberg, G. (2012). Pedagogical documentation: A practice for negotiation and democracy. In C. Edwards, L. Gandini, & G. Forman (Eds.), *The hundred languages of children: The Reggio Emilia experience in transformation* (3rd ed.). Santa Barbara, CA: Praeger.

Dahlberg, G., & Moss, P. (2005). *Ethics and politics in early childhood education.* London: Routledge.

Dewey, J. (1964). What psychology can do for the teacher. In R. Archambault (Ed.), *John Dewey on education: Selected writings.* New York, NY: Random House.

Disraeli, B. (1841). *Amenities of literature: Consisting of sketches and characters of English literature.* London: Edward Moxon.

Duckworth, A. L., Peterson, C., Matthews, M. D., & Kelly, D. R. (2007). Grit: Perseverance and passion for long-term goals. *Journal of Personal and Social Psychology, 92*(6), 1087–1101.

Durlak, J. A., Weissberg, R. P., Dymnicki, A. B., Taylor, R. D., & Schellinger, K. B. (2011). The impact of enhancing students' social and emotional learning: A meta-analysis of school-based universal interventions. *Child Development, 82*(1), 405–432.

Dweck, C. S. (1999). *Self-theories.* Philadelphia, PA: Psychology Press.

Dweck, C. S. (2006). *Mindset: The new psychology of success.* New York, NY: Random House.

Dweck, C. S. (2012). *Mindset: How you can fulfill your potential.* London: Constable & Robinson.

CHAPTER 7

Eisner, E. W. (2010). Does experience in the arts boost academic achievement? *Arts Education Policy Review.* http://dx.doi.org/10.1080/10632919809599448

Elias, M., Leverett, J. C. D., Humphrey, N., Stepney, C., & Ferrito, J. (2016). *How to implement social and emotional learning at your school.* https://www.edutopia.org/blog/implement-sel-at-your-school-elias-leverett-duffell-humphrey-stepney-ferrito

Eze, M. O. (2010). *Intellectual history in contemporary South Africa.* London: Palgrave Macmillan.

Gilligan, C. (1982). *In a different voice: Psychological theory and women's development.* Cambridge, MA: Harvard University Press.

Goleman, D. (1995). *Emotional intelligence.* New York, NY & London: Bantam Books. https://www.slideshare.net/JavedIqbal105/emotional-intelligence-by-daniel-goleman

Goleman, D. (1998). *What makes a leader?* http://www.sdcity.edu/Portals/0/CMS_Editors/MESA/PDFs/Generic/WhatMakesALeader.pdf

Goleman, D. (2017). Emotional intelligence. http://www.danielgoleman.info/topics/emotional-intelligence/

Goodwall. (2017). Website. https://www.goodwall.org/

Hughes, C. (2017). *Understanding prejudice and education: The challenge for future generations.* Oxford: Routledge.

Hughes, C., & Acedo, C. (2017). *Guiding principles for learning in the 21st century.* Educational Practices Series 28. Geneva: UNESCO International Bureau of Education & International Academy of Education. http://www.ibe.unesco.org/sites/default/files/resources/practices_series_28_v3_002.pdf

IB [International Baccalaureate] (2013a). *IB Learner profile booklet.* Cardiff: IB.

IB (2013b). *Theory of knowledge guide* (Course guide). Cardiff: IB.

Keller, H. (1938). *Helen Keller's journal: 1936–1937.* New York, NY: Doubleday, Doran.

Kiel, F. (2015). *Return on character.* Boston, MA: Harvard Business Review Press.

Kohlberg, L. (1976). Moral stages, moralization: The cognitive developmental approach. In T. Lickona (Ed.), *Moral development and behavior.* New York, NY: Holt, Rinehart & Winston.

Kohlberg, L. (1981). *Essays on moral development.* New York, NY: Harper & Row.

Kohlberg, L., & Hersch, R. H. (1977). Moral development: A review of the theory. *Theory into Practice, 16*(2), 53–59.

Maugham, W. S. (1919). *The moon and sixpence.* London: Heineman.

Newton, D. (2014). *Thinking with feeling: Fostering productive thought in the classroom.* Oxford: Routledge.

OECD (2015). *Skills for social progress: The power of social and emotional skills.* http://www.oecd.org/edu/ceri/skills-for-social-progress-key-messages.pdf

Perry, W. G. (1970). *Forms of intellectual and ethical development in the college years: A scheme.* New York, NY: Holt, Rinehart & Winston.

Piketty, T. (2014). *Capital in the twenty-first century.* Cambridge, MA: Harvard University Press.

Podulka Coe, D., Pivarnik, J. M., Womack, C. J., Reeves, M. J., & Malina, R. M. (2006). Effect of physical education and activity levels on academic achievement in children. *Medicine & Science in Sports & Exercise, 38*(8), 1515–1519.

Poole, R. (1991). *Morality and modernity.* London: Routledge.

Power, F. C., Higgins, A., & Kohlberg, L. (1989). *Lawrence Kohlberg's approach to moral education.* New York, NY: Cambridge University Press.

Salovey, P., & Mayer, J. D. (1990). Emotional intelligence. *Imagination, Cognition, and Personality, 9*, 185–211.

Skinner, M. E. (2002). College students with learning disabilities speak out: What it takes to be successful in postsecondary education. *Journal of Postsecondary Education and Disability, 17*(2), 91–104.

Steiner, G. (1967). *Language and silence: Essays 1958–1966.* London: Faber.

Transparency International (2016). Overview. http://www.transparency.org/research/cpi/overview

UWC [United World Colleges International] (2017). Website. http://www.uwc.org

Waldorf Education (2017). FAQs: About Waldorf education. https://waldorfeducation.org/waldorf_education/faqs#anthro

Wilson, E. O. (1998). *Consilience: The unity of knowledge.* New York, NY: Knopf.

Zins, J. E., Bloodworth, M. R., Weissberg, R. P., & Walberg, H. J. (2007). The scientific base linking social and emotional learning to school success. *Journal of Educational and Psychological Consultation, 17*(2–3), 191–210.

CHAPTER 8

CONCLUSION

The Framework

In today's volatile, uncertain, complex, ambiguous, paradoxical world, the educational experience we give young people must respond to the challenges of the century. At the same time, some of education's age-old precepts must remain intact. Subject offerings will differ from system to system, degree to degree; and pedagogical approaches will be equally diverse. However, the fundamental societal goal of education – to contribute to the human experience and legacy in a positive, meaningful way, remains the same.

What has changed dramatically in the last centuries is the scope of what that societal goal entails. Concretely, what does it mean to contribute to the human experience and legacy in the first third of the twenty-first century? Educators from the ancients all the way to those who designed a vision for education in the mid-eighteenth century saw the role of education as local and bound to a culturally and historically specific set of circumstances, and thus they created fields such as national history and local citizenship. Today, however, we view educational standards from a global perspective, comparing scores on international assessments, designing frameworks through international organisations such as UNESCO and UNICEF, grappling with challenges and problems at an international scale. When governments, ministries, schools, universities and examination boards create curriculum standards, they inspect each other, contrast, compare and collaborate at a global scale.

In looking at global challenges, my purpose in this book is not to address matters of international education per se – since there is a specific field of international education and groups of schools that call themselves international schools – but rather to address general matters that concern all those involved in education, matters intrinsically international in nature. I believe that in the twenty-first century, all schools are international schools, since all educate young people whose fate and future will without doubt involve many countries, organisations and relationships, directly (if they travel the world) or indirectly through the professional lives they will lead and all the ramifications these will entail. Even as simple consumers, every young person is, and will continue to be, part of a global market, taking decisions that have a global impact.

Those who design and implement a quality, meaningful education must feature, consciously and explicitly, the challenges that I have identified. We all know how fundamental education is as a tool for economic, social, cultural, individual and group development, and therefore we cannot bury our heads in the sand and decide to focus only on the bare bones (subjects and academic achievement). There must be a thrust to make young people aware, proficient and committed to the world in which they live in ways that are moral, dispositional and practical. Such a result will point the powerful tool of education in the direction of changing the world, as said in the well-known adage by Nelson Mandela ("Education is the most powerful weapon which you can use to change the world").

The seven challenges discussed in this book (mindfulness, terrorism, singularity, post-truth politics, sustainability, knowledge in the twenty-first century and character) are all relevant for all types of education, irrespective of students' ages, stations, contexts and traditions. They are challenges that we face today and will almost definitely face tomorrow.

THE PURPOSE OF THE FRAMEWORK

This final chapter synthesises the seven challenges into educational strategies that institutions might consider, strategies that equip learners with experiences and tools that will help them face the future confidently. For subject each area, I enumerate core educational strategies, give examples of tasks or assessments that could take place in the classroom, mention examples related to the practice in question and share references that offer some theoretical or empirical grounding to the strategies in question.

This framework can be used by teachers, curriculum designers, heads of school, students and researchers. The framework can be applied to different subjects and cultures depending on opportunities. Many of the strategies involve debates, discussions, sharing of ideas and imparting of information. What this means is that if educational institutions are dedicated to curriculum coverage with no time or space for supplemental work, it will be difficult to achieve these aims. Indeed, schools must offer opportunities for students to reach into these twenty-first century learning experiences in meaningful ways.

It might be that an entire, distinct subject needs to be offered to allow for these goals to be achieved. For example, at my school (La Grande Boissière, International School of Geneva), we run a programme that gives us time to address many of these objectives. The course runs once a week and involves debates, guest speakers, a service learning programme, mentoring and assemblies. Through this, we are able to address the core areas of mindfulness and character.

A subject that can allow for the necessary time, scope and learning climate to address many of these challenges is philosophy, a subject that unites many of the higher-order thinking skills and ethical questions that need to be developed in today's world. Through the study of philosophy, especially if it goes beyond purely theoretical study of the great philosophical traditions and takes students into debates about the contemporary world and personal decisions they will take in their lives, students can approach the subject of post-truth politics.

Table 1. Framework table

Area	Subdivision	Learning experiences for students and advice for instructors	Examples	Resources & research
Character	Discipline	Modelling self-discipline as a teacher. Clear routines and systematic fairness in decision-making. Stretching students academically, socially and intellectually. Clear and regular classroom protocols, emphasising patience. A strong sports programme. A strong arts programme	Many schools exhibit these elements. Notable examples of schools with strong arts programmes include Los Angeles County High School; the Professional Performing Arts High School in New York; Philadelphia High School for the Creative and Performing Arts; the International School of Geneva's La Grande Boissière in Switzerland; Queen's College Somerset in the UK. Examples of schools with strong sports programmes include Millfield, Whitgift and Guilford in the UK and the Kamehameha Schools in Hawaii.	Schools or groups of schools that emphasise character development, to mention a few, include the United World Colleges movement (www.uwc.org), the Geelong Grammar School (www.ggs.vic.edu.au), Wellington College (https://www.wellingtoncollege.org.uk/) and the Round Square association of schools (www.roundsquare.org). Resource centres dedicated specifically to education and character include character.org with its "framework for school success" through 11 principles of effective character education, as follows: Promotes core values; Defines "character" to include thinking, feeling, and doing. Uses a comprehensive approach. Creates a caring community. Provides students with opportunities for moral action.

(Continued)

CHAPTER 8

Table 1. (Continued)

Area	Subdivision	Learning experiences for students and advice for instructors	Examples	Resources & research
	Ethics	Openly communicating institutional values to the whole community through assemblies, communiqués and public events. Dialogue as a basis for living together and learning. Strong service learning throughout the school. Ethical role models. Stimulating and modelling ethically conscientious social commentary. Most especially, leading students by example and by doing rather than by preaching alone.	Religious education can be found in different expressions throughout the world. The International Baccalaureate places emphasis on a values-based approach and puts into practice elements of Kohlberg's stages of moral development. Values-based schools such as the United World Colleges, with an emphasis on service learning; the Waldorf schools, with a strong philosophy of advocacy and dialogue; the Reggio Emilia schools, with a focus on student voice and active listening to children – all further express an ethical approach to education. Educational companies and fora such as Goodwall and Ashoka do this further.	Offers a meaningful and challenging academic curriculum. Fosters students' self-motivation. Engages staff as a learning community. Fosters shared leadership. Engages families and community members as partners. Assesses the culture and climate of the school (http://character.org/more-resources/11-principles/). A good resource for the development of social and emotional intelligence is the OECD's Skills for Social progress (http://www.keepeek.com/Digital-Asset-Management/oecd/education/skills-for-social-progress_9789264226159-en#.WZVo4CgjE2w).

154

CONCLUSION

Area	Subdivision	Learning experiences for students and advice for instructors	Examples	Resources & research
				A comprehensive discussion of character education is the Centre for Curriculum Redesign's Character Education for the 21st Century (http://curriculumredesign.org/wp-content/uploads/CCR-CharacterEducation_FINAL_27Feb2015.pdf).
	Emotional intelligence	Social and Emotional Learning programmes. Modelling emotional intelligence as a leader and teacher. Studying the nature and impact of emotions as part of the curriculum. Professional development. A strong arts programme.	For a character programme that develops emotional intelligence, the International School of Geneva (see further in this chapter); the International Baccalaureate Diploma Programme's Theory of Knowledge course allows for the study of emotions in the classroom for 16–18 year olds.	
Mindfulness	Disconnect	Off-screen moments in the learning day. An emphasis on explicitly face-to-face interaction between students. Monitoring and controlling the number of hours spent in front of a screen per day (more than four is excessive).	A number of schools control and monitor screen time, particularly for younger children. Better-known examples include the Waldorf School in Silicon Valley (http://waldorfpeninsula.org/).	Fractus Learning (https://www.fractuslearning.com/2014/05/07/teaching-without-technology/).

(Continued)

155

CHAPTER 8

Table 1. (Continued)

Area	Subdivision	Learning experiences for students and advice for instructors	Examples	Resources & research
	Walking and running	Daily cardiovascular physical exercise. Outdoor lessons. Hikes or extended walks with students.	The Walking Classroom (http://www.thewalkingclassroom.org/); the White Mountain School in the USA.	WHO (2016); Kramer, Erickson, and Colcombe (2006); Lambourne and Tomporowski (2010).
	Mind wandering	Moments in learning when students can cut away from the task at hand and come back with fresh perspectives. Intense, demanding moments should be interspersed with lower order cognitive tasks allowing for mind wandering. Being conscious of the negative effects of over-burdening students with tasks. Learning through play.	Metalab (https://labs.psych.ucsb.edu/schooler/jonathan/); the Lego Foundation.	Singer and Antrobus (1963); Mooneyham and Schooler (2013); Oppezzo and Schwartz (2014); Seli, Risko, and Smilek, 2016; Szpunar, Moulton, and Schacter (2013).
	The arts	Ensuring students appreciate artistic traditions from around the world. Practicing the performing arts.	For the performing arts: LAMDA (https://www.lamda.org.uk/); for schools with strong arts programmes, see the table in the chapter of this book on character.	Merritt (2016); Rich and Goldberg (2009); Hallam (2010); Stuckey and Nobel (2010); Malchiodi (2008).

Area	Subdivision	Learning experiences for students and advice for instructors	Examples	Resources & research
Terrorism	Educating for peace explicitly as a value and superordinate goal	Modelling and encouraging peaceful processes within the educational institution. Discussing peace openly as a superordinate value. Teaching about peace building and figures who have lobbied for peace through the humanities.	Education 4 Peace (http://www.education4peace.org/); Education for Peace (http://www.educationforpeace.com/).	Hughes (2017); UNESCO guidelines for integrating an education for peace (http://unesdoc.unesco.org/images/0023/002336/233601e.pdf).
	Teaching dialogue, mediation and negotiation skills	Structured classroom talk allowing for student voice to be expressed. Dialogic classroom practice; Philosophy for Children mediation techniques. Creating a culture of debating within the educational institution. Ensuring that ground rules for the structuring of formal dialogue are designed, communicated and understood.	Philosophy for Children UK (http://www.philosophy4children.co.uk/); Dialogic Teaching by Robin Alexander (http://www.robinalexander.org.uk/dialogic-teaching/); "Debate and Forensics" competitions are a good example of structured dialogue; Model United Nations; Students' League of Nations (https://www.ecolint.ch/beyond-classroom/students-league-nations).	Alexander (2006); Lipman (2003); Allport (1954); Pettigrew and Tropp (2008).

(Continued)

Table 1. (Continued)

Area	Subdivision	Learning experiences for students and advice for instructors	Examples	Resources & research
	Teaching democracy and human rights as intrinsic truths	Teaching the Universal Declaration of Human Rights. Teaching various cultural expressions of human rights so as to de-center a purely Western approach	Human Rights Resource Centre (http://hrlibrary.umn.edu/edumat/activities.shtm); UN Human Rights Training and Education Materials (http://www.ohchr.org/EN/PublicationsResources/Pages/TrainingEducation.aspx); The Global Human Rights Education and Training Centre (http://www.hrea.org/programs/human-rights-teaching/).	United Nations (1948).
	Ensuring a context-specific approach to the explanation of terrorism	Explaining geopolitical and historical contexts behind terrorist attacks for deeper understanding. Avoiding sweeping universalist generalisations about terrorism.	Roots of Terrorism teachers' guide (Frontline, 2016); Zinn education project (2016); US Department of State curriculum guide on terrorism (Office of the Historian, 2016).	Brockhoff, Krieger, and Meierrieks (2015); Webb, (2012); Elu and Price (2015); Malik (2008).
	Offering spiritual transcendence through education	Teaching philosophy with an emphasis on soteriology (the spiritual, salvatory aspect of a philosophy of life). Encouraging the posing of, and working through, big existential questions.	For an example of big existential questions, see: Simon, K. G. (2002). "The Blue Blood is Bad, Right?" *Educational Leadership*, 60(1). For an approach to philosophy with an emphasis on soteriology, see Ferry, L. (2010). Learning To Live. Edinburgh: Canongate.	Ferry (2010); Simon (2002).

Area	Subdivision	Learning experiences for students and advice for instructors	Examples	Resources & research
	Security	Clear lockdown procedures. Routine identity checks. Badging of visitors. Good relationship with local authorities. Surveillance cameras.		Ruz (2015).
	Counselling	Having a trained post-trauma therapist on site. Making the school psychologist visible in the community so that students have full awareness of, and access to, him/her.	University of Virginia guidelines (2015); American Academy of Child & Psychiatry guidelines (2015).	University of Virginia (2015); Ochberg (1987); Ehlers et al. (2005); Silver et al. (2005); Josman et al. (2006).
	Spiritual responses to terrorism	Nurturing stoical responses through the teaching of philosophy. One-on-one coaching. Student discussion groups.	A good book that deals with stoicism is Marcus Aurelius' masterpiece *The Meditations*; good examples of 1:1 counselling can be found on university websites such as those of Dublin and Bristol.	Farkas and Hutchison-Hall (2008); Meisenhelder and Marcum (2009).

(Continued)

CHAPTER 8

Table 1. (Continued)

Area	Subdivision	Learning experiences for students and advice for instructors	Examples	Resources & research
Singularity	Ethical, consequential STEM	Assessment (see further in this chapter)	Challenge questions from Edutopia (2015) focussing on physics[1]; projects emphasising engineering from NASA's Mars Education (2016)[2]; activities touching on the ethical implications of STEM from TeachEngineering (2016).[3]	MIT Blossoms (http://blossoms.mit.edu/resources/mit_resources); the book *How to Clone a Mammoth* (Shapiro, 2015); the FIRST robotics competition (http://www.firstinspires.org/); MASTER Tools, developed by the Shodor Education Reform, George Mason University and the National Centre for Supercomputing Applications (http://www.shodor.org/master/). The National Science Foundation's K-12 projects (http://www.gk12.org/resources/stem-activities-and-resources-for-k-12-teachers-and-students/).

CONCLUSION

Area	Subdivision	Learning experiences for students and advice for instructors	Examples	Resources & research
	Integrated technology	Using robots to measure distance over time in physics (allowing students to learn about coding while they do this). Encouraging the use of 3D printers, coded robots for tessellations, photography software or computerised simulations for art projects. Reconstructing historical encounters (such as the exploration of the so-called New World or the expansion of the Roman Empire) through computerised presentations involving software allowing for cutting-edge visuals. Using robots for early years writing lessons (for example, EPFL's co-writer project). Using computerised logarithms for graphing in economics. Using computerised random selection-generating software for debating (meaning that speakers' names are identified at random). Making films or documentaries using cutting-edge technology for presentations in literature or the humanities.	NASA's Mars for Students (https://mars.nasa.gov/participate/students/); FIRST robotics competitions (https://www.firstinspires.org/robotics/frc); Carnegie Mellon's Medical Robotics Technology Center; Pennsylvania College of Technology.	http://study.com/articles/Top_Schools_for_Robotics_Technologies.html https://www.edutopia.org/technology-integration-guide-description

(Continued)

161

CHAPTER 8

Table 1. (Continued)

Area	Subdivision	Learning experiences for students and advice for instructors	Examples	Resources & research
	Post-singularity higher-order thinking	A school-wide character programme. Learning experiences that push students to apply new technologies in creative, analytical and ethical ways. Emphasising non-automatable facets of being, such as kindness, empathy, deep reflection.	The International School of Geneva, La Grande Boissière's Character Programme pushes students to explore and express post-singularity higher order thinking; examples of strategies heightening empathy can be found in my book, *Understanding Prejudice and Education: The Challenge for Future Generations* (2017).	Hughes (2017).
	Confidence and STEM	Ensuring staff gender diversity in STEM subjects to offer girls role models. Teaching mathematical resilience.	Mathematical resilience programme (http://www.mathematicalresilience.org/).	Goodall and Johnston-Wilder (2015); Hughes (2017).

Area	Subdivision	Learning experiences for students and advice for instructors	Examples	Resources & research
Post-truth politics	The teaching of truth theories (correspondence, coherence, pragmatic)	Logic (syllogism and fallacies). An exploration of the fallibility of human memory. Discussion of the philosophy of science and an overview of subject learning in terms of truth formation (art=convention, mathematics=axioms, science=laws, social science=theories, etc). The study of philosophy, particularly epistemology (the structure of knowledge). The study and understanding of scientific experimental methodology that is more or less rigorous.	The International Baccalaureate's Theory of Knowledge course allows instructors opportunities to explore logical syllogisms, Bertrand Russell's theories of truth and the philosophy of science.	Loftus (1979); Russell (1918); Kuhn (1962); Peirce (1868); Ash (1951); Milgram (1963); Torgeson, Torgeson, and Brown (2010).
	Grappling with historical revisionism	Being aware of Holocaust denialism. Viewing established discourses on colonialism with critical distance. Understanding that history and social science textbooks represent truth in ideologically slanted ways. The study of political fiction that deals with truth in politics, such as Machiavelli's *The Prince* (1532) and Orwell's *1984* (1949).	The Holocaust Educational Trust (https://www.het.org.uk/lessons-from-auschwitz-programme); La Maison d'Izieu (http://www.memorializieu.eu/souscrivez-pour-la-maison-dizieu/); UNESCO's Education about the Holocaust (http://en.unesco.org/holocaust-remembrance).	Owen (2016); Akçam (2006); Hickling-Hudson (2016); Orwell (1949).

(Continued)

CHAPTER 8

Table 1. (Continued)

Area	Subdivision	Learning experiences for students and advice for instructors	Examples	Resources & research
	Understanding propaganda	Teaching the mechanics of propaganda and ensuring students understand how propaganda works. The study of historical examples of propaganda, particularly during the World Wars, followed by application to contemporary examples.	Any good history course should address and deconstruct well-known examples of historical propaganda. This is often the case for curriculum board approaches to WWI and WWII but broader, structural analyses of the role of propaganda in the discourse of history are more frequent at university level.	Wooddy (1935); Frugaldad (2011); Herman and Chomsky (1988).

Area	Subdivision	Learning experiences for students and advice for instructors	Examples	Resources & research
	The study of contemporary examples of relativism and attacks on the notion of objective truth	An examination of the ascendance of US president Donald Trump (the role of the media, political campaigning techniques, how facts and statistics were presented during the campaign and presidency). A critical study of the Brexit campaign in the UK (the role of the media, the promises that were made and to whom, different strains of propaganda and inaccurate information, arguments for and against). Discussion and study of climate change discussions and controversies.	Some United World Colleges run a weekly "global affairs" club, where students debate contemporary issues (see, for example, http://www.uwcrobertboschcollege.de/en/college-life/global-affairs).	Orwell (1949).
	Debates about whistleblowing	Analysis of, and debate about, Julian Assange's Wikileaks (whether such an approach is ethically correct or not). Case study analysis of the Edward Snowden affair.		

(Continued)

Table 1. (Continued)

Area	Subdivision	Learning experiences for students and advice for instructors	Examples	Resources & research
	Philosophical discussions on relativism and absolutism	Discussions about what relativism and absolutism are as concepts. Pressing students to form opinions on areas sometimes relegated to the domain of sheer subjectivity (such as the arts) for them to understand canons of beauty and standards of excellence. Critically investigating philosophical positions on subjectivity, such as those of Nietzsche, as well as positions on objectivity, such as those of Kant.	The teaching of philosophy and theory of knowledge. In the International Baccalaureate's Theory of Knowledge Course, students have opportunities to study aesthetics.	Blackburn (2001).
	Striving for clarity of expression	Communicating the necessity of writing and speaking clearly. Examples of obscurantist and clear rhetoric. Studies of essays on the importance of clarity and thought, such as Orwell's *Politics and the English Language* or *On the Sublime* by Longinus. Exercises in speech making and the writing of texts requiring maximum clarity, such as instruction manuals, speeches, resolutions, position papers and manifestos.	The International Baccalaureate's Language and Literature course; oratorical contests such as the Lawrence Campbell Oratory Competition in Australia; student council elections involving speech-making and general campaigning for students to improve their diction and rhetorical skills in a real life setting.	Lanham (1979); Provost (1985).

CONCLUSION

Area	Subdivision	Learning experiences for students and advice for instructors	Examples	Resources & research
Sustainability	Understanding the dynamics of a consumer society	Facilitating classroom discussions on consumerism at a student level through analysis of elements such as intergroup dynamics and peer pressure. Making students aware of the economic and media-driven cycle of consumerism. Educating students in the historic traditions of revolt against mass consumerism such as Communism and ideological oppositions in Europe and the United States from the 1960s up until the end of the 1980s. Educating students to understand alternative socioeconomic models such as degrowth and microcredit. Understanding the potential impact of social media activism as a response to excessive consumerism but also the dangers of "clicktivism" and a passive armchair activism.	Consumerism: Lessons for Kids (http://study.com/academy/lesson/consumerism-lesson-for-kids.html).	http://unesdoc.unesco.org/images/0024/002463/246352e.pdf Asara et al. (2015); Herman and Chomsky (1988); Baudrillard (1970); Cohen (2012); Klein (1999, 2007).

(Continued)

167

CHAPTER 8

Table 1. (Continued)

Area	Subdivision	Learning experiences for students and advice for instructors	Examples	Resources & research
	Learning to love nature	Open discussion and analysis of animal rights. Deep reflection on the eating of meat and the institutionalisation of "no meat days". The study of different cultural paradigms in which nature and animals are central and venerated (such as India). Striving to give students direct access to virgin natural landscapes such as those found in Africa. The study of literature in which natural cycles and environments are closely intertwined with day-to-day life. Creation and use of vegetable patches for younger students. Creation and use of areas of wild nature, such as woods, pathways through unspoilt patches of nature. Greening educational institutions by planting trees and respecting existing flora. Fieldtrips or exchanges that put students into direct contact with unspoilt nature.	Forest Schools ("some forest kindergartens have the children outside 80 to 90% of the time" [Forest and Nature School in Canada: A Head, Heart, Hands Approach to Outdoor Learning, 2014. FSC-Guide_Web]); no meat days in the cafeteria; the Nelson Mandela University Nature Conservation Course.	http://forestschools.com/training-help/forest-schools-level-1-to-level-4/; http://snrm.mandela.ac.za/Nature-Conservation

168

Area	Subdivision	Learning experiences for students and advice for instructors	Examples	Resources & research
	Studying indigenous knowledge systems	The study of indigenous knowledge systems holistically with an overview of anthropological patterns that unite different strands of this approach. Ensuring the knowledge and understanding of specific instances of indigenous knowledge systems, such as those elaborated by the Yanomani, Kho San and Aboriginal peoples.	The International Baccalaureate's Theory of Knowledge course with a section on Indigenous Knowledge Systems;	Berkes et al. (2003); Mazzocchi (2006); Semchison (2001); Roué and Molnar (2016); United Nations (1992). http://www.ibo.org/programmes/diploma-programme/curriculum/theory-of-knowledge/what-is-tok/
	Thinking and acting locally	Facilitating student engagement in local environmental projects such as litter pickups, and the cleaning of local resources. Encouraging and modelling the use of public transport. Awareness raising and action programmes for local flora and fauna that are threatened by extinction.	The Coolbinia Independent Public School (Australia) engages in local sustainability work.	http://www.sustainabilityinschools.edu.au/thinking-globally-acting-locally http://www.csiro.au/en/Education/Programs/Sustainable-Futures

(Continued)

CHAPTER 8

Table 1. (Continued)

Area	Subdivision	Learning experiences for students and advice for instructors	Examples	Resources & research
	Modelling and teaching regenerative systems	Classes share books, resources and devices (for example in groups of four but with pedagogically sound rules for group interaction). Students are taught recycling as part of a design cycle process with emphasis on sustainability and environmental impact. Historical, economic and geographic examples of sustainable practice at a number of levels are taught and modelled as case studies. Students are brought to look at economic expansionism, industrialisation, urbanisation and production-line development with a critical eye, always aware of externalities and environmental impact associated with such models. Schools ensure that they model recycling of paper, glass and other materials. Schools avoid the use of plastic, unnecessary and wasteful water and electricity consumption. Students are given natural spaces on campus to practice regenerative ecology (compost heaps, small-scale agriculture and so on).	The International Baccalaureate and United World Colleges both work with the Ellen MacArthur Foundation on circular economy models. The Ellen MacArthur Foundation runs courses on Life Cycle Assessments (analysing products' life cycle and global footprint) as well as courses on ecological use of technology, energy and production. The Solar Impulse Foundation has produced educational materials on clean technologies, particularly photovoltaic electricity.	https://www.ellenmacarthurfoundation.org/ http://aroundtheworld.solarimpulse.com/join-us

170

Area	Subdivision	Learning experiences for students and advice for instructors	Examples	Resources & research
Knowledge	*Ensuring strong knowledge consolidation*	Repeats to ensure memorisation; typically, following Ebbinghaus, this will involve repeats the next day, the following three days, a week later and then a month later. Designing an educational experience that begins with knowledge so that this knowledge can then be applied in meaningful ways to different contexts and through more creative and critical instances of learning (in other words, building up knowledge towards skill). Ensuring that teachers' professional development allows for the consolidation of their own mastery of academic knowledge. Designing and administering quality knowledge tests that assess knowledge acquisition and understanding.	ED Hirsch's core curriculum	Timperley et al. (2007); Blank and de las Alas (2009); Sadler et al. (2013); Cotton (1988); Tuytens and Devos (2011); Christodolou (2014); Kirschner, Sweller, and Clark (2006); Chase and Simon (1973); Chi, Feltovich, and Glaser (1981); Larkin, McDermott; Bahrick, Bahrick, Bahrick, and Bahrick (1993).

(Continued)

CHAPTER 8

Table 1. (Continued)

Area	Subdivision	Learning experiences for students and advice for instructors	Examples	Resources & research
	Ensuring essential knowledge is covered in STEM and geography	*Biology* The biology of life (photosynthesis, respiration and the cardiovascular system, digestion), systems and biological taxonomies (kingdoms, species, phenotypes), microbiology (cells, bacteriology, viruses), biochemistry (processes within cells), genetics, evolution. *Chemistry* Stoichiometry (moles), salt formation (ionic structures, acids and bases), atomic theory, analytical chemistry (measurements), organic chemistry (carbon), periodicity (elements), energetics (electrical chemistry), metals. *Physics* Forces and motion (speed, velocity, gravity, acceleration), the electromagnetic spectrum (radioactivity, light, waves and quantum physics), astrophysics, atomic theory (at a deeper level than chemistry).	Partnership for 21st Century Skills; US Department of Education's STEM Programs; STEM 101 resources.	http://www.p21.org/our-work/p21-framework https://www2.ed.gov/about/inits/ed/green-strides/stem.html https://www.stem101.org/

Area	Subdivision	Learning experiences for students and advice for instructors	Examples	Resources & research
		Mathematics Number and arithmetic, functions (graphing), algebra, calculus, trigonometry, geometry, statistics, logic. *Geography* Physical (environments, desertification, climate, weather, geology, ecology, plate tectonics); human (urbanisation, agriculture, globalisation, immigration, demographics).		
	Designing an international, 21st century humanities and arts curriculum	Texts and historical events should cover all of the continents, with some emphasis on issues of global significance, such as slavery, colonisation, the World Wars and Cold War. Ensuring that students grapple with the more substantive of cultural expressions, such as foundational myths, religious texts or archetypes. Leading students to understand and appreciate artistic expressions from around the world within the meaning of their cultural contexts.	In my book, *Understanding Prejudice and Education: The Challenge for Future Generations* (2017), I suggest what sort of choices schools can make to ensure that the arts and humanities address contemporary geopolitical tensions. Harari's book, *Sapiens*, covers salient historical, geopolitical and economic fault lines that explain the 21st century well. The book can be read by students 15+ years old. Another book that does this is Jared Diamond's *Guns, Germs and Steel*.	Hughes (2017); Harari (2011); Diamond (1997).

CHAPTER 8

The area of sustainability can be integrated into subjects such as the sciences and geography. The area of terrorism relates well to history, sociology and politics. The question of the role of knowledge in a twenty-first century education and how it relates to skills is a generic one that spans all subjects and educational experiences: it is a question for those who teach and design education.

However, possible approaches are manifold, and any of these areas can be integrated into a number of subjects according to context and situations: it is ultimately for the user to decide how to adopt them.

NOTE 1: ON CHARACTER

At the International School of Geneva's *La Grande Boissière*, the world's first International School, students are assessed on their character, as in Table 2.

Table 2. Character reports at the International School of Geneva (ISG, 2017)

Self-Mastery	Comes to class on time, ready to work, with the necessary materials.
	Pays attention and resists distractions during class.
	Remembers and follows instructions promptly, including submitting homework in a timely fashion.
Curiosity	Displays engagement with the subject matter and with others in the class.
	Demonstrates a willingness to learn new skills and an interest in new knowledge.
	Asks questions to deepen understanding where appropriate.
Tenacity	Reacts positively to feedback given by teachers and peers.
	Consistently seeks high standards
	Works productively, even without teacher support, on difficult tasks.
Social Intelligence	Contributes to a productive learning environment through demonstrated politeness, sensitivity, and respect for others in the class.
	Works effectively with peers, demonstrating leadership and an ability to learn from others.
	Shows an awareness of the values of the school through acts of kindness, and demonstrates a willingness to interact with those who think, look and act in ways different from himself or herself.

NOTE 2: ON STEM CRITERIA

Each of the above areas could be broken down into more granular descriptors of the course and would depend on the nature of the task at hand. The "Analysis of ethical implication" band, for example, could be expanded into the following:

- *Analysis* of the impact of the project on the environment (water, earth, air, fossil fuels, living creatures, space)

CONCLUSION

> - Scientific knowledge
> - Mathematical knowledge
> - Technological skill
> - Use of engineering principle
> - Integration of interdisciplinary concept or "big idea"
> - Collaborative problem-solving behaviour
> - Innovative thinking
> - Staying power
> - Analysis of ethical implications

Figure 2. Essential STEM assessment criteria

- *Evaluation* of the potential consequences for human behaviour (social patterns, wealth distribution, family and professional life)
- *Reflection* on what could happen were this project to fall into the wrong hands (potential uses for conflict, destruction, control)
- *Synthesis* of all the possible knock-on effects that might be caused by this project's development (first, second, third causes, domino effects, what decisions or powers might load onto the project)
- *Study* of similar projects historically and their ethical uses

Students could also use frameworks to map and guide their project development such as the United Nations' Development Goals (UN, 2016), thereby ensuring that environmental, social capital and ethical questions are asked along each stage of development. Big existential questions could also initiate projects: for example, "Why would we want to go to Mars in the first place?" or "Where will the materials needed for this project come from, and how are they manufactured?"

NOTES

[1] Questions from Edutopia (2015):
- What are the characteristics of Earth's atmosphere as you ascend up to near space? That's 30,500 meters or 100,000 feet! At that altitude, you are above 95% of the Earth's atmosphere.
- How will those characteristics affect the efficiency of a solar panel?
- What will happen to party balloons inflated to different sizes?
- How fast does a weather balloon travel as it rises through the atmosphere?

[2] NASA (2016) projects:
- Students will create a space mission which requires them to balance the return of their science data with engineering limitations such as power, mass and budget.
- Students will learn the limitations of operating a planetary rover and problem solving solutions by using this hands-on simulation (Grade 5–8).
- Students will use research to develop their criteria for determining if something is alive… They will then use their criteria to determine whether there is anything alive in three different "soil" samples.

[3] TeachEngineering (2016) activities:

175

CHAPTER 8

- 3RC (Reduce, Reuse, Recycle and Compost): Students look at the effects of packaging decisions (reducing) and learn about engineering advancements in packaging materials and solid waste management. Through an associated activity, they observe biodegradation in a model landfill (composting) (Grade 4).
- Able Sports: This activity focuses on getting students to think about disabilities and how they can make some aspects of life more difficult. The students are asked to pick a disability and design a new kind of sport for it (Grade 8).
- Above Ground Storage Tank Design Project: Students have learned about Pascal's law, Archimedes' principle, Bernoulli's principle, and why above-ground storage tanks are of major concern in the Houston Ship Channel (Texas, USA) and other coastal areas. In this culminating activity, student groups act as engineering design teams to derive equations to determine the stability of specific above-ground storage tank scenarios with given tank specifications and liquid contents. With their flotation analyses completed and the stability determined, students analyze the tank stability in specific storm conditions. Then, teams are challenged to come up with improved storage tank designs to make them less vulnerable to uplift, displacement and buckling in storm conditions. Teams present their analyses and design ideas in short class presentations (Grade 9).

REFERENCES

Akçam, T. (2006). *A shameful act: The Armenian genocide and the question of Turkish responsibility.* New York, NY: Metropolitan Books.

Alexander, R. (2006). *Towards dialogic teaching: Rethinking classroom talk* (3rd ed.). Cambridge: Dialogos.

Allport, G. (1954). *The nature of prejudice.* Cambridge, MA: Addison-Wesley.

Asara, V., Otero, I., Demaria, F., & Corbera, E. (2015). Socially sustainable degrowth as a social-ecological transformation: Repoliticizing sustainability. *Sustainability Science, 10*(3), 375–384.

Asch, S. E. (1951). Effects of group pressure upon the modification and distortion of judgment. In H. Guetzkow (Ed.), *Groups, leadership and men.* Pittsburgh, PA: Carnegie Press.

Bahrick, H. P., Bahrick, L. E., Bahrick, A. S., & Bahrick, P. E. (1993). Maintenance of foreign language vocabulary and the spacing effect. *Psychological Science, 4*, 316–321.

Baudrillard, J. (1970). *La société de consommation.* Paris: Folio.

Berkes, F., Colding, J., & Folke, C. (2003). *Navigating social-ecological systems: Building resilience for complexity and change.* Cambridge: Cambridge University Press.

Blackburn, S. (2001). *Think: A compelling introduction to philosophy.* New York, NY: Oxford University Press.

Blank, R. K., & de las Alas, N. (2009). *Effects of teacher professional development on gains in student achievement: How meta analysis provides scientific evidence useful to education leaders.* Washington, DC: Council of Chief State School Officers.

Brockhoff, S., Krieger, T., & Meierrieks, D. (2015). *More education = less terrorism? Studying the complex relationship between terrorism and education.* https://politicalviolenceataglance.org/2015/12/04/more-education-less-terrorism-studying-the-complex-relationship-between-terrorism-and-education/

Chase, W. G., & Simon, H. A. (1973). Perception in chess. *Cognitive Psychology, 1*, 33–81.

Chi, M. T. H., Feltovich, P. J., & Glaser, R. (1981). Categorization and representation of physics problems by experts and novices. *Cognitive Science, 5*, 121–152.

Christodolou, D. (2014). *Seven myths about education.* London: Routledge.

Cohen, D. (2012). *Homo economicus: Prophète (égaré) des temps nouveaux.* Paris: Albin Michel.

Cotton, K. (1988). *Classroom questioning.* Portland, OR: Education Northwest. http://educationnorthwest.org/sites/default/files/ClassroomQuestioning.pdf

Diamond, J. (1997). *Guns, germs, and steel: The fate of human societies.* New York, NY: Norton.

Ehlers, A., Clark, D. M., Hackmann, A., McManus, F., & Fennell, M. (2005). Cognitive therapy for post-traumatic stress disorder: Development and evaluation. *Behaviour Research and Therapy, 43*(4), 413–431.

CONCLUSION

Elu, J., & Price, J. (2015). Causes and consequences of terrorism in Africa. In C. Monga & J. Yifu Lin (Eds.), *The Oxford handbook of Africa and economics: Context and concepts.* Oxford: Oxford University Press.

Farkas, Z. D., & Hutchison-Hall, J. (2008). Religious care in coping with terrorism. *Journal of Aggression, Maltreatment & Trauma, 10*(1–2), 565–576.

Ferry, L. (2010). *Learning to live.* Edinburgh: Canongate.

Frugaldad (2011). Media consolidation: The illusion of choice (infographic). http://www.frugaldad.com/media-consolidation-infographic/

Goodall, J., & Johnston-Wilder, S. (2015). Overcoming mathematical helplessness and developing mathematical resilience in parents: An illustrative case study. *Creative Education, 6,* 526–535. http://dx.doi.org/10.4236/ce.2015.65052

Hallam, S. (2010). The power of music: Its impact on the intellectual, social and personal development of children and young people. *International Journal of Music Education, 28*(3), 269–289. http://ijm.sagepub.com/content/28/3/269.full.pdf+html

Harari, Y. (2014). *Sapiens: A brief history of humankind.* London: Vintage.

Herman, E. S., & Chomsky, N. (1988). *Manufacturing consent: The political economy of the mass media.* New York, NY: Pantheon Books.

Hickling-Hudson, A. (2006). Cultural complexity, post-colonialism and educational change: Challenges for comparative educators. *International Review of Education, 52*(1–2), 201–218.

Hughes, C. (2017). *Understanding prejudice and education: The challenge for future generations.* Oxford: Routledge.

ISG [International School of Geneva] (2017). *Character reports: La Grande Boissière community handbook.* Geneva: ISG. https://www.ecolint.ch/campus/la-grande-boissiere

Josman, N., Somer, E., Reisberg, A., Weiss, P. L. T., Garcia-Palacios, A., & Hoffman, H. (2006). BusWorld: Designing a virtual environment for post-traumatic stress disorder in Israel: A protocol. *CyberPsychology & Behavior, 9*(2), 241–244. doi:10.1089/cpb.2006.9.241

Kirschner, P. A, Sweller, J., & Clark, R. E. (2006). Why minimal guidance during instruction does not work: An analysis of the failure of constructivist, discovery, problem-based, experiential, and inquiry-based teaching. *Educational Psychologist, 41*(2), 75–86.

Klein, N. (1999). *No logo.* Toronto: Knopf Canada.

Klein, N. (2007). *The shock doctrine.* Toronto: Knopf Canada.

Kramer, A. F., Erickson, K. I., & Colcombe, S. J. (2006). Exercise, cognition, and the aging brain. *Journal of Applied Physiology, 101,* 1237–1242. doi:10.1152/japplphysiol.00500.2006

Kuhn, T. (1962). *The structure of scientific revolutions.* Chicago, IL: University of Chicago Press.

Lambourne, K., & Tomporowski, P. (2010). The effect of exercise-induced arousal on cognitive task performance: A meta-regression analysis. *Brain Research, 1341,* 12–24. doi:10.1016/j.brainres.2010.03.091

Lanham, R. (1979). *Revising prose.* London: Longman.

Larkin, J. H., McDermott, J., Simon, D. P., & Simon, H. A. (1980). Expert and novice performance in solving physics problems. *Science, 208,* 1335–1342.

Lipman, M. (2003). *Thinking in education* (2nd ed.). Cambridge: Cambridge University Press.

Loftus, E. (1979). *Eyewitness testimony.* Cambridge, MA: Harvard University Press.

Malchiodi, C. (2008). Drawing on the effort-driven rewards circuit to chase the blues away. *Psychology Today.* https://www.psychologytoday.com/blog/arts-and-health/200808/drawing-the-effort-driven-rewards-circuit-chase-the-blues-away

Malik, J. (Ed.) (2008). *Madrasas in South Asia: Teaching terror?* London: Routledge.

Mazzocchi, F. (2006). *Western science and traditional knowledge: Despite their variations, different forms of knowledge can learn from each other.* https://www.ncbi.nlm.nih.gov/pmc/articles/PMC1479546/

Meisenhelder, J. B., & Marcum, J. P. (2009). Terrorism, post-traumatic stress, coping strategies, and spiritual outcomes. *Journal of Religion and Health, 48*(1), 46–57. doi:10.1007/s10943-008-9192-z

Merritt, S. (2016). Squeezing out arts for more 'useful' subjects will impoverish us all. *The Guardian.* https://www.theguardian.com/commentisfree/2016/jun/25/squeezing-out-arts-for-commercially-useful-subjects-will-make-our-culture-poorer

CHAPTER 8

Milgram, S. (1963). Behavioral study of obedience. *Journal of Abnormal and Social Psychology, 67*(4), 371–378. doi:10.1037/h0040525

Mooneyham, B. W., & Schooler, J. W. (2013). The costs and benefits of mind-wandering: A review. *Canadian Journal of Experimental Psychology, 67*(1), 11–18.

Ochberg, F. (1987). *Post-traumatic therapy and victims of violence*. New York, NY: Brunner/Mazel.

Oppezzo, M., & Schwartz, D. L. (2014). Give your ideas some legs: The positive effect of walking on creative thinking. *Journal of Experimental Psychology: Learning, Memory, and Cognition, 40*(4), 1142–1152.

Orwell, G. (1949). *Nineteen eighty-four*. London: Secker & Warburg.

Owen, J. (2016). British Empire: Students should be taught colonialism 'not all good', say historians. *The Independent*. http://www.independent.co.uk/news/education/education-news/british-empire-students-should-be-taught-colonialism-not-all-good-say-historians-a6828266.html

Peirce, C. S. (1868). Some consequences of four incapacities. *Journal of Speculative Philosophy, 2*, 140–157.

Pettigrew, T. F., & Tropp, L. R. (2008). How does intergroup contact reduce prejudice? Meta-analytic tests of three mediators. *European Journal of Social Psychology, 38*, 922–934.

Provost, G. (1985). *100 ways to improve your writing*. Harmondsworth: Penguin.

Rich, B. R., & Goldberg, J. (Eds.) (2009). *Neuroeducation: Learning, arts and the brain: Findings and challenges for educators and researchers from the 2009 Johns Hopkins University summit*. New York, NY: Dana Press. http://steam-notstem.com/wp-content/uploads/2010/11/Neuroeducation.pdf

Roué, M., & Molnar, Z. (Eds.) (2016). *Knowing our lands and resources: Indigenous and local knowledge of biodiversity and ecosystem services in Europe and Central Asia*. Paris: UNESCO.

Russell, B. (1918). The philosophy of logical atomism. In J. G. Slater (Ed.), *The collected papers of Bertrand Russell, 1914–19* (Vol. 8, p. 228). London: Routledge.

Ruz, C. (2015, November 19). What should you do in an attack? *BBC*. http://www.bbc.com/news/magazine-34844518

Sadler, P. M., Sonnert, G., Coyle, H. P., Cook-Smith, N., & Miller, J. L. (2013). The influence of teachers' knowledge on student learning in middle school physical science classrooms. *American Educational Research Journal, 50*(5), 1020–1049.

Seli, P., Risko, E. F., & Smilek, D. (2016). On the necessity of distinguishing between unintentional and intentional mind wandering. *Psychological Science, 27*(5), 685–691.

Semchison, M. R. S. (2001). Ways of learning: Indigenous approaches to knowledge: Valid methodologies in education. *The Australian Journal of Indigenous Education, 29*(2), 8–10.

Silver, S. M., Rogers, S., Knipe, J., & Colelli, G. (2005). EMDR therapy following the 9/11 terrorist attacks: A community-based intervention project in New York City. *International Journal of Stress Management, 12*(1), 29–42. http://dx.doi.org/10.1037/1072-5245.12.1.29

Singer, J. L., & Antrobus, J. S. (1963). A factor-analytic study of daydreaming and conceptually- related cognitive and personality variables [Monograph Supplement 3-V17]. *Perceptual and Motor Skills, 17*, 187–209. doi:10.2466/pms.1963.17.1.187

Stuckey, H. L., & Nobel, J. (2010). The connection between art, healing, and public health: A review of current literature. *American Journal of Public Health, 100*(2), 254–263. http://doi.org/10.2105/AJPH.2008.156497

Szpunar, K. K., Moulton, S. T., & Schacter, D. L. (2013). Mind wandering and education: From the classroom to online learning. *Frontiers in Psychology, 4*, 495. http://doi.org/10.3389/fpsyg.2013.00495 https://www.ncbi.nlm.nih.gov/pmc/articles/PMC3730052/

Timperley, H., Wilson, A., Barrar, H., & Fung, I. (2007). *Teacher professional learning and development: Best evidence synthesis iteration*. Wellington: Ministry of Education. http://www.educationcounts.govt.nz/publications/series/2515/15341

Torgerson, D. J., Torgerson C. J., & Brown, C. (2010). Randomized Controlled Trials (RCTs) and non-randomized designs. In J. S. Wholey & H. P. Hatry (Eds.), *The handbook of practical program evaluation* (3rd ed.). Chichester: Jossey-Bass.

Tuytens, M., & Devos, G. (2011). Stimulating professional learning through teacher evaluation: An impossible task for the school leader? *Teaching and Teacher Education, 27*(5), 891–899.

United Nations (1948). *Universal declaration of human rights.* Paris: United Nations. http://www.un.org/en/universal-declaration-human-rights/
United Nations (1992). *Convention on biological diversity* (No. 30619). Rio de Janeiro: United Nations.
University of Virginia (2015). *Talking to children about terrorism.* http://curry.virginia.edu/research/projects/threat-assessment/talking-to-children-about-terrorism
Webb, A. (2012). *Teaching the literature of today's Middle East.* London: Routledge.
WHO [World Health Organisation] (2016). *Global strategy on diet, physical activity and health.* http://www.who.int/dietphysicalactivity/factsheet_young_people/en/
Wooddy, C. (1935). Education and propaganda. *Annals of the American Academy of Political and Social Science, 179*, 227–239. http://journals.sagepub.com/doi/abs/10.1177/000271623517900129

ABOUT THE AUTHOR

Conrad Hughes holds a PhD in English from the University of the Witwatersrand, and a Master's in Comparative Literature from Université Paul Valéry Montpellier 3. He also holds a Doctorate in Education (EdD) from Durham University.

He was a university lecturer in English and an English teacher and diploma program coordinator in schools in India and the Netherlands, before starting to work at the International School of Geneva (Ecolint), the oldest international school in the world.

Conrad has been at the Ecolint for ten years, first as an English and Theory of Knowledge teacher, then as Director of Education, prior to taking up the role of Campus Principal at La Grande Boissière, in 2015.

During his tenure as Director of Education, Conrad had numerous articles published on a variety of topics, including the IB Middle Years Programme, the Theory of Knowledge component of the IB Diploma, child-centered pedagogy, the role of education in combating prejudice and the English syllabus for the IB Diploma. Conrad also led the work to articulate the *Guiding Principles for Learning in the 21st Century*, which was jointly published with IBE UNESCO in 2014.

His latest book is *Understanding Prejudice and Education: The Challenge for Future Generations*, Routledge, 2017.

Printed in the United States
By Bookmasters